Firebrands

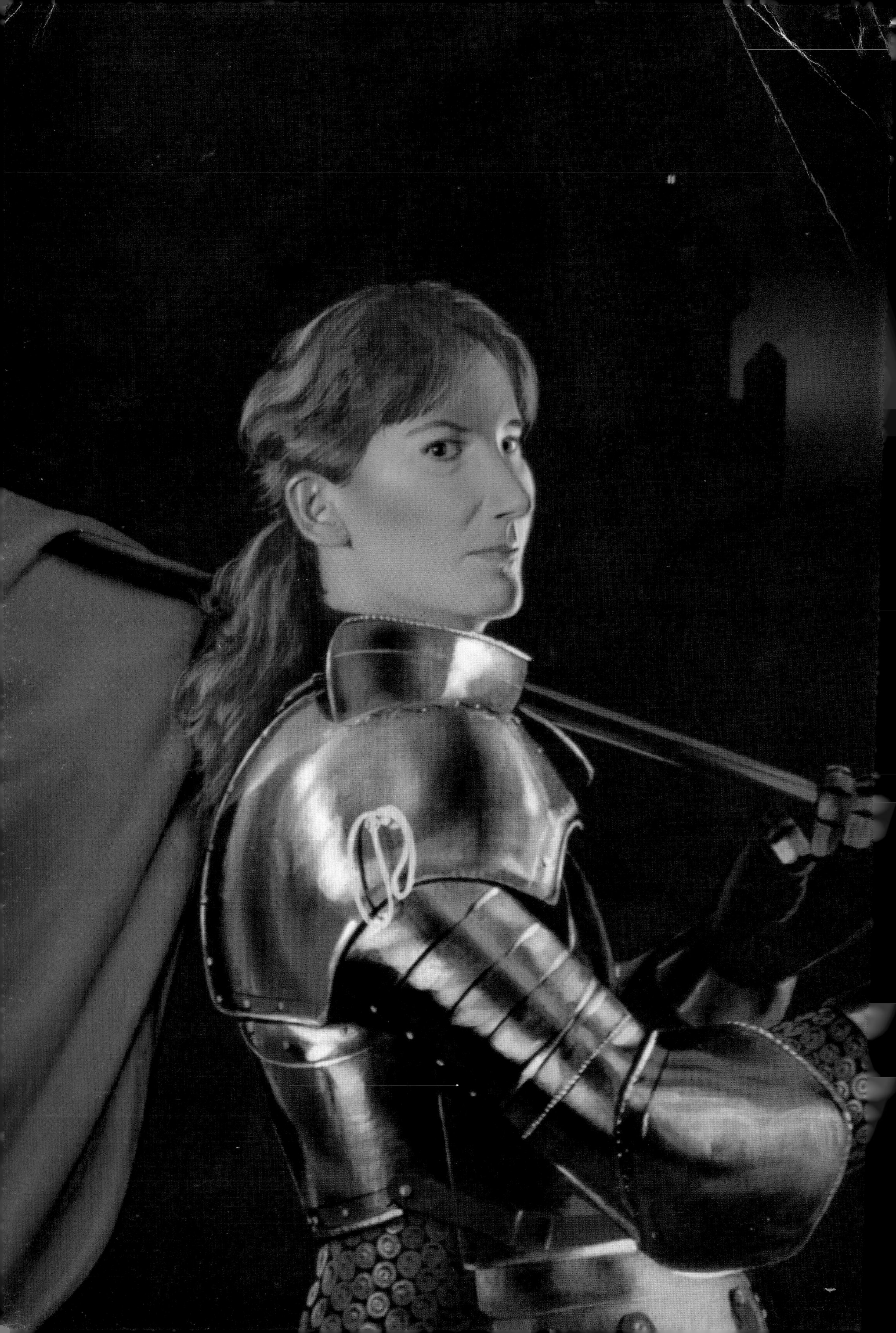

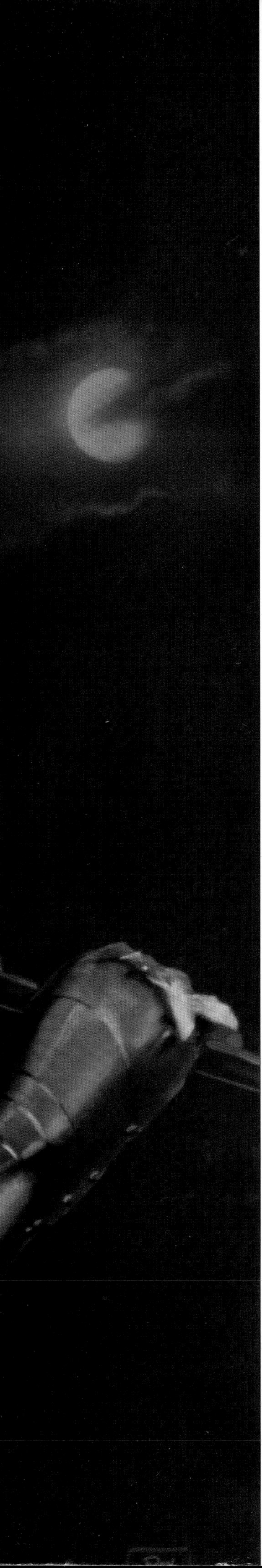

Firebrands

The heroines of science fiction and fantasy

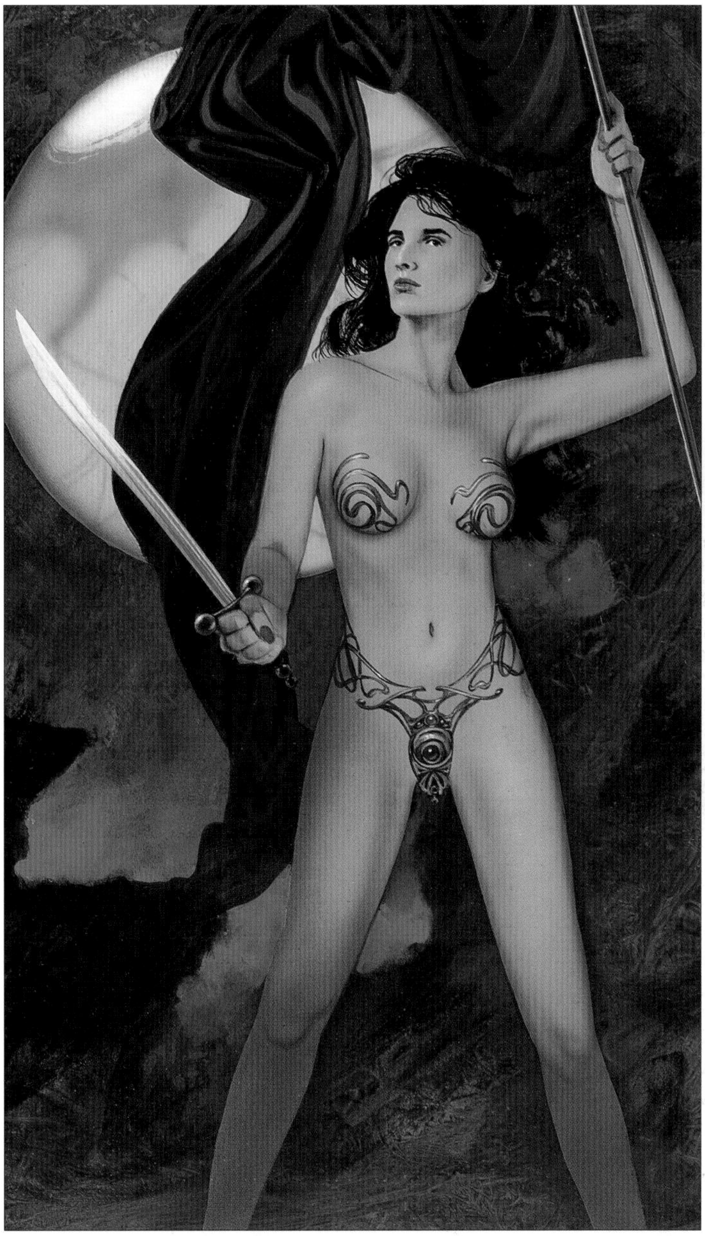

Ron Miller
Text by Pamela Sargent

THUNDER'S MOUTH PRESS

This book is for
Polly Freas,
science fiction heroine

THUNDER'S MOUTH PRESS

Published in the UNITED STATES By
Thunder's Mouth Press
841 Broadway, Fourth Floor
New York, NY 10003

First published in Great Britain in 1998
by Paper Tiger
An imprint of Collins & Brown Limited

Library of Congress Catalog card number:
98-85761

ISBN 1 56025-164-6

Designed by Kevin Williams

Reproduction by Hong Kong Graphic & Printing Ltd
Printed and bound in Singapore by Kyodo Printing Co (S'pore) Pte Ltd

Bronwyn Tedeschiiy (page 1)
(*Palaces & Prisons, Silk & Steel,
Hearts & Armor, Mermaids &
Meteors*, Ron Miller, 1991-1995)
*The pampered, self-interested and head-
strong Princess Bronwyn is thrust into a
world where she must fight not only for
her life but also in defence of what she
believes to be right. Bronwyn also
appears on pages 104 and 106.*

Jirel of Joiry (page 2)
('The Black God's Kiss', 1934,
C. L. Moore; also *Jirel of Joiry* (six
stories) 1982)
*Warrior-commander of Joiry, the strongest
fortress in the kingdom, Jirel is a powerful
leader who does not hesitate to confront
Hell itself to bring back a deadly kiss for
her most hated enemy. Jirel is the first
female sword-and-sorcery character to
be featured in her own series.*

Thuvia (page 3)
(*Thuvia, Maid of Mars*, Edgar Rice
Burroughs, 1916)
*Thuvia is a princess of Ptarth and ex-
slave of the therns. With John Carter and
Tario, Jeddak of Lothar, she rescues Kulan
Tith, Jeddak of Kaol, from a band of
green Torquasians.*

Contents

Wilma Deering (left)
(Armageddon 2419 A.D., Philip
Francis Nowlan, 1928)
*Wilma lives in the 25th century where,
after the collapse of Western civilization,
she becomes a member of the
'Wyoming Gang'. Her duties alternate
between military or police work and fac-
tory work. The 'gangs' – all that remain
of America – have to be on constant
alert for raiding parties of their evil Han
conquerors. She discovers Anthony 'Buck'
Rogers – a citizen of the 20th century
who had fallen into a state of suspended animation – and together they succeed in eventually destroying the Han
dynasty. In the long-running comic strip
inspired by the novel, Wilma's adventures continue into interplanetary space.*

Introduction

MEMORABLE HEROES are numerous in science fiction. The first were Dr Frankenstein and his monster, the central characters of Mary Shelley's *Frankenstein* (1818) which writer and critic Brian Aldiss, in his history of the genre, described as 'the first real novel of science fiction' (*Billion Year Spree*, 1973). Other heroes range from John Carter of Edgar Rice Burroughs's Mars series to more complex and varied figures such as Isaac Asimov's future police detective Lije Baley in *The Caves of Steel* (1954) and *The Naked Sun* (1958), Robert A. Heinlein's Michael Valentine Smith of *Stranger in a Strange Land* (1961) and Lazarus Long of *Methuselah's Children* (1958) and *Time Enough for Love* (1973), Frank Herbert's Paul Atreides of *Dune* (1965) and William Gibson's Case in *Neuromancer* (1984). Screen and television science fiction heroes have included such instantly recognizable characters as Buck Rogers, Flash Gordon, Luke Skywalker and Han Solo of Star Wars and Star Trek's Captain Kirk, Mister Spock and Captain Picard. Anyone with even a passing acquaintance with science fiction is likely to assume that the genre is largely a literature directed at men and boys in which female characters are rare and of little importance.

There is some justice to this assumption. The history of female characters in science fiction and fantasy might superficially be summed up as follows. In the beginning, women characters in science fiction could be characterized largely by their absence. During the Thirties and Forties, when most science fiction was confined to pulp magazines, any female in a story was likely to be a damsel in distress, shown in accompanying illustrations as a skimpily clad beauty in a brass brassière being carried off by a monster, or a deadly opponent of the hero and depicted as an exotic woman in seductive clothing. During the Fifties, science fiction's female characters were generally confined to the roles of mother, wife or daughter and generally stayed in the background; the occasional female scientist who might appear in a story was usually there to provide a love interest for the hero.

In the Sixties, a revolution of sorts occurred. The British writers J.G. Ballard, Brian Aldiss and Michael Moorcock and the American writers Samuel R. Delany, Roger Zelazny and Harlan Ellison, among others, were experimenting with both subject matter and style. These writers, loosely grouped together under the somewhat misleading term 'New Wave', rejected the elements of pulp fiction and often viewed technology and the future with pessimism. Not surprisingly, the female characters created by these writers were quite different from earlier depictions of women; for one thing, they were allowed to have a sex life. The Seventies, during which a number of women writers influenced by the feminist movement began to write science fiction, saw the emergence of more varied and complex female characters, many of whom played roles once restricted to males. Today, readers can find an abundance of female characters in science fiction and many would find it odd if there were no women playing important parts in a story.

This brief summary contains some truth, but also misses much. The fact is that women of strength and power have been important characters in science fiction and the related genre of fantasy almost since their beginnings. They may have been greatly outnumbered by their male counterparts, but they were present and the depictions of these characters in earlier works may have helped to lay the groundwork for those that appeared in the stories of later writers.

Violet Ray (opposite)
(The Golden Amazon series, John Russell Fearn, 1939-1954)
Violet Ray had been turned into a superwoman by the atmosphere of Venus. In her first appearance in a novel, however, in 1944, a surgeon changed her glandular structure so that she would have superhuman strength.

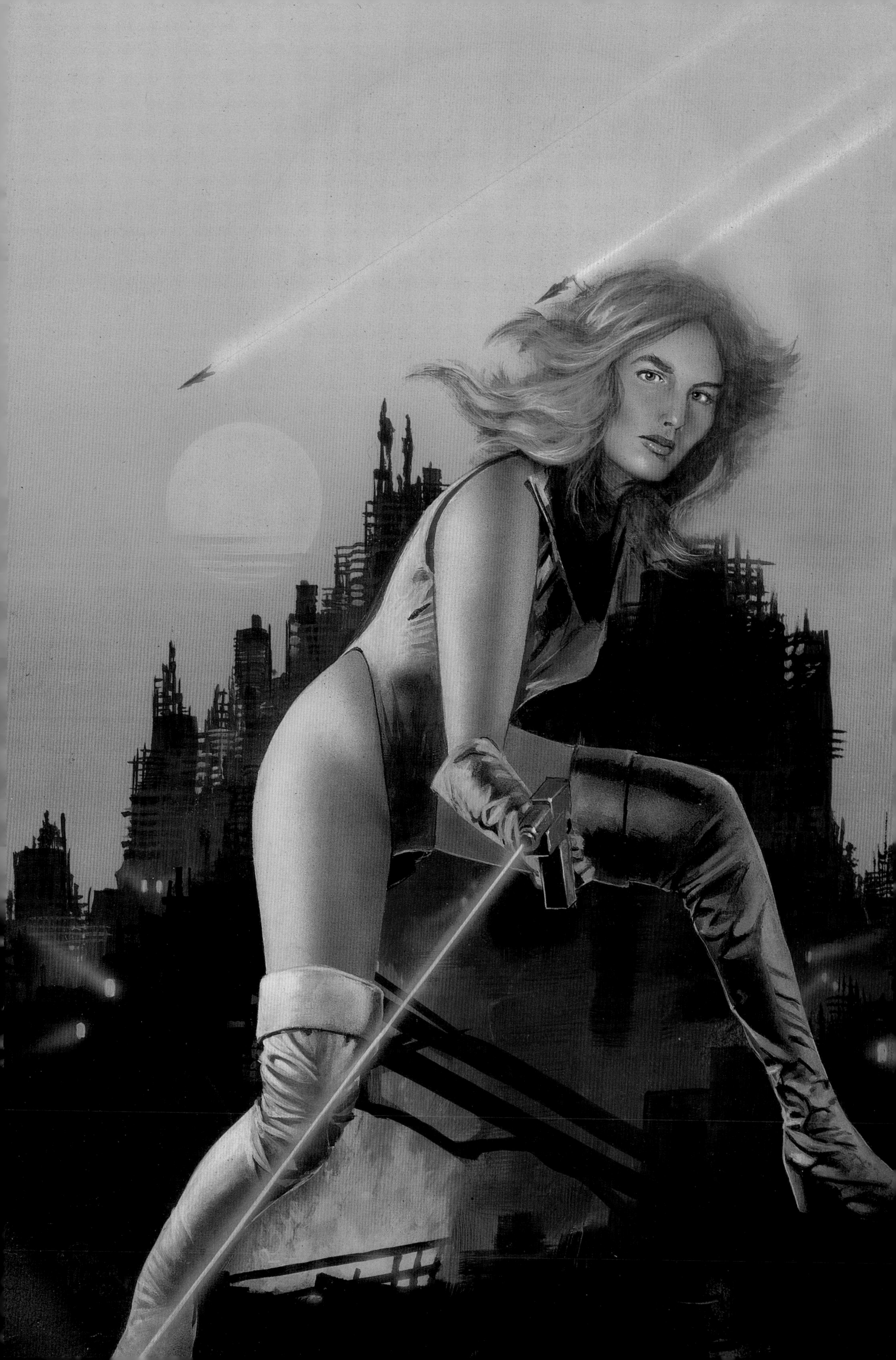

Chapter 1
The Beginnings to
the 1930s

Brynhild (below)
(*The Volsunga Saga*,
also appears as
Brünnhilde in *Die
Walküre*, by Richard
Wagner, 1856)
*The powerful Valkyrie
Brynhild disobeys her
father, Wotan, and is
condemned to mortality,
when she then falls in
love with the equally
heroic Siegfried.*

When considering characterization in science fiction, it is important to remember the roots of the genre. Two springs have fed those roots: the tradition of myth and fantasy, and in more recent times, the pulp magazines and the plot devices of adventure fiction. In both of these forms, characters tend to be larger than life and archetypal rather than realistically drawn. Many of the heroines in these sorts of science fiction stories are indeed stereotypes and the same can be said of the heroes.

Early science fiction characters are not especially notable for their realism, but instead for their out-sized stature and exaggerated traits. Heroes are often handsome, brilliant, physically imposing men who command skills far beyond the mastery of most human beings, while equally skilled and brilliant villains do their best to create havoc for the heroes. Often such characters can be seen as the projection of their creators' fears and desires, and the same is also true of the female characters.

Veronica Cody
(opposite)
(*Return to Skull
Island*, R. Milnikov,
1938)
*Grandniece of Buffalo
Bill and cousin of the
famous aviator, Veronica
Cody spearheads a
return expedition to
the fabulous island
home of the late
King Kong.*

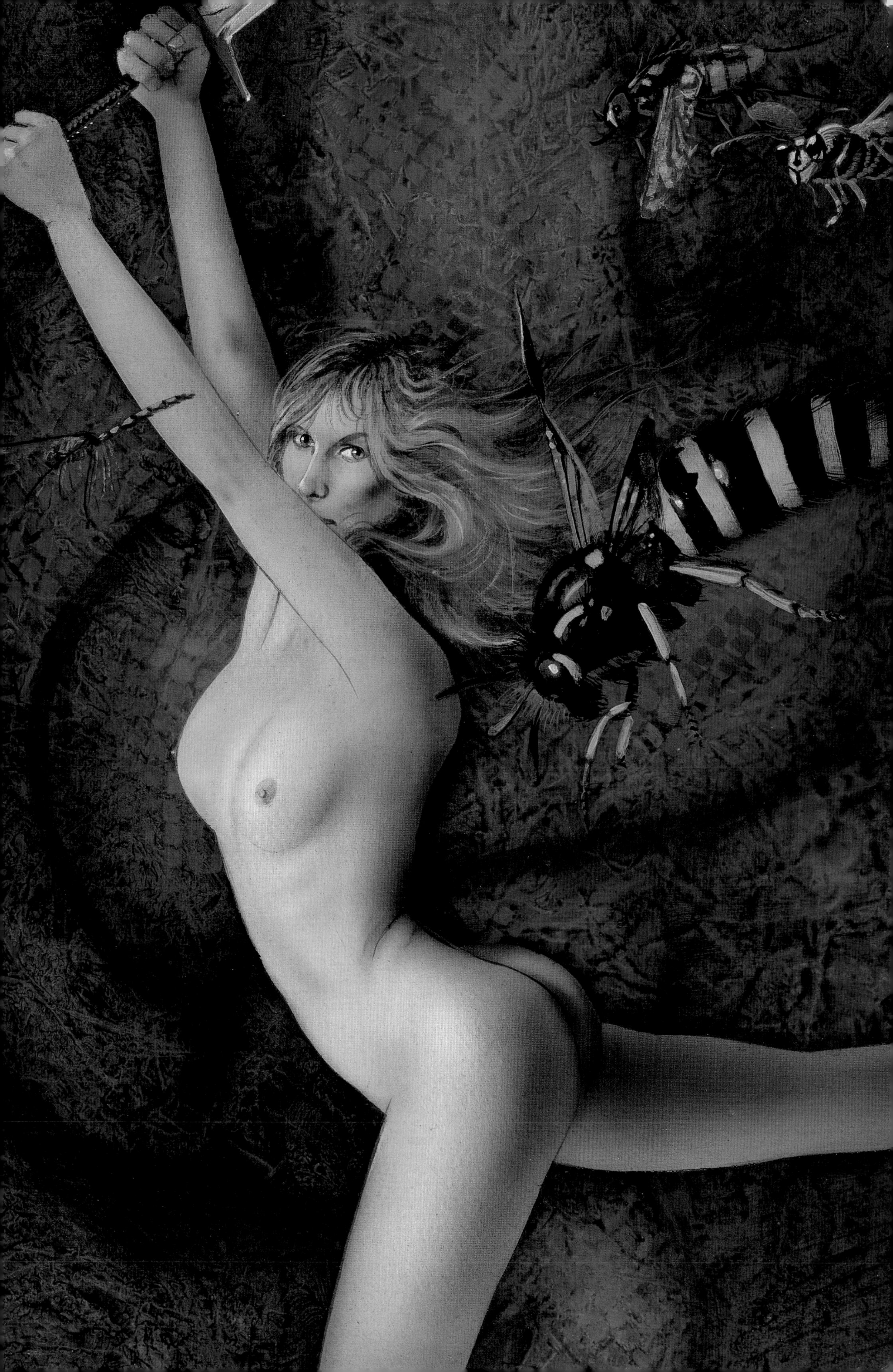

Figures such as Bradamant in Ariosto's fantasy masterpiece *Orlando Furioso* (1516) and Ayesha in H. Rider Haggard's *She* (1887) are not meant to be realistic depictions of women. Interestingly, they are equals, even the superiors, of the male characters around them, although immortal Ayesha is finally undone by her passion for her long-lost lover, Kallikrates, whom she killed in a fit of jealousy two thousand years before the novel begins. When the explorer Leo Vincey makes his way to the African land where Ayesha rules, she sees that he is the reincarnation of Kallikrates. Wanting to give Leo the immorality that she possesses, she leads him to a cave that contains the flaming pillar of life and enters the flame, in order to encourage him to do the same, but this time, the flame that originally gave her immorality makes her rapidly wither and die. Before her death, Ayesha promises to return to the grief-stricken Leo.

A somewhat more plausible and realistic female character, Weena, is featured in H. G Wells's classic novel *The Time Machine* (1895). Wells meant to comment on the class divisions of his own society and their possible evolutionary consequences in this tale of a future in which the descendants of humankind have become two species, the gentle but decadent Eloi, descendants of the parasitical rich, and 'the bestial, apelike' Morlocks, who are the descendants of the labouring classes. Weena, an Eloi, is saved from drowning by the Time Traveller: no one among the passive Eloi watching her struggles in the water even thinks of trying to save her. She rewards the Time

Mitaine (left)
(*Legend of Croquemitaine*, Ernest l'Epine, 1863)
Mitaine is a female knight in the days of Charlemagne – freely modelled on Bradamant of Orlando Furioso – indulging in adventures no less fantastic. She is the daughter of Miton, a friend of Roland, and Mita, sister of Oliver.

Britomart (opposite)
(*The Faerie Queene*, Edmund Spenser, 1589-1596)
Inspired by Ariosto's Orlando Furioso, Spenser wrote an Anglicized version, with female knight Britomart taking on a role similar to Bradamant's. Each of Spenser's 6 great knights represent some virtue.. In Book III, Britomart, representing Chastity, rescues Amoret (Wifely Devotion) from Busirane (Unlawful Love).

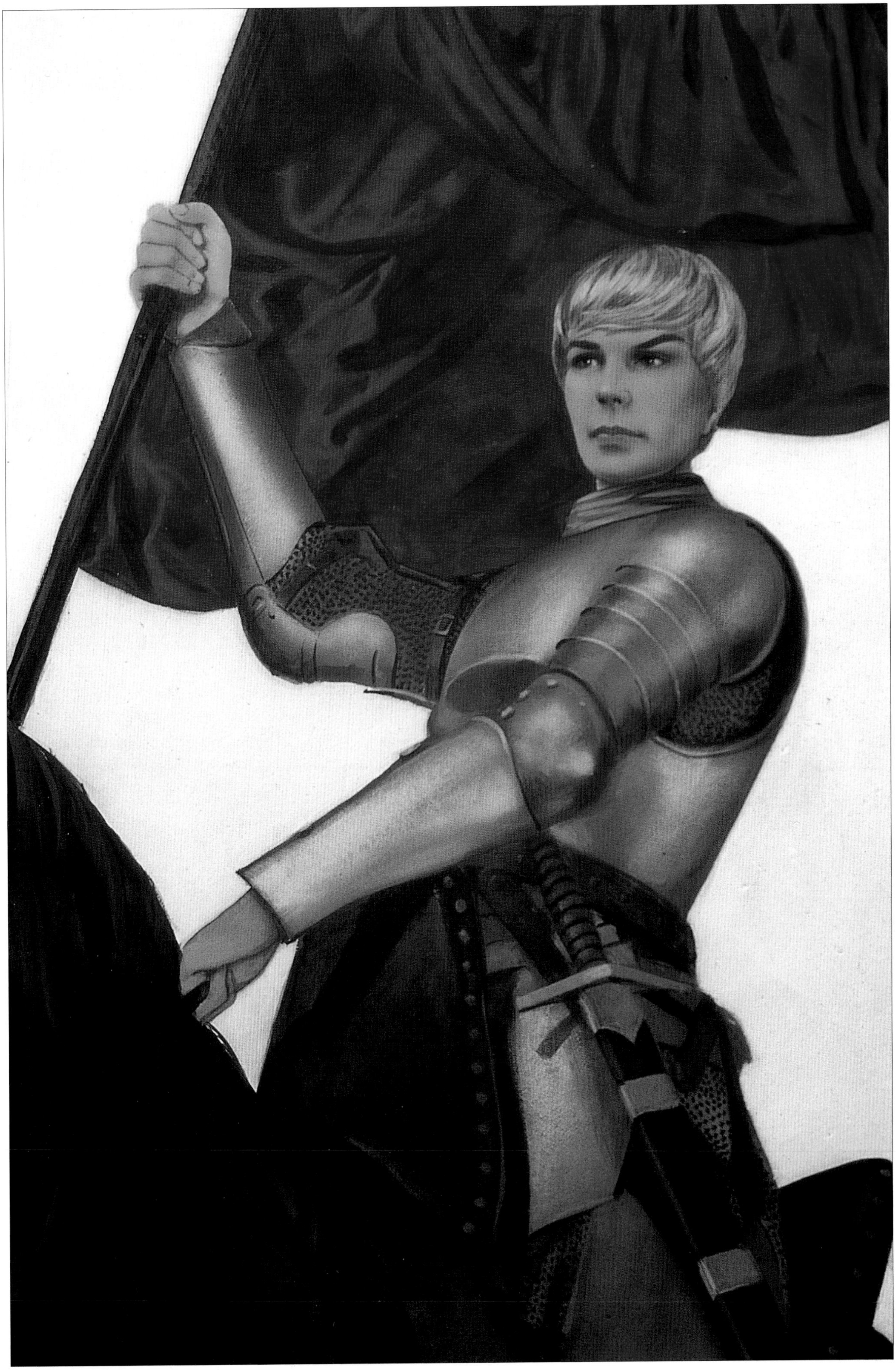

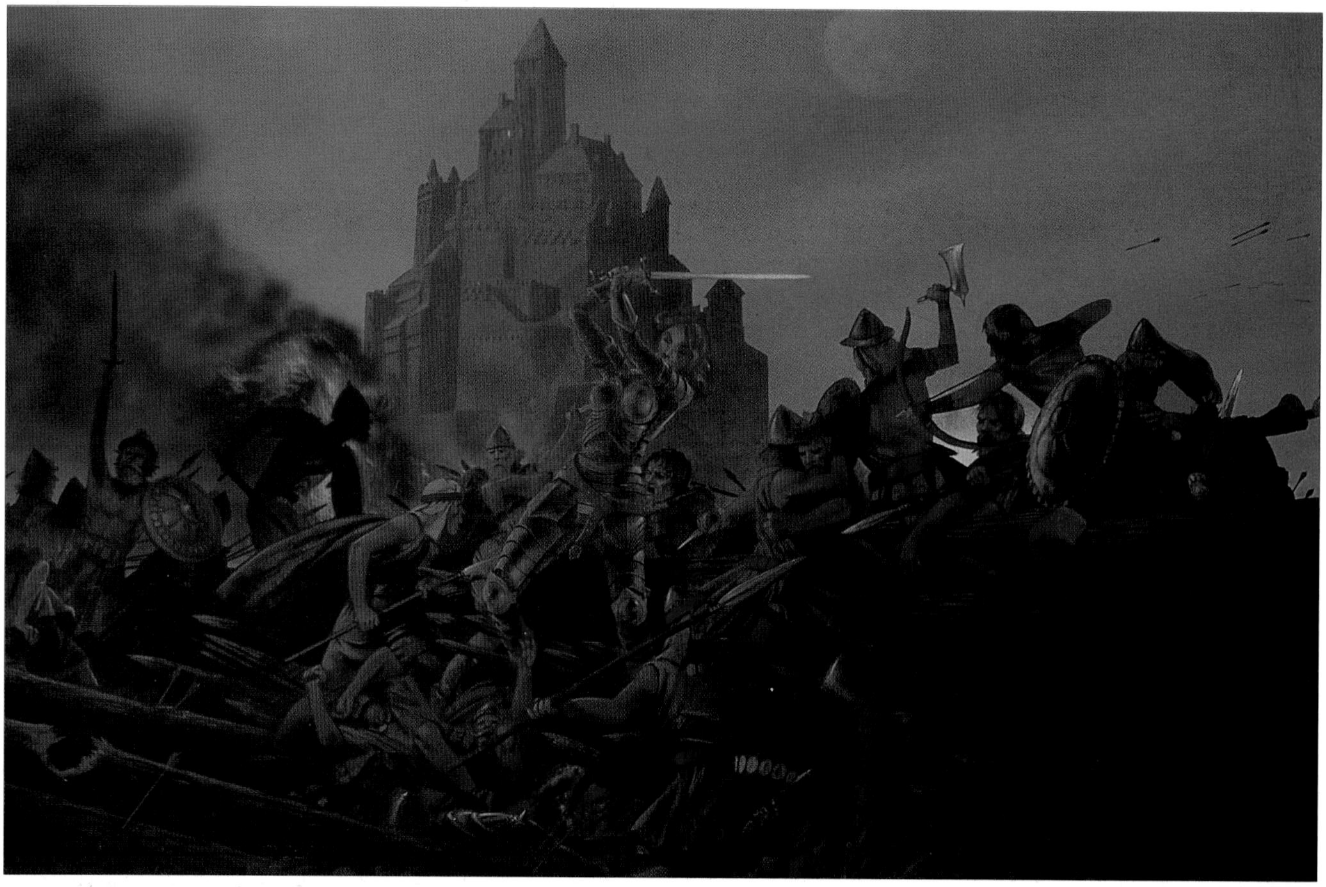

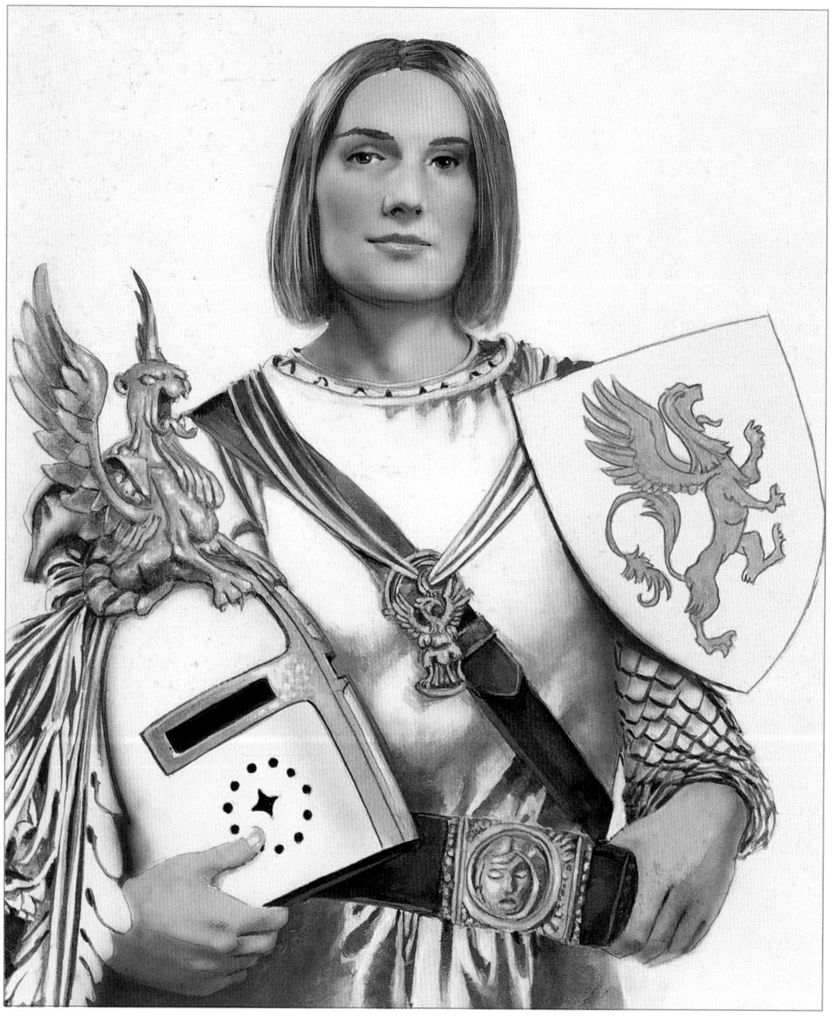

Bradamant (above and left)
(*Orlando Furioso*, Ludovico Ariosto, 1516)

The fabulous Bradamant, daughter of Duke Amon, sister of Renaud and cousin of the incredible Roland, is perhaps the first great heroine of fantasy. Like her brothers and cousins, she is one of Charlemagne's most valued knights and her unbelievable exploits occupy much of Ariosto's epic, 46-canto poem, in which she not only defeats other warriors but entire armies virtually single-handedly. As reknowned for her beauty as for her prowess at arms, her eventual marriage to the Saracen hero Ruggiero not only inaugurates peace between the Christians and the Moors, but establishes a future dynasty of heroes, kings and popes.

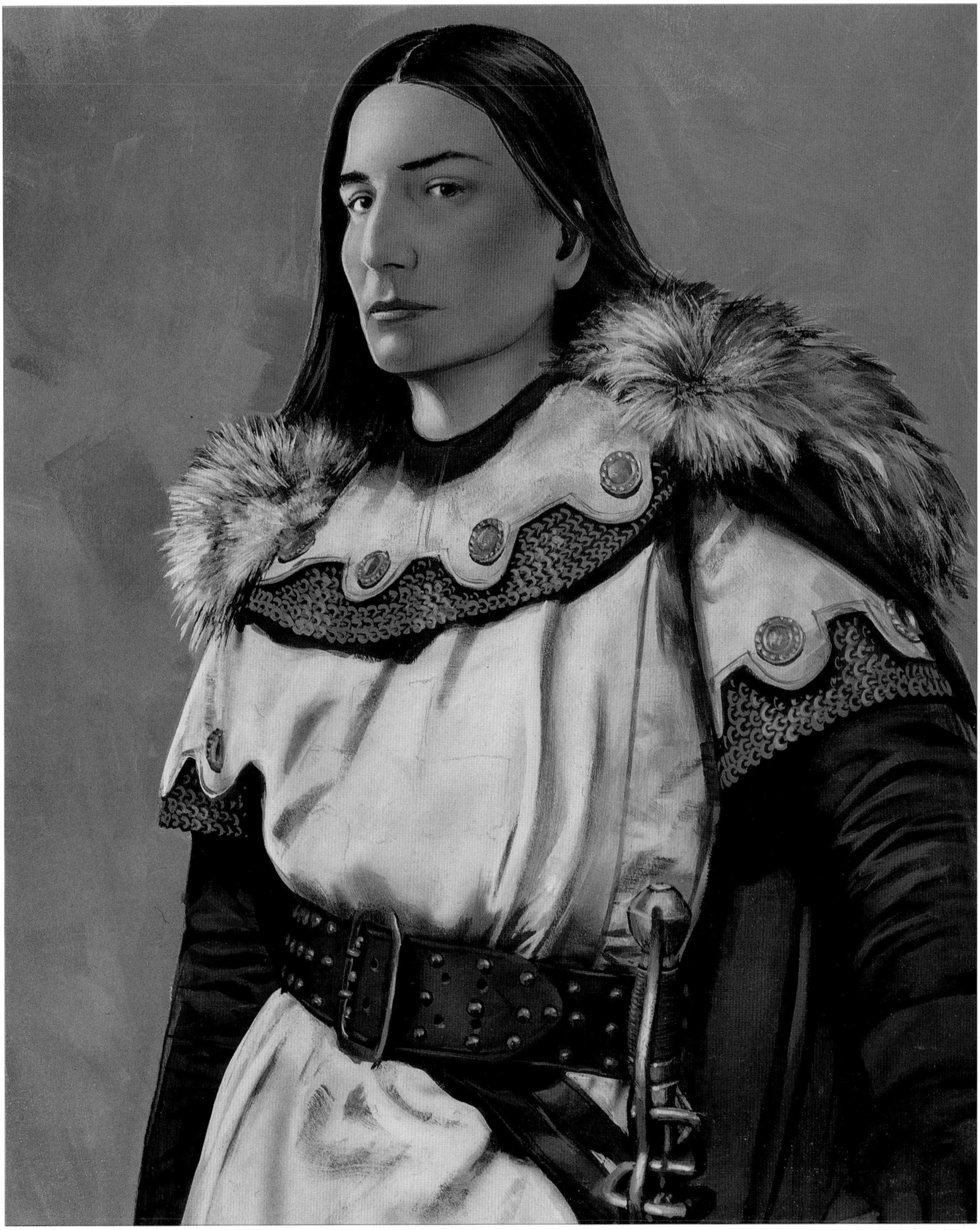

Marfisa (above)
(*Orlando Furioso*, Ludovico Ariosto, 1516)
Marisa is the Saracen equivalent of the redoubtable Bradamant, and for much of Ariosto's epic poem her bitter enemy – until Bradamant discovers that Marfisa is, in fact, her lover's sister. Joining forces, they form an almost invincible team before which whole armies melt.

Traveller with her utter, almost mindless devotion. Weena is hardly a character of strength and power, but then neither are the male Eloi, all of whom are helpless against the Morlocks who prey upon them. Weena may seem to embody some male fantasies of feminine helplessness, but she (as are the Morlocks, who feed upon those whose ancestors exploited them) is also meant as a warning of what evolution and increasing divisions among social classes might hold for humankind's future.

Wells's Weena has one feature in common with most of the early heroines of science fiction. She seems to have no ties to other females, but instead exists largely in isolation from them; no other female Eloi has much of a role in *The Time Machine*. There were some early exceptions to this lone-woman model in early science fiction, particularly in utopian fiction written by women; *Mizora* (1890) by Mary Bradley Lane and *Herland* (1915) by Charlotte Perkins Gilman are two notable examples. *Mizora* is a depiction of an all-woman society that by eliminating men, has also rid itself of crime. *Herland*, a long-neglected and recently

The Little Mermaid (above and opposite)
('The Little Mermaid', Hans Christian Andersen, 1835)
The beautiful sea maiden willingly sacrifices her life for the happiness of the man she loves. Though by today's standards this act may on the face of it seem less than feminist, the real point is that the mermaid gave her life willingly and on her own volition, with much the same sense of self-sacrifice that a soldier exhibits when he dies to save a comrade.

rediscovered book that is now viewed as a feminist classic, reveals a gentler all-female society through the eyes of three male visitors, one of whom adores and idealizes women while the second looks down on them: the third man tells the story.

Such tales necessarily show a variety of females with different kinds of relationships. In general, however, female characters were usually isolated figures. Ayesha may not be the only woman with an important role in *She*; there is also the kindly Ustane, who accompanies Leo Vincey to Ayesha's kingdom. But no bond exists between these two very different char-

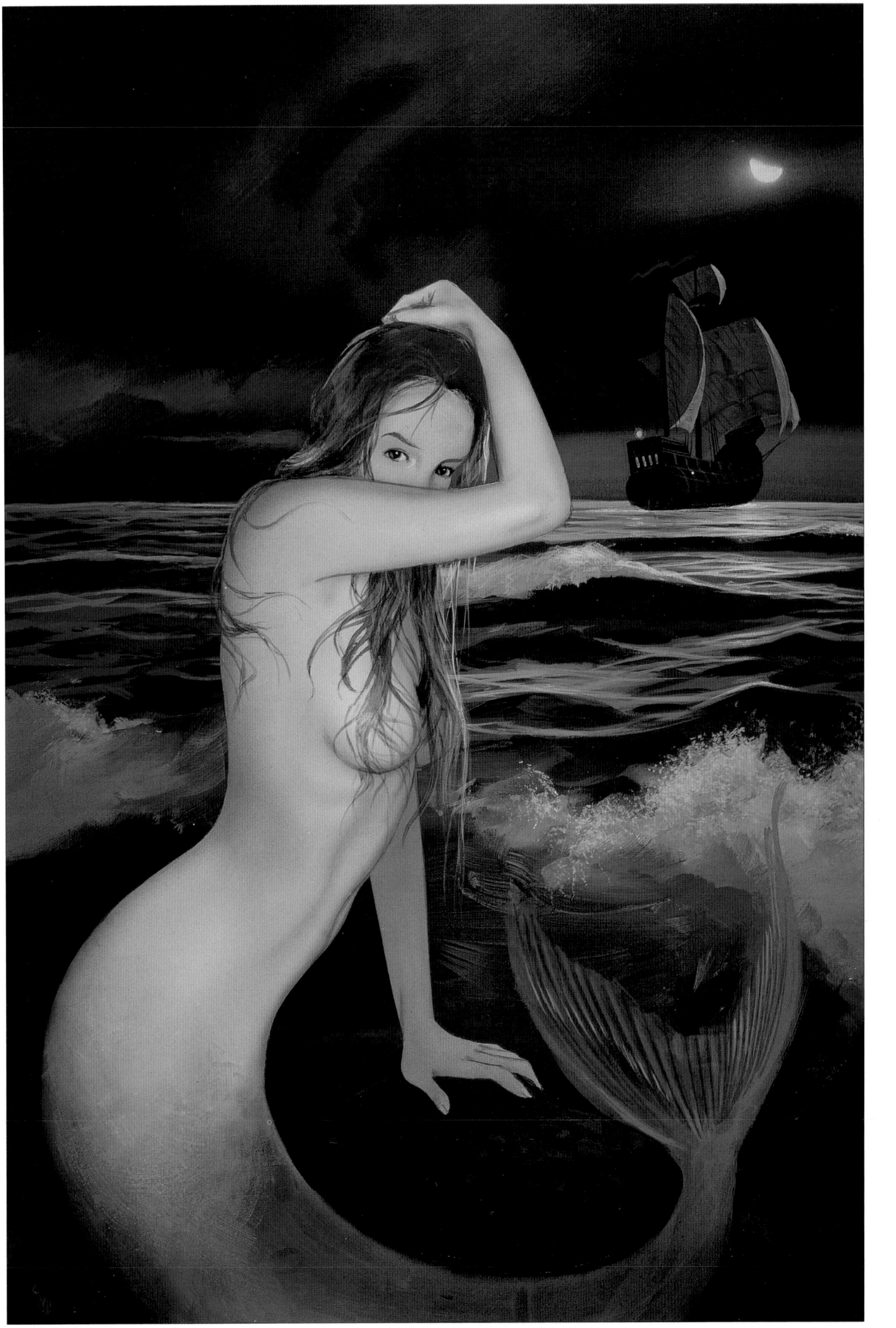

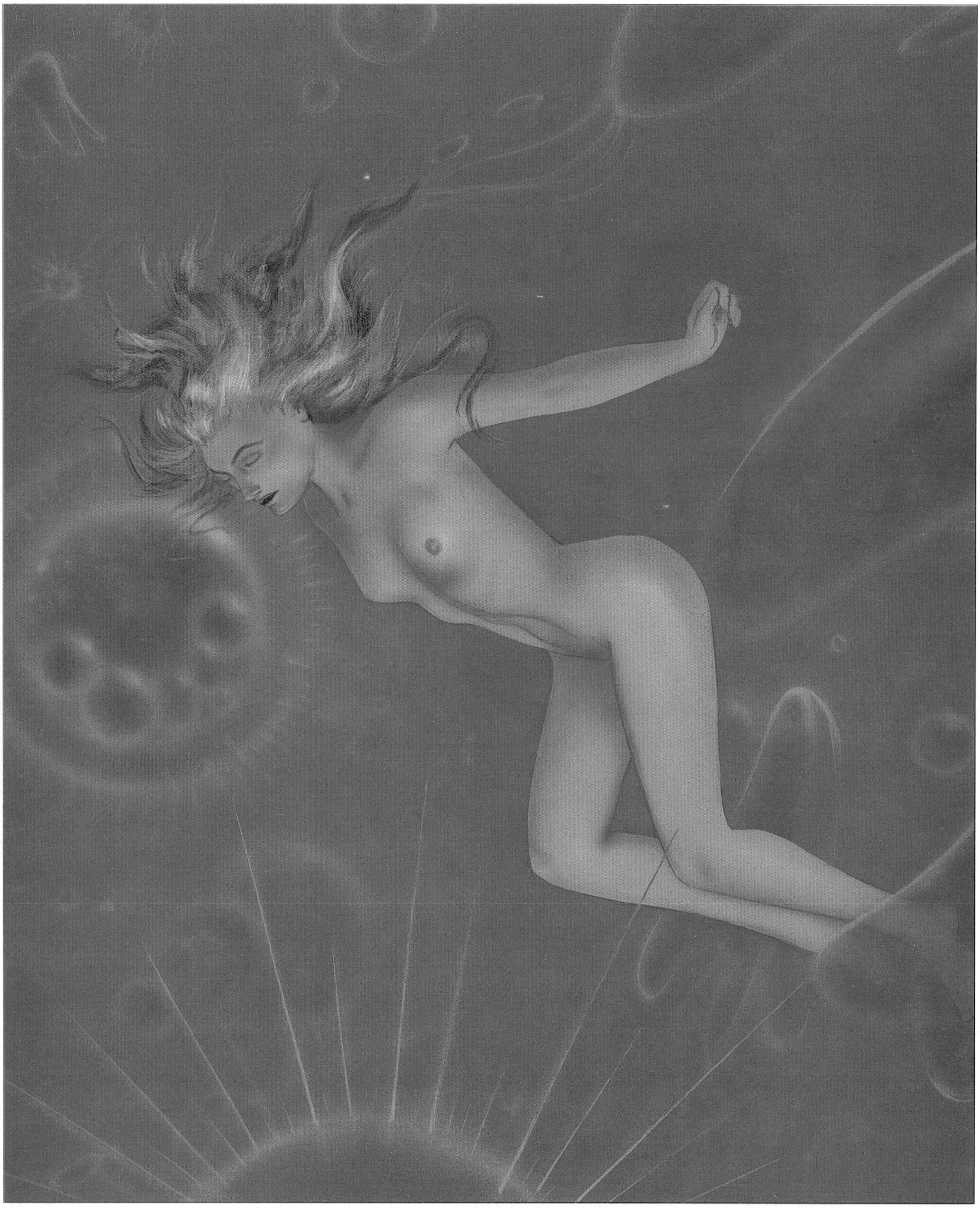

Animula (above)
('The Diamond Lens', Fitz-James O'Brien, 1858)
Animula may not be a heroine in any sense that the other women in this collection are heroic, but her story is perhaps the most tragic. A microscopic creature found in a drop of water by an obsessed, criminal inventor, her discoverer falls in love with her. Unfortunately, through his negligence, she dies when he allows the drop to evaporate.

Ayesha (opposite)
(*She*, H. Rider Haggard, 1887; also *Ayesha*, 1905)
4,000-year-old Ayesha, She-Who-Must-Be-Obeyed, the despotic Queen of Kôr, has remained alive and youthful via the incredible Flame of Life, while awaiting the reincarnation of her long-dead lover, Kallikrates.

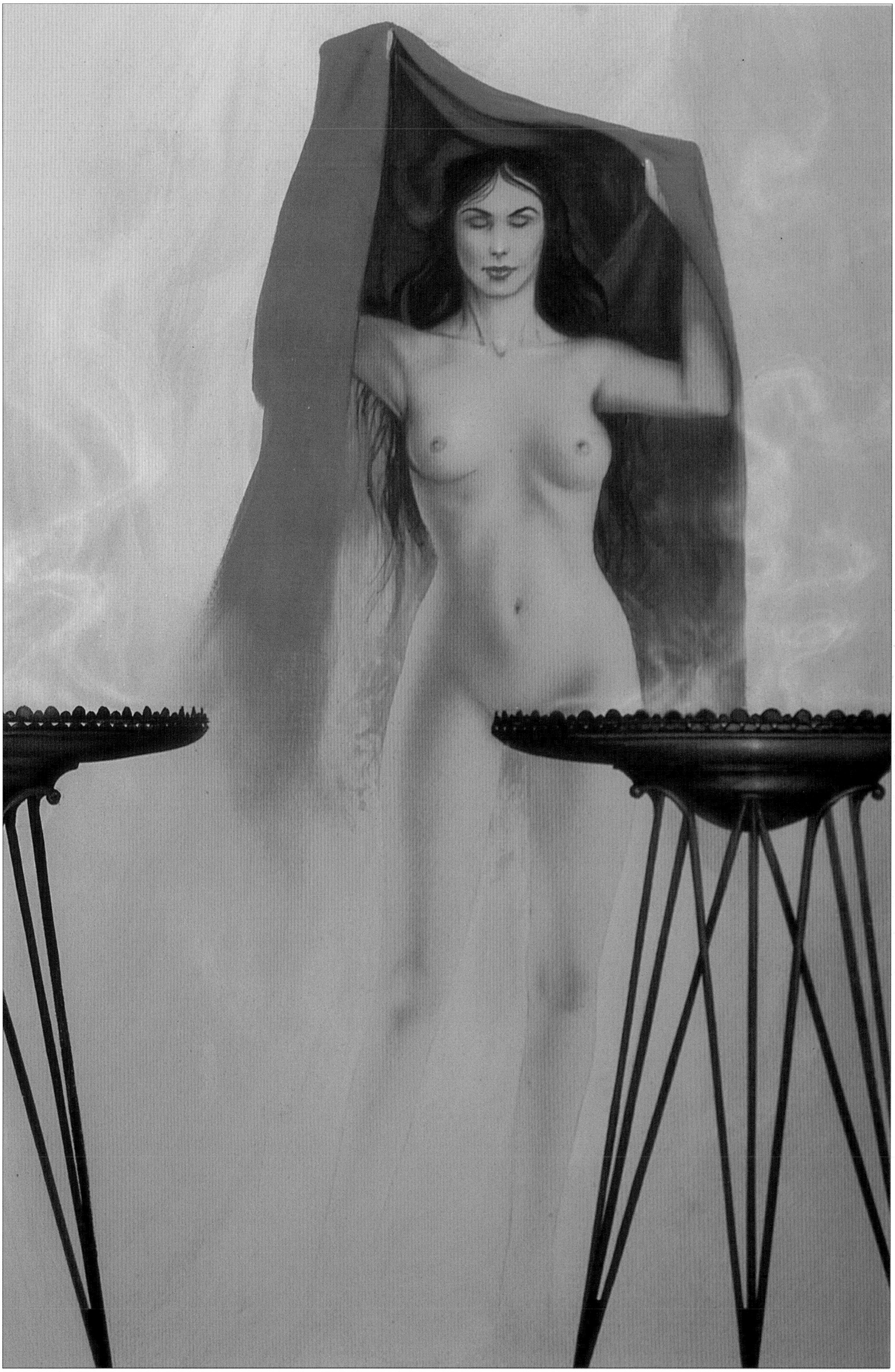

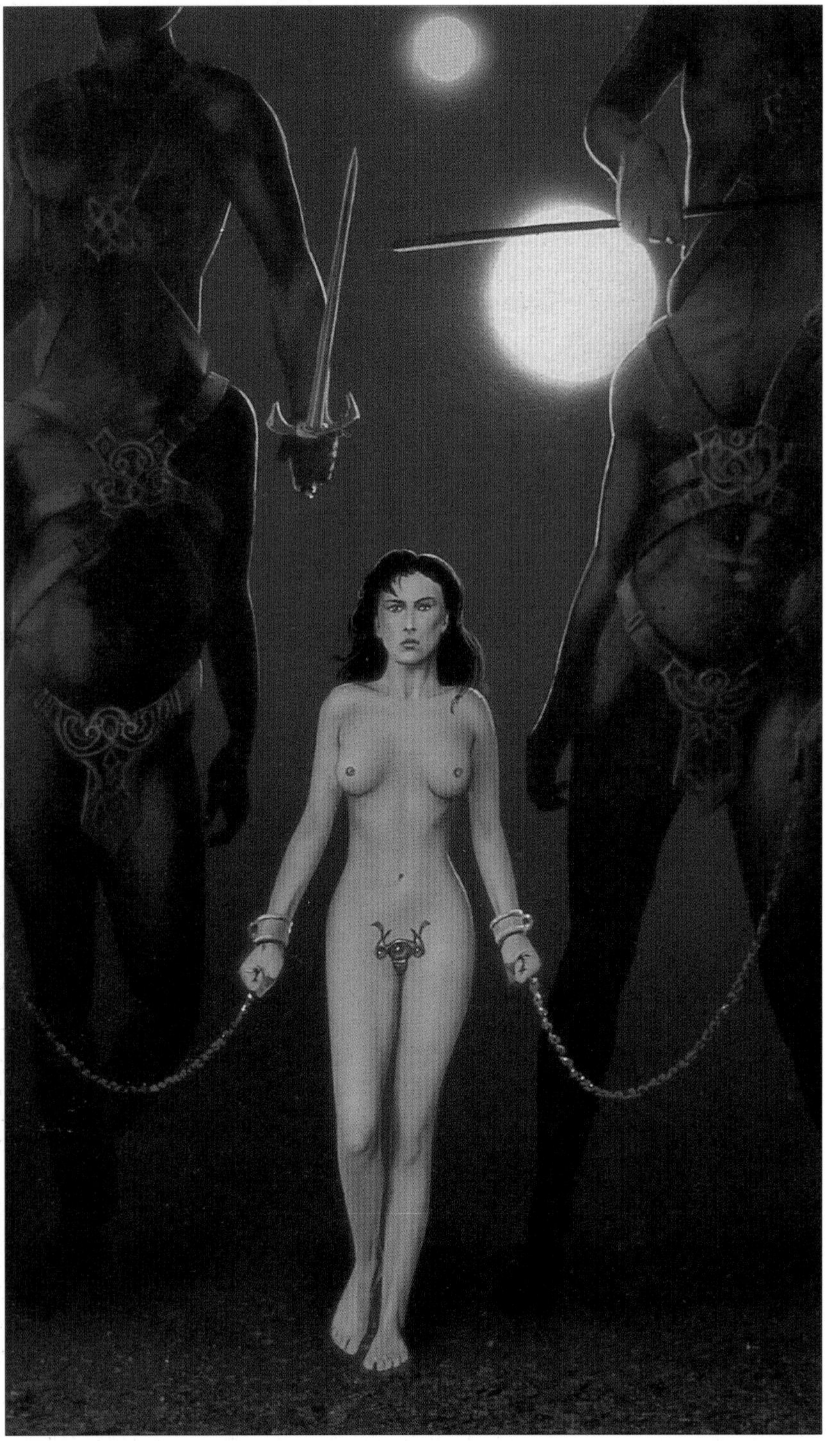

Dejah Thoris (left)
(*A Princess of Mars*, Edgar Rice Burroughs, 1912)
Dejah Thoris is the Princess of Helium, daughter of Mors Kajak and granddaughter of Tardos Mors, Jeddak of all Helium. Although often dismissed as existing for the sole purpose of being rescued by hero John Carter, she does indeed prevail in a number of adventures in her own right, such as when she sets out on a pilgrimage that takes her from one pole of Mars to the other.

Titania (opposite)
(*A Midsummer Night's Dream*, William Shakespeare, 1595-1596)
Titania, queen of the fairies, has turned poor amateur thespian, Bottom, into a jackass. Titania is the only fictional heroine to have a moon named after her.

acters, and ultimately Ustane becomes the victim of Ayesha's jealousy. A sequel, *Ayesha* (1905) introduces another strong female character, Atene, who becomes a rival of Ayesha's ghost for the love of Leo. Rivalry between women is not uncommon among characters in early fantastic tales; bonds of friendship or esteem are more rarely depicted.

C. L. Moore's character Jirel of Joiry, who first appeared in stories published during the Thirties, can be seen as a descendant of the female knight Bradamant. C. L. Moore (the initials stand for Catherine Lucille) was one of the first women science fiction writers to make a mark on the field; her heroine Jirel is strong, beautiful, skilled in the use of weapons, and capable of leading armies of men into battle. But along with such women as Robert E. Howard's Red Sonja and E. E. Smith's Clarrissa MacDougall, Jirel is one of a kind, with few ties to other women. In 'Jirel Meets Magic' (1935), two other female characters appear, but in the familiar roles of victim and antagonist,: Irsla is a dryad who dies when a witch, Jarisme, cuts down her life-tree: Jirel must defeat Jarisme with the aid of a crystal talisman given to her by Irsla. To show a heroine as someone without many connections to other females is not so strange, perhaps, for women depicted as extraordinary, except that male heroes were allowed to have male sidekicks, friends, colleagues, and comrades-in-arms. (To E. E. Smith's credit, he gives Clarrissa MacDougall and her four daughters roles of equal importance to the men in his Lensmen series, published in magazine form between 1934 and 1942 and in book form between 1948 and 1954. In fact,

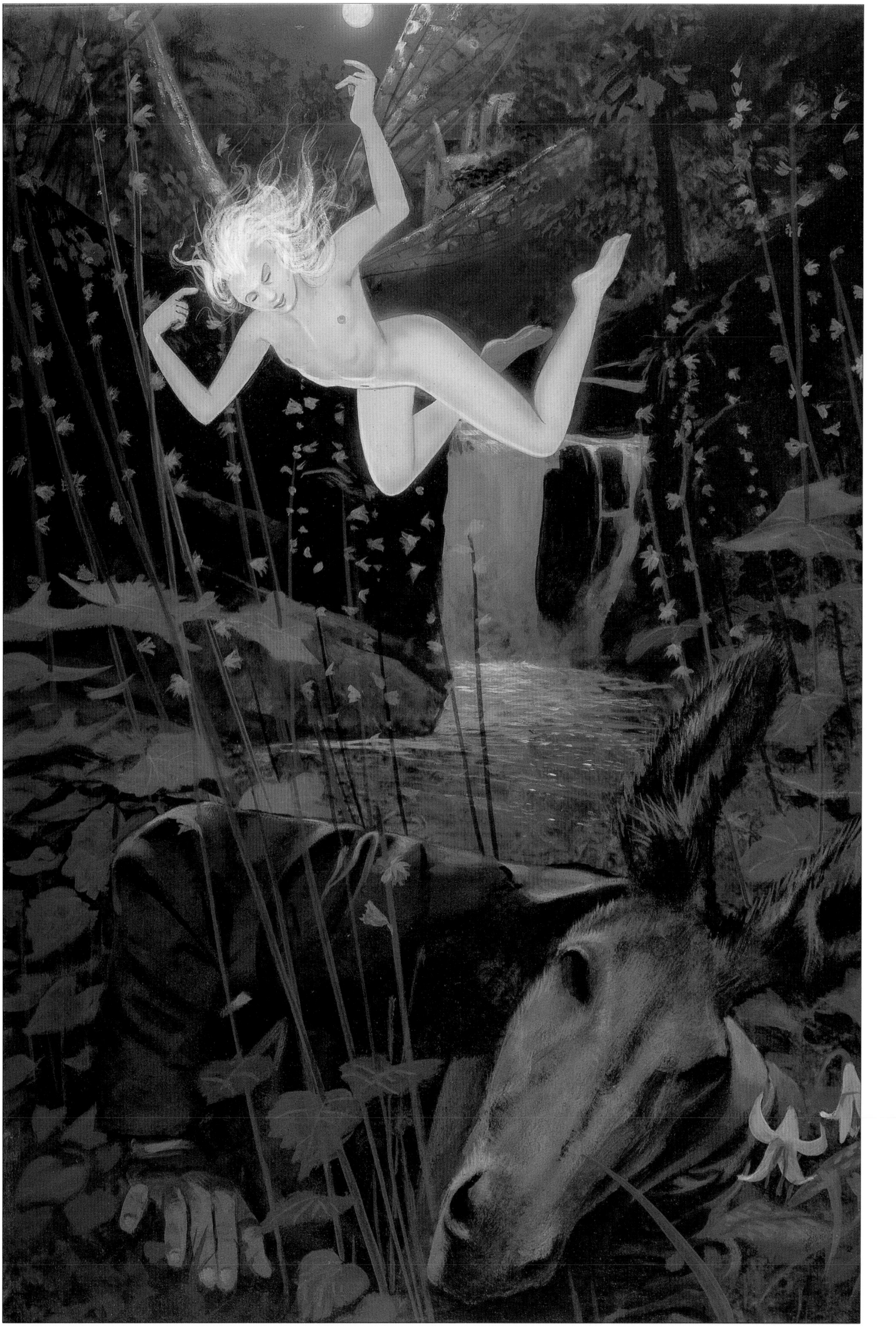

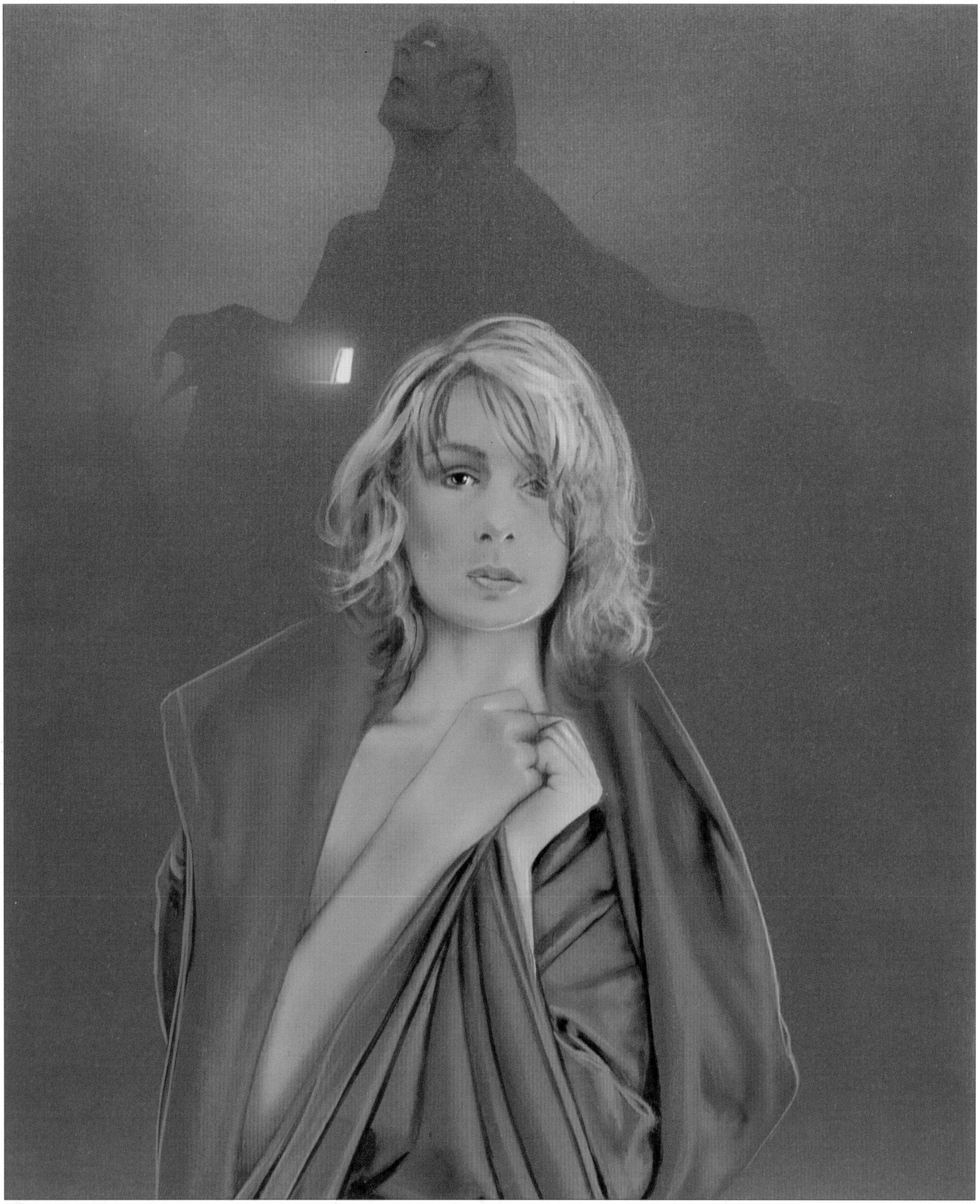

Weena (above)
(*The Time Machine*, H. G. Wells, 1895)
Innocent, naïve, elfin Weena, of the Eloi, is a pampered inhabitant of the world of 802,000 AD. Nevertheless, she is willing to abandon a life of paradisical comfort and luxury to confront and defy the horror of the troglodytic Morlocks.

Rima (opposite)
(*Green Mansions*, W. H. Hudson, 1904)
Rima, the Bird Girl, is discovered in the Amazonian jungle by vagabond Abel. She is unspoiled and wild, like the animals she lives with, knowing neither evil nor guile. This gives her an almost supernatural stature in the eyes of worldly Abel, who falls in love with her. But his dream ends tragically when Rima is burned to death by hostile Indians.

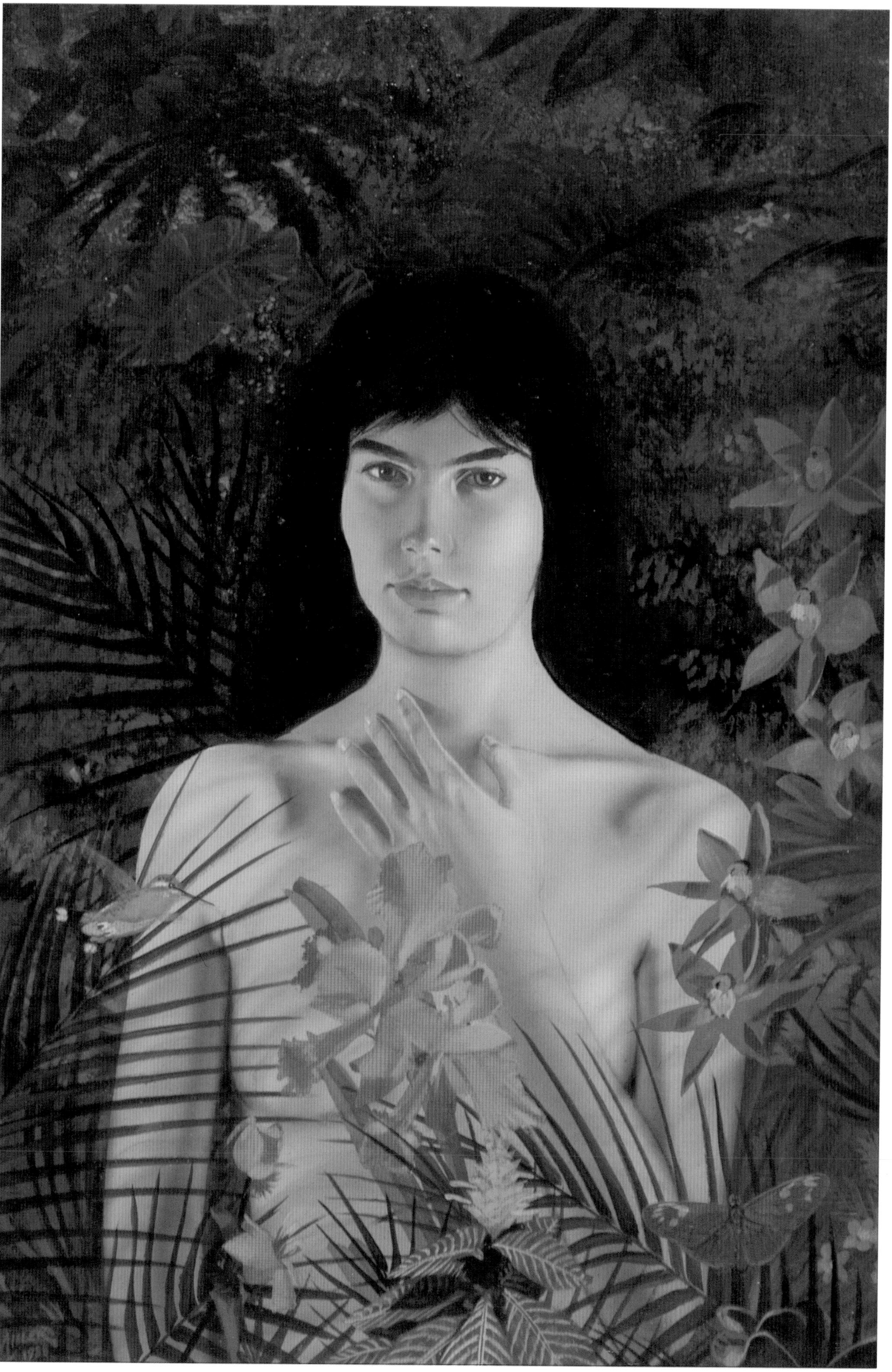

Clarrissa, along with her male counterpart, Kimball Kinnison, is the product of an eons-long breeding plan by benevolent aliens, the Arisians. She becomes the first female to wear the Lens, a device that is a partially alive entity attuned to only one being and which serves as a universal translator; Clarrissa is needed by the Lensmen to work with an alien matriarchy, the Lyranians).

However powerful the female characters in early science fiction were, the message often was that they were exceptions. The same was true for the male protagonists in many early works, but the unspoken assumption seemed to be that there were more such exceptions among men than among women. Female characters, however admirable, heroic, or awe-inspiring, often ended up suffering because of their superior abilities, the implication being that they might have been happier and better off had they been less exceptional. Ayesha loses her immorality and dies (she is, in the novel *Ayesha*, eventually reunited with her love, but only after death). After causing the death of

Naïs (above)
(The Lost Continent, C. J. Cutcliffe Hyne, 1899)
The barbarian girl Naïs is introduced in Cutcliffe Hyne's great Atlantean epic in an arena where she not only faces down a giant sabre-toothed tiger, but also manages to beat the monster – by chewing a bone into a makeshift knife with her own teeth – and make her escape – taking the ostensible hero of the novel with her. Ultimately, after more unbelievable adventures and travails, she remains one of the only two survivors of the cataclysm that overwhelms Atlantis.

Guillaume, a man she has regarded as her enemy, Jirel realizes that she felt some love for him after all (in 'Black God's Kiss', 1934), and regrets her deed; later, she must free Guillaume's soul from the netherworld where it is imprisoned, at great risk to herself (in 'Black God's Shadow', 1934). Dejah Thoris, the Martian princess of Edgar Rice Burroughs's *A Princess of Mars* (1912) and its sequels, is constantly beset by dangers from which John Carter, the hero (and eventually her husband) must rescue her.

Phorenice (above)
(*The Lost Continent*, C. J. Cutcliffe Hyne, 1899)
The warlike, despotic Empress of Atlantis, Phorenice, ultimately redeems herself heroically as civil and natural catastrophe overwhelm her empire. Originally a swineherd's daughter, she raised herself to her exalted position by sheer force of will and physical courage. She was as adept in the arts of war and the use of weapons as any man – and found herself – 'a mere slip of a girl' – leading troops into battle.

Two memorable early heroines of science fiction were created during the Thirties by Stanley G. Weinbaum, whose career as a writer was cut tragically short. After writing for little longer than a year, acquiring many devoted readers, and showing every sign of becoming a major figure in science fiction, he died at the age of thirty-three. Weinbaum was a pioneer in his treatment of aliens, creating alien characters who 'had their own reasons for existing', as Isaac Asimov put it, instead of existing only to effect the human characters as either a menace or as a benevolent force. It may be no coincidence that Weinbaum was also innovative in his treatment of female characters.

The eponymous heroine of Weinbaum's *The Red Peri* (1935), a female space pirate, has both male and female followers, although the women tend to resent Peri's marked ability to attract the love and devotion of men. Peri also chooses a life of freedom over the love of Frank Keene, despite her strong feelings for him. Black Margot, another of Weinbaum's female creations, who appears in *Dawn of*

Flame (1939), is intellectually gifted and immortal. Weinbaum had intended to write a series about the Red Peri, but his death prevented him from doing so. One has to wonder how many more heroines he might have created, and how much he might eventually have influenced science fiction's treatment of female characters.

Olaf Stapledon deserves mention here, although memorable female characters or, indeed, vividly depicted human characters of either sex, are not usually considered a stan-

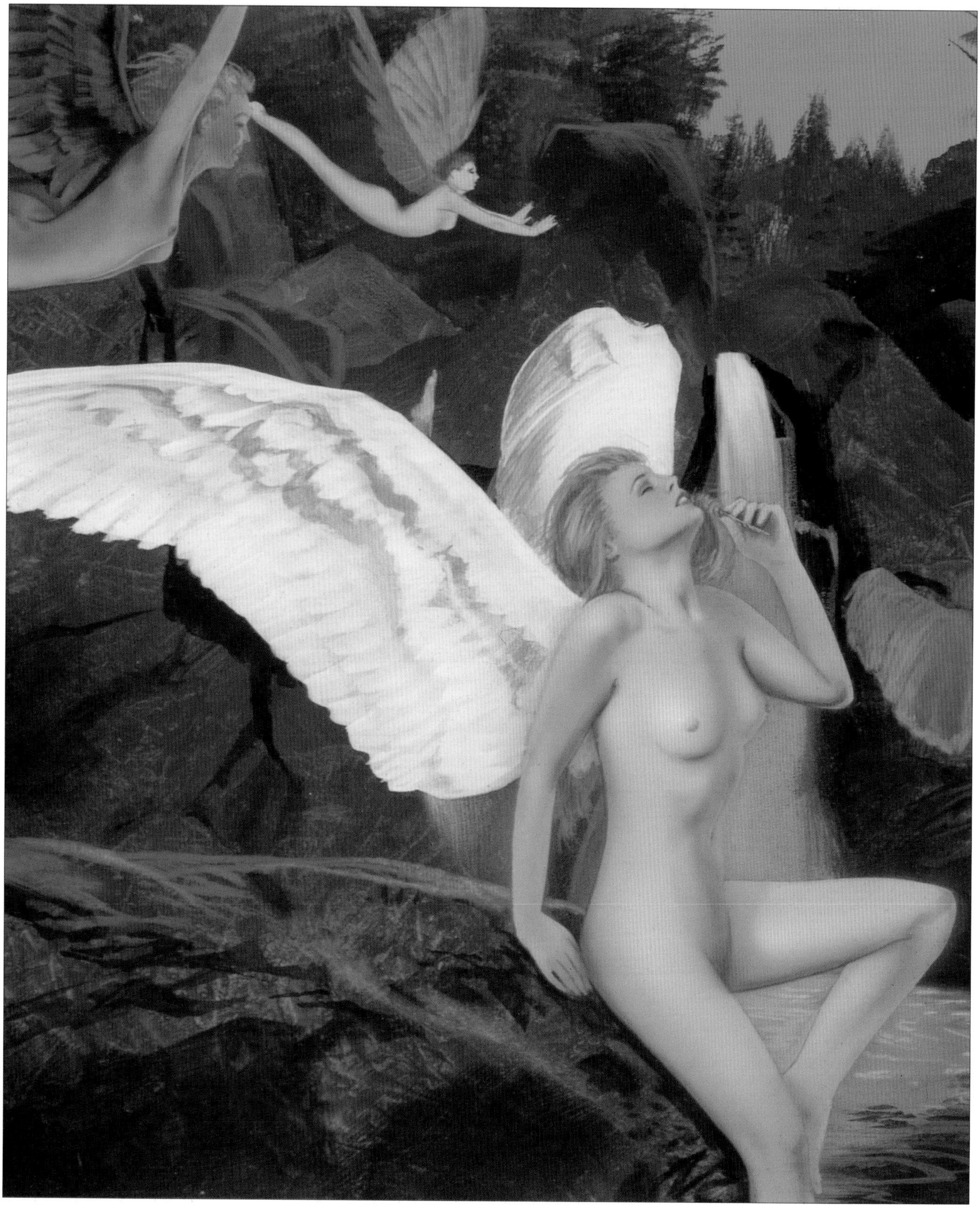

The Angels (above)
(*Angel Island*, Inez Haynes Gillmore, 1914)
The five nameless 'angels' – beautiful, nameless winged women – have always lived unmolested on their paradisical island. . . until the shipwrecked men arrive. Although three of the men respect the women in their own peculiar fashion, the others have different ideas. Eventually, resenting the women's freedom, the men mutilate them.

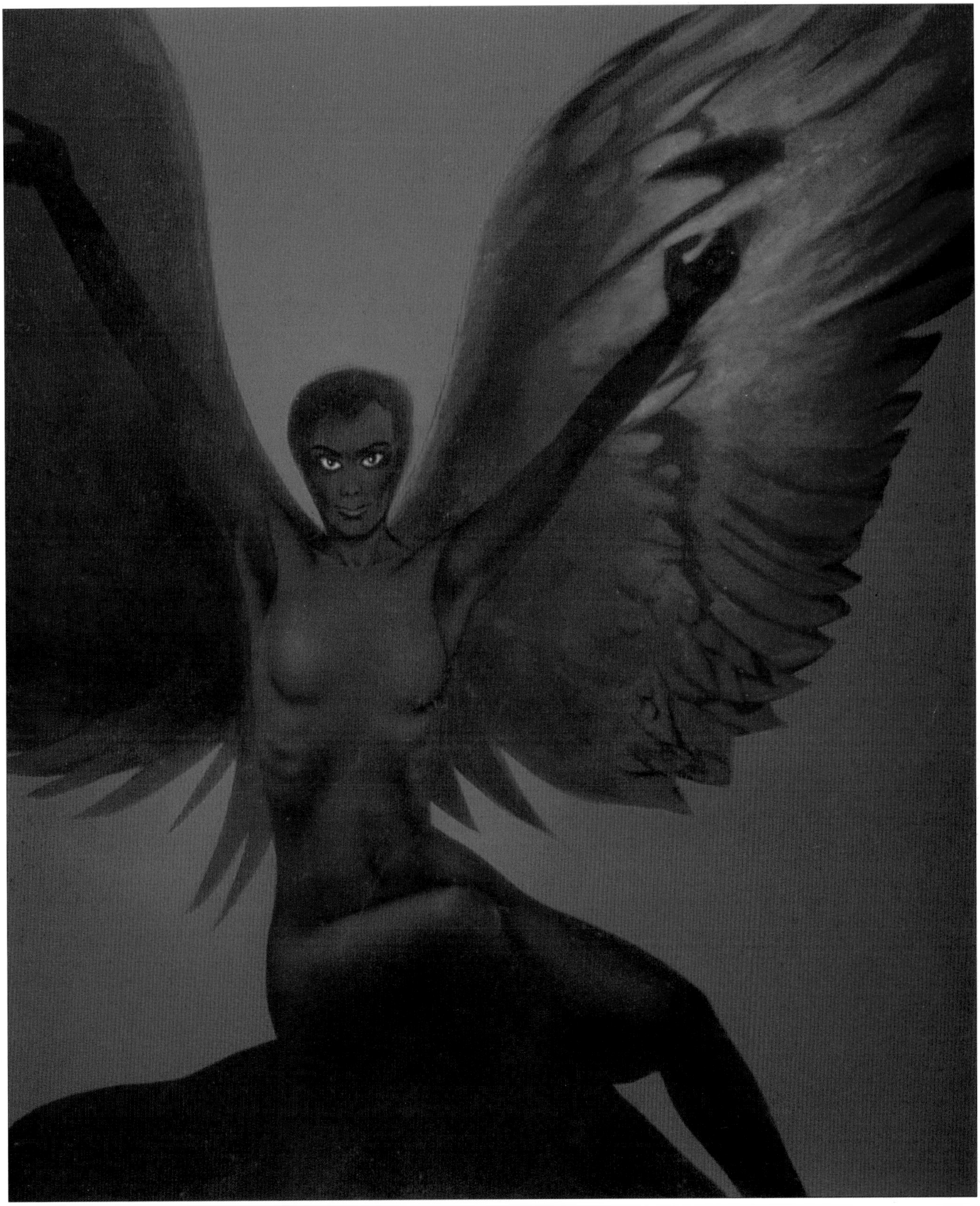

Yahnah (above)
(*The Bird of Time*, Wallace West, 1952)
Young Martian Princess Yahnah is suddenly burdened with problems of a magnitude that never faced any of her ancestors – the invasion of Mars by creatures from the earth – and the fate of her race and her planet depend upon her solution.

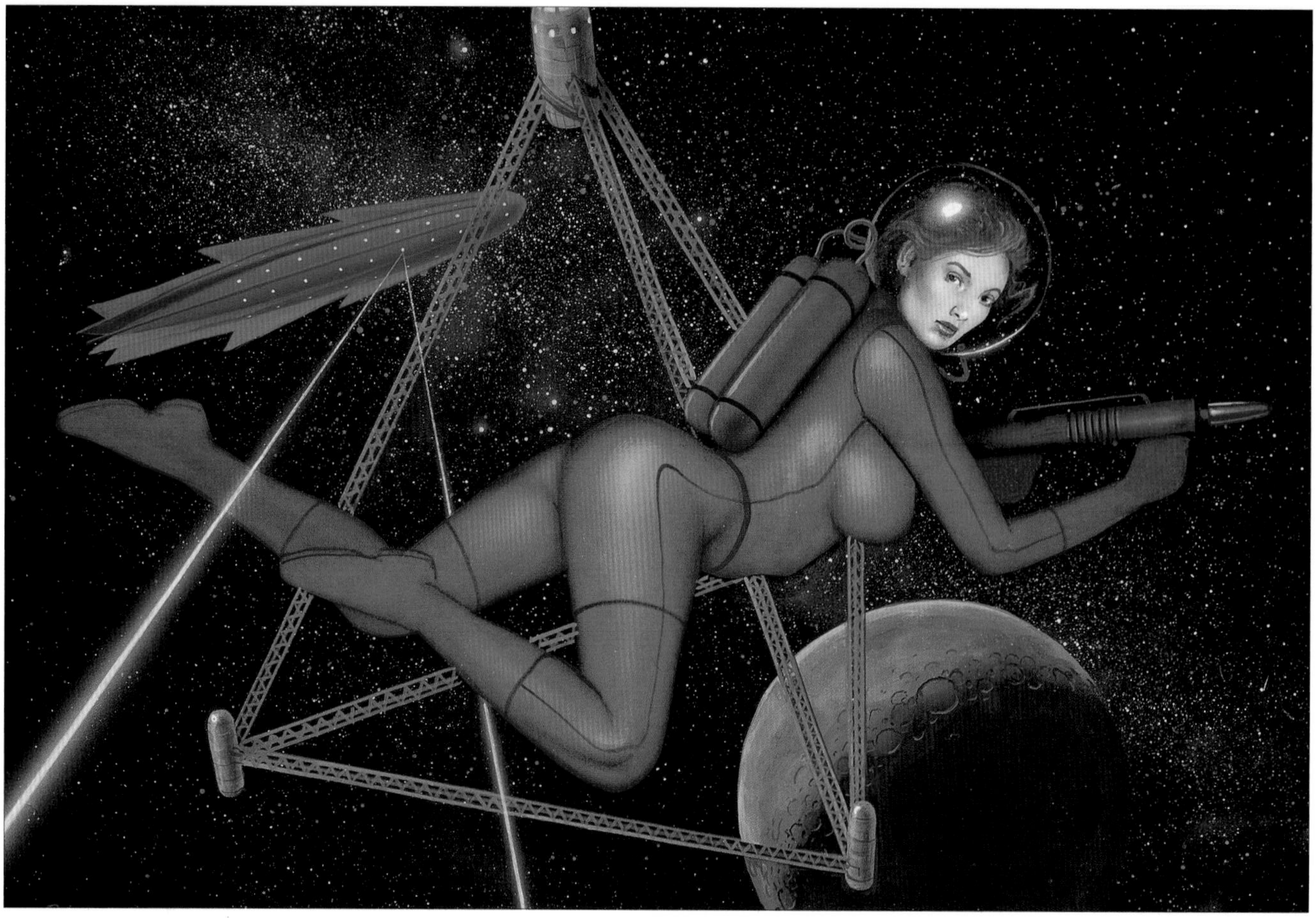

Red Peri Maclane (above)
('The Red Peri', Stanley G. Weinbaum, 1935)
Super-space pirate Red Peri is the scourge of the spaceways. She maintains a secret base on Pluto that is only accidentally discovered by a scientific expedition. The men are astonished to discover that the dreaded pirate is a woman – and a beautiful one at that.

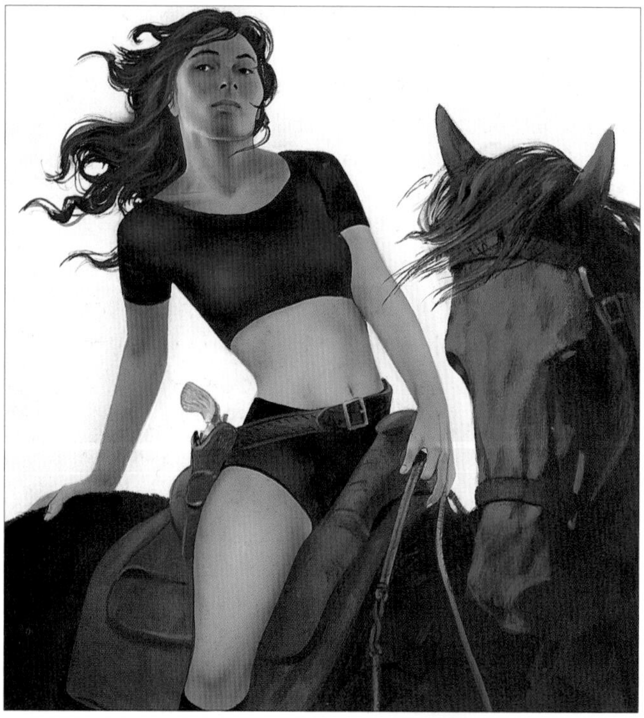

dard feature of his work. Trained as a philosopher at Oxford, Stapleton drew upon none of science fiction's pulp magazine tropes, preferring a cooler, more intellectual speculation about the future. He won critical praise for his novels *Last and First Men* (1930) and *Star Maker* (1937), which were notable for their cosmic scale and scope. Brian Aldiss, in *Trillion Year Spree* (an updated and revised version of *Billion Year Spree*, 1986), described reading Stapledon as being like 'standing on the top of a high mountain. One can see a lot of planet and much of the sprawling uncertain works of man, but little actual human activity; from such an altitude, all sense of the individual is lost.' In fact, Stapledon wrote close-up character-driven stories in his novels *Odd John* (1935) and *Sirius* (1944), as a contrast to his cosmic works.

Black Margot (left)
(*Dawn of Flame*, Stanley G. Weinbaum, 1939; also *The Black Flame*, 1949)
Margaret Smith, also known as Black Margot and Margaret of Urbs, is a bloodthirsty ruler. She was granted immortality by her scientist brother and as one of the only two such immortals, she leads an army of global conquest.

Adala (above)
(*The Face in the Abyss,* Abraham Merritt, 1923;
also *The Snake Mother,* 1930)
*The last survivor of an ancient race, Adala, the Snake
Mother, is custodian of secrets and wisdom far beyond the
achievement of humans.*

In *Sirius*, Stapledon created the memorable figure of Plaxy Trelone, the young woman who comes to love the sheep dog Sirius, who is part of an experiment and has the thoughts and perceptions of a human being. The love of Plaxy and Sirius crosses the boundaries between species. The realism and human detail of this novel offer a fine example of what science fiction could be in the hands of a thoughtfully speculative writer.

As the Thirties drew to a close, the influence of a new editor at one science fiction magazine was changing the way in which some science fiction writers approached their material. In 1937, John W. Campbell became editor of *Astounding* (later *Analog*) Magazine; among the writers he discovered were Isaac Asimov, A. E. van Vogt, Robert A. Heinlein, and Theodore Sturgeon. The critic Leon Stover, writing in the *St. James Guide to Science Fiction Writers* (Fourth Edition, edited by Jay P. Pederson, 1995) about Campbell's influence, asserts: 'Had it not been for John W. Campbell, Jr, science fiction as a publisher's category might have perished with the demise of the pulp industry. As editor of *Astounding* . . . he

demanded good writing and sometimes got it. That is his achievement.'

Specifically, Campbell insisted on realism in his stories, as well as better writing, and this was to have a profound effect on the genre. He fed ideas to his writers and insisted on what he regarded as sound thinking about the future and its possibilities. More realistic characters were preferred to the larger-than-life figures of the older stories; heroes were more often intelligent, educated, competent, and quick to resolve crises, rather than superhuman. This demand for realism also affected the ways in which female characters were depicted, although not always for the better. Realistic female characters, by the standards of the day, were more likely to be limited to traditional roles, since those were the roles most women played in real life. The world of science and

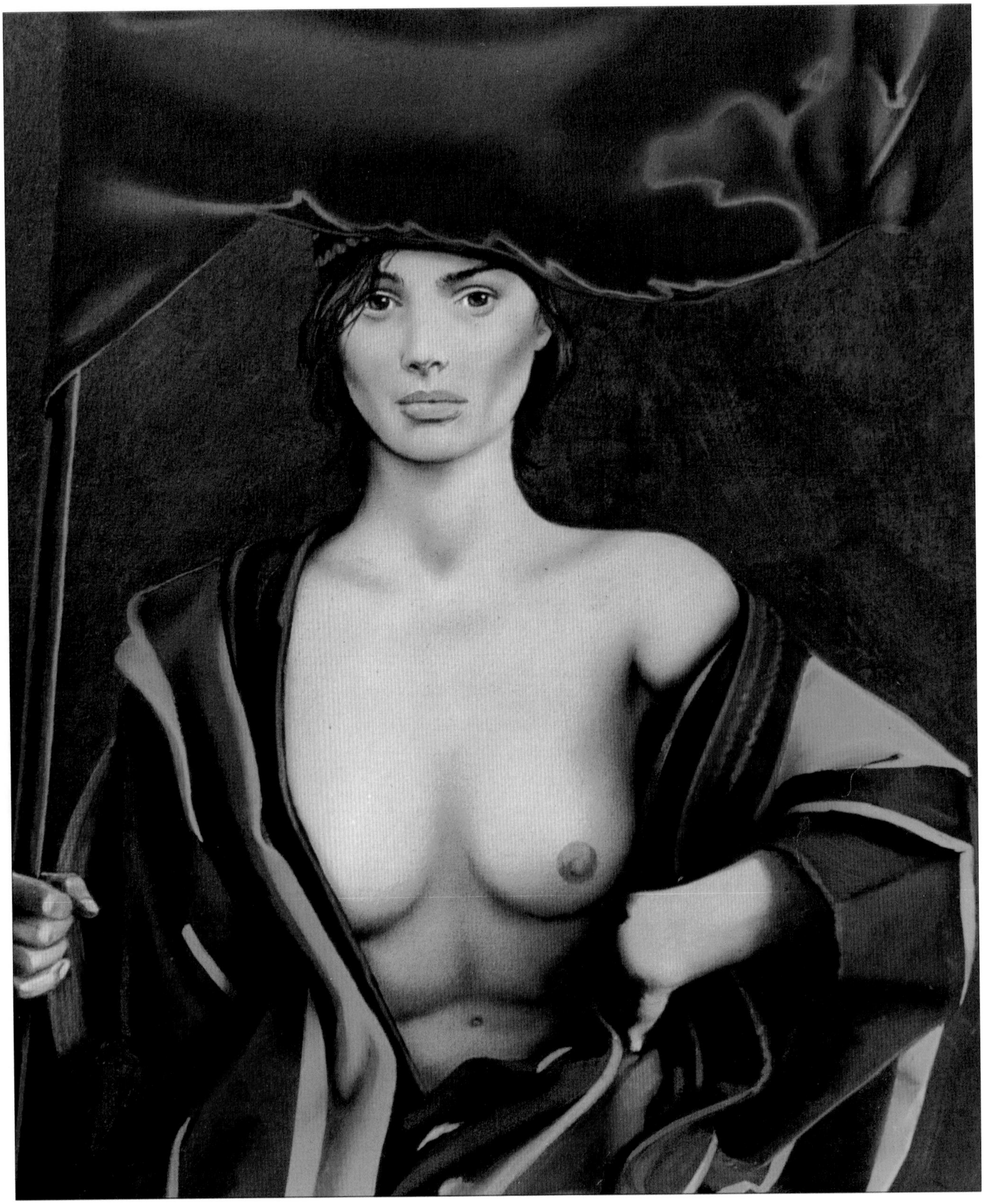

Antinea (above)
(*Atlantida*, Pierre Benoit, 1920)
Antinea, like She's Ayesha, is the immortal queen of a lost kingdom – in this case, the remnants of the city of Atlantis, buried beneath the sands of the Sahara Desert. All of her many scores of husbands are carefully preserved in a special sort of museum, all neatly labelled and numbered.

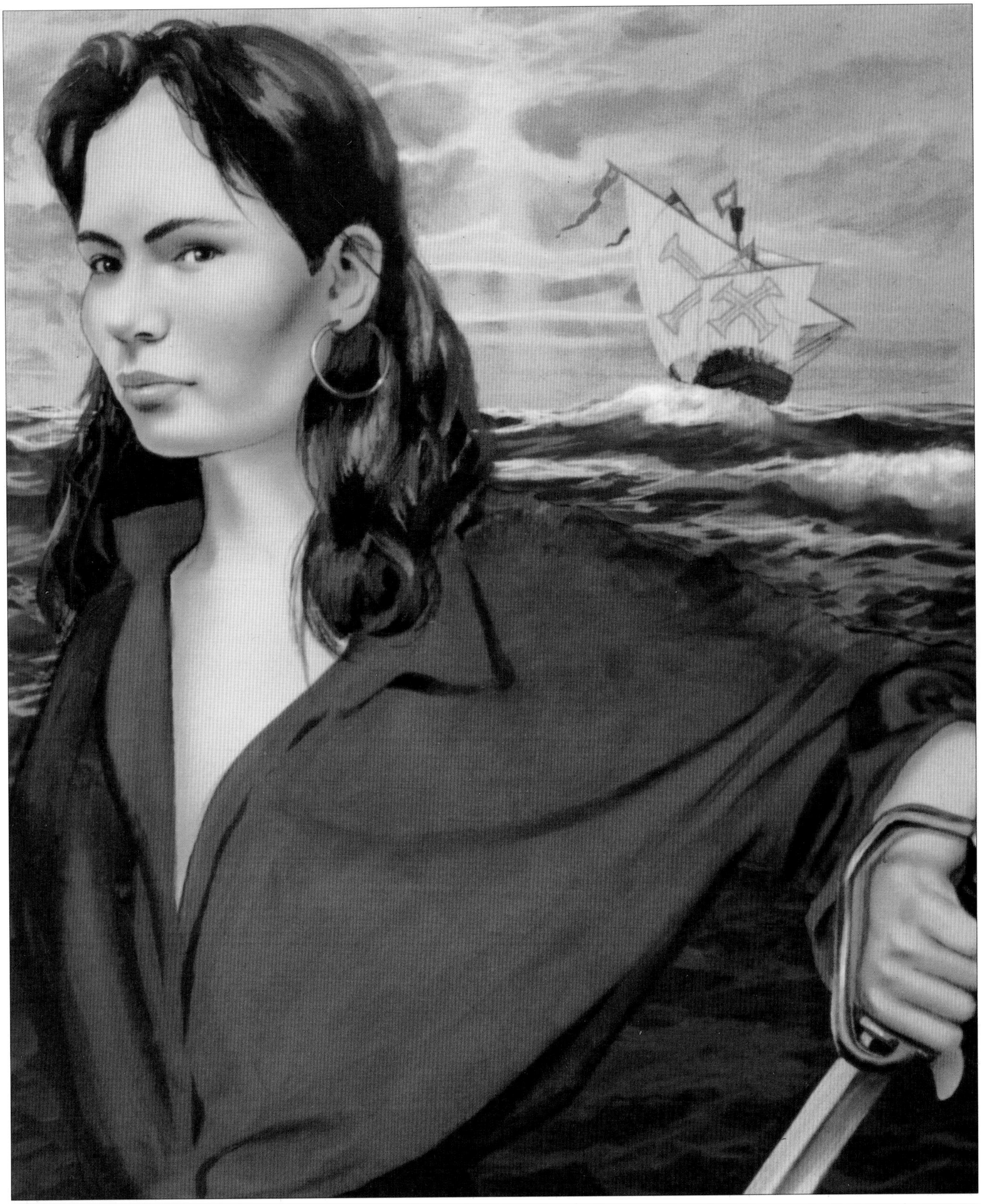

Captain Krista (above)
(*Pirate Queen of Venus*, R. Molnar, 1920)
Mistress of the shoreless world-ocean of Venus, Captain Krista discovers that she is an anachronism when Earth, which had long abandoned space travel, rediscovers her planet and she has to defend her way of life with centuries-out-of-date technology: wooden ships and cannons versus spacecraft and ray guns.

technology, then and (to a lesser extent) now, was seen as male territory.

Campbell also had practical reasons for wanting stories that would feature male characters. As Paul A. Carter reports in his book *The Creation of Tomorrow: Fifty Years of Magazine Science Fiction* (1977): 'In 1949 John Campbell tabulated three thousand reader questionnaires and reported that the typical *Astounding* reader by that time was "just over thirty" . . . he remained, however, overwhelmingly – 93.3 per cent – male.' Carter goes on to discuss the covers of science fiction pulp magazines; although they 'have a reputation for gaudy cover paintings that featured attractive young women struggling in the clutches of bug-eyed monsters … for the first four or five years, the magazines' covers all but ignored women as a possible subject.' As for *Astounding*, the early magazine that was to have the most lasting effect on the genre, Carter points out that a woman did appear on the cover of its

Patricia Savage (above and left)
(*Doc Savage* magazine – Pat first appears in 1934 and in 37 succeeding Doc Savage novels, with her last adventure in 1948)

'I don't want to be safe,' Pat said.

Pat Savage, cousin of the fabulous Doc Savage, comes by her extra-ordinary abilities honestly: by picking the right ancestors – at least according to her biographer, Philip José Farmer. Some of her more illustrious – and infamous – relatives include Sherlock Holmes, John Clayton Lord Greystoke, Phileas Fogg, Professor John Moriarty and Fu Manchu. Beautiful enough to be a fashion model, Pat operates a very chic and very expensive Park Avenue beauty parlour/gymnasium, 'Patricia, Incorporated', which she abandons at the slightest hope of joining her illustrious cousin in an adventure. Adept at handling almost any weapon, she habitually carries a nickel-plated six-shooter in her purse. She is accomplished at jiu jitsu, boxing and dirty street fighting; she is a pilot, fluent in sign language, Morse, French and Mayan, able to lip-read as well as being the ticketed captain of her own three-masted schooner: the Patricia.

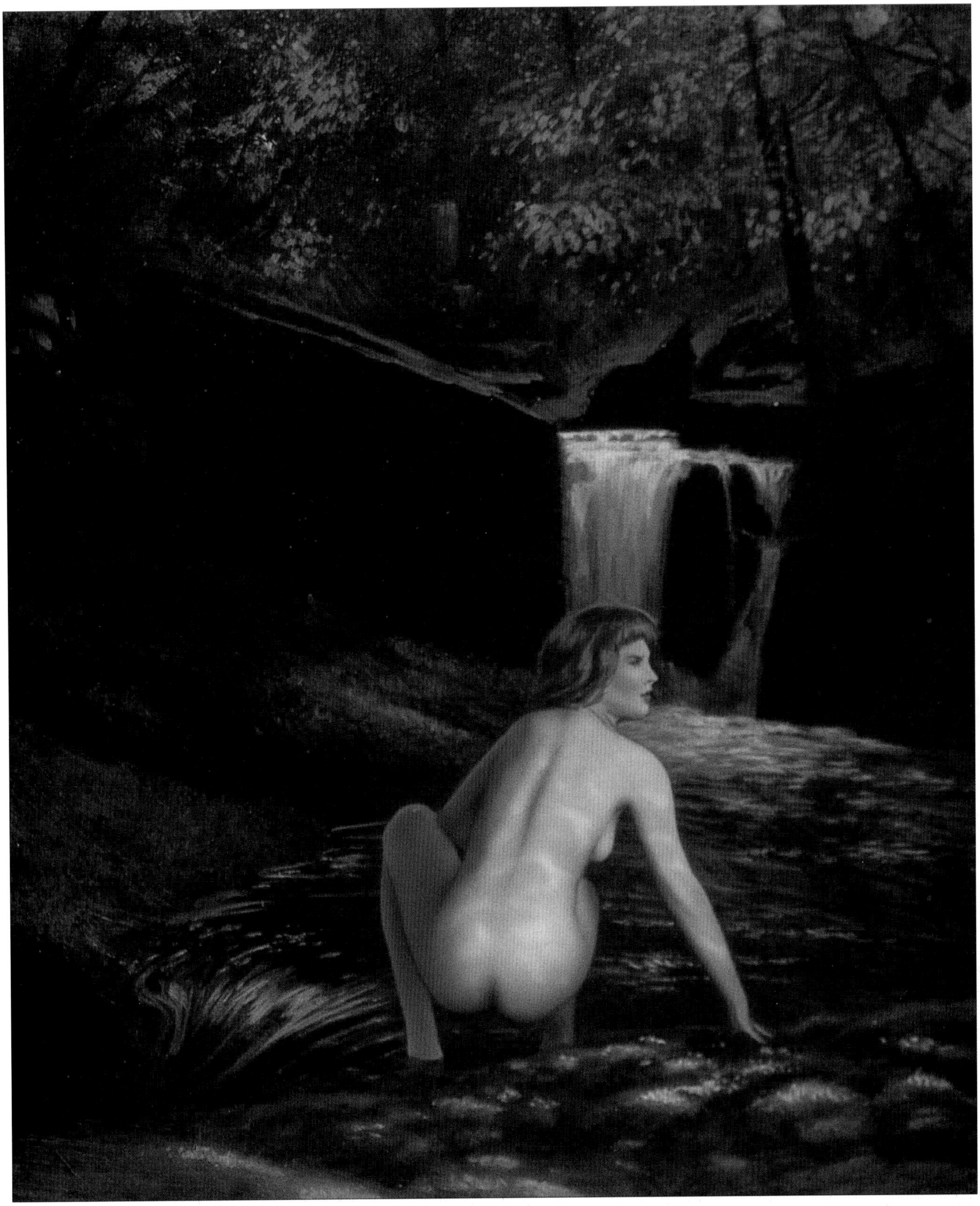

Marcelle (above)
(*The Island of Captain Sparrow*, S. Fowler Wright, 1928)
Charlton Foyle is thrown onto a mysterious island populated not only with pirates, but also with strange creatures that resemble the satyrs of classical mythology. Is the creature he knows as Marcelle a magical being, a dryad, or is she a human castaway, like himself?

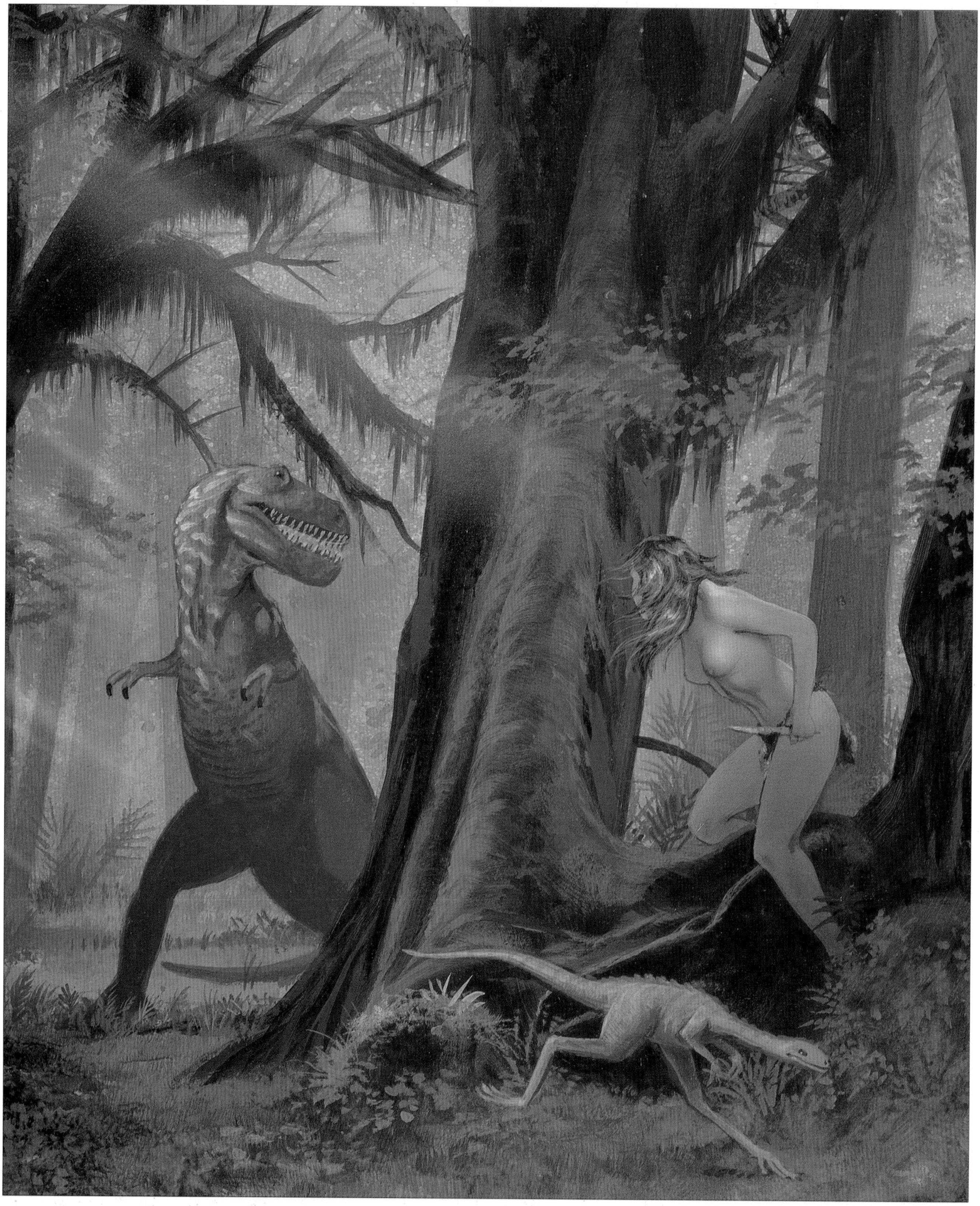

Dian the Beautiful (above)
(*At the Earth's Core*, Edgar Rice Burroughs, 1922)
Dian, Queen of Pellucidar, the fabulous, prehistoric world that occupies the interior of the hollow earth.

La-Ja (opposite)
(*Back to the Stone Age*, Edgar Rice Burroughs, 1936)
An inhabitant of Pellucidar, the aggressively hostile prehistoric world that exists in the hollow centre of the earth, La-Ja is only able to survive by the exercise of her intelligence, quick wit and strength – qualities she tries to encourage in Wilhelm von Hurst, the alien visitor from the unknown surface world.

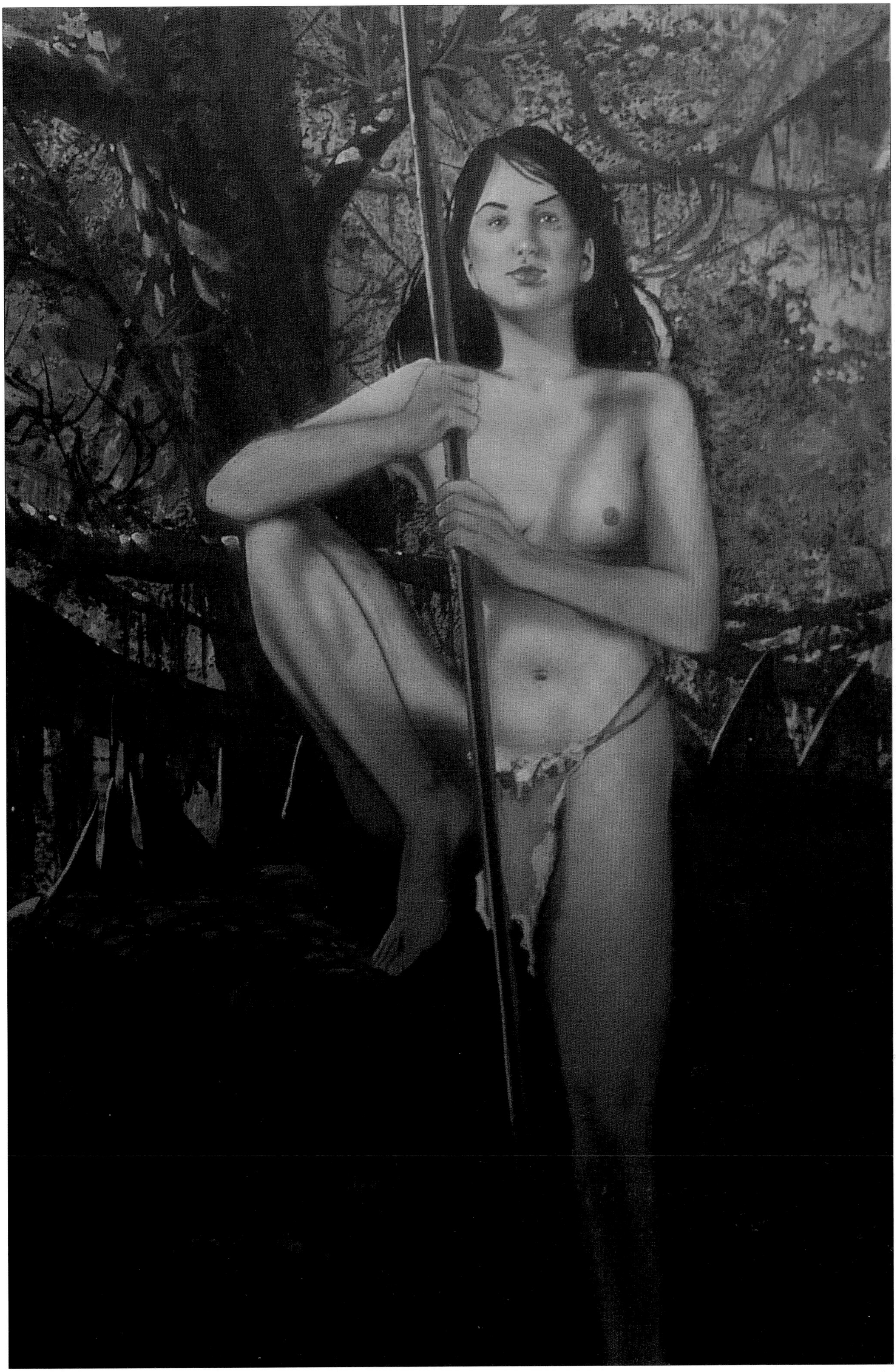

Norhala of the Lightnings (above)
(*The Metal Monster*, Abraham Merritt, 1920)
*In a fabulous city of metal beings who exist in geometrical
forms, the Persian woman, Norhala, has a mysterious bond
with the gigantic sphere that seems to control this city.
Only she can protect the explorers who have discovered
the metal metropolis.*

first issue in January, 1930, 'although in pictorial
interest she was a subordinate to a man and a
giant beetle. In December of that year, cover
artist H. W. Wesso introduced what was to
become science fiction's version of the eternal
triangle: the man, the woman, and the monster
all sharing space on the cover more or less
equally.' After 1933, the covers usually featured
alien landscapes and strange machines rather
than human figures; Campbell continued this
tradition while insisting upon realistic and
astronomically accurate cover paintings. As
Carter puts it: 'The message for the boys
seemed to be: look not to the other sex for
inspiration, but to the stars.'

It can be argued that such vigorous characters as Ayesha, Dejah Thoris, Sharane (of A.
Merritt's 1924 novel *The Ship of Ishtar*), and the

Red Peri were as much female fantasy figures
for their male creators as they were strong
female characters, while Jirel of Joiry can
appeal to female readers as wish-fulfilment and
to male readers as the kind of beautiful and
strong woman some men might fantasize
about dominating. Even so, these characters
could also be appreciated for themselves, and
were of heroic stature. The female characters
in more realistic science fiction lived smaller,
more modest lives, as did most of their counterparts in real life. Both the heroic figures and
the female characters who filled more modest
roles did have one feature in common.
They were perceived by a largely male reader-
ship as 'the other' beings who could often
seem to male readers to be as alien as
any extraterrestrial.

Sharane (opposite)
(*The Ship of Ishtar*, Abraham Merritt, 1924)
*Sharane is priestess of Ishtar, one of the two deities – the
other being the evil Nergal – that are at war on a great
slave galley divided equally between them, doomed to
wander the endless seas of its world forever.*

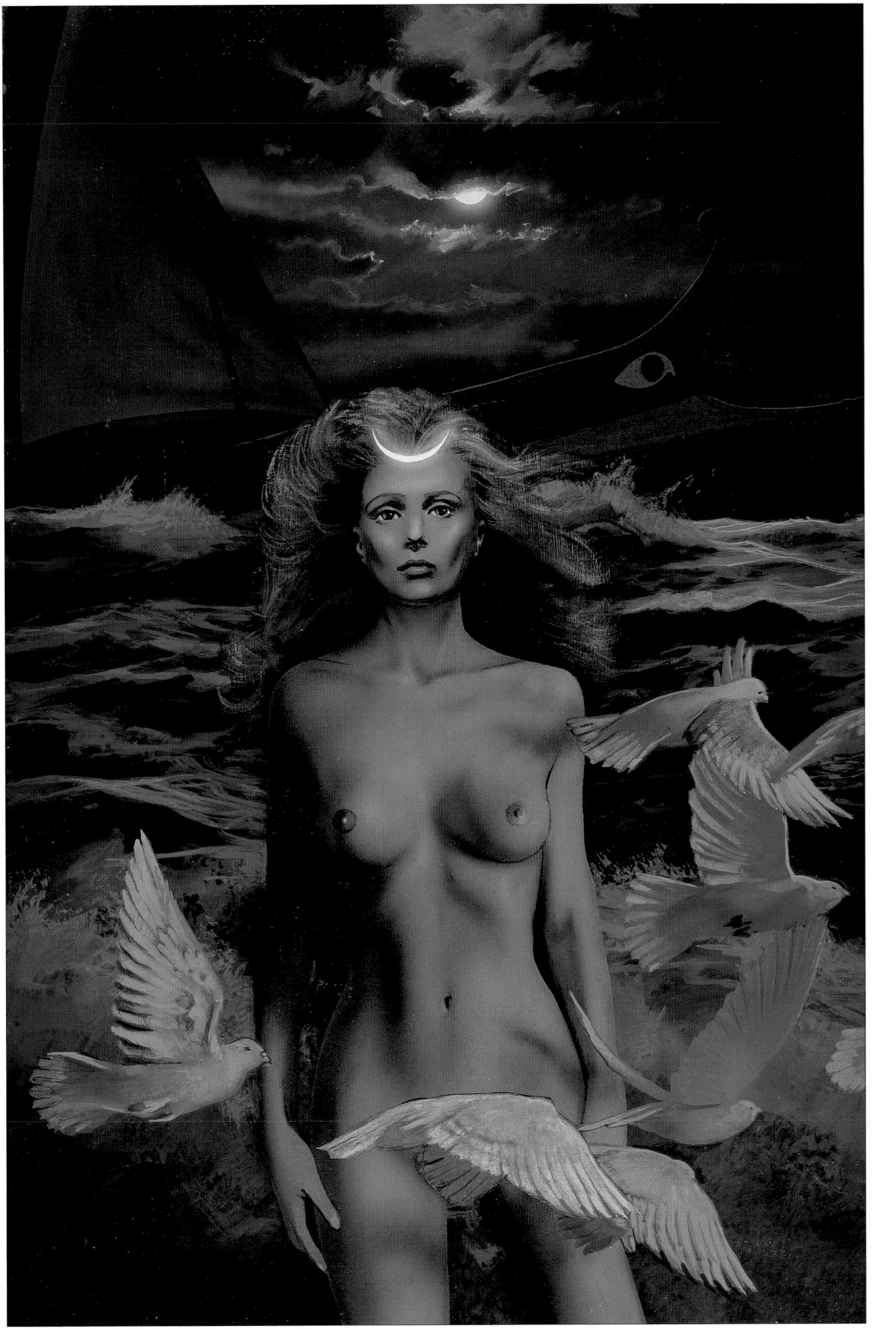

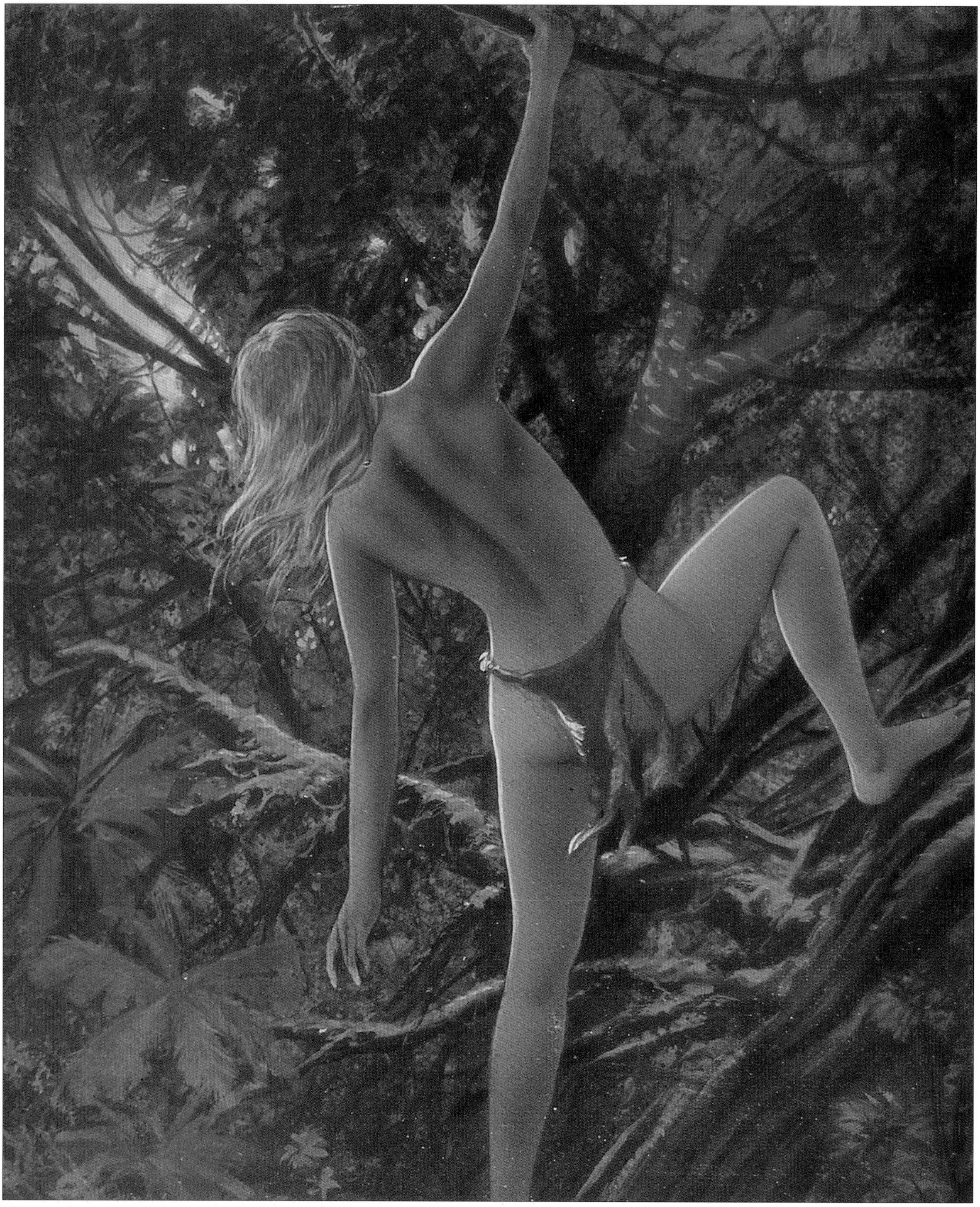

Jane (above)
(*Tarzan the Untamed*, Edgar Rice Burroughs, 1920)
Like her husband, Tarzan, but very much unlike the Jane sterotyped by countless motion pictures, she is perfectly capable of surviving the jungle entirely on her own. Starting bare-handed, she creates her own weapons, utensils and treehouse shelter.

Nadara de la Valois (opposite)
(*The Cave Girl*, Edgar Rice Burroughs, 1913)
When physical and moral weakling Waldo Emerson Smith-Jones is cast away on a desert island, his only companion is Nadara – a sort of female Tarzan. She had been marooned herself for nearly twenty years but has managed to flourish on her own. With her aid, Waldo not only survives but is transformed into a kind of Tarzan himself.

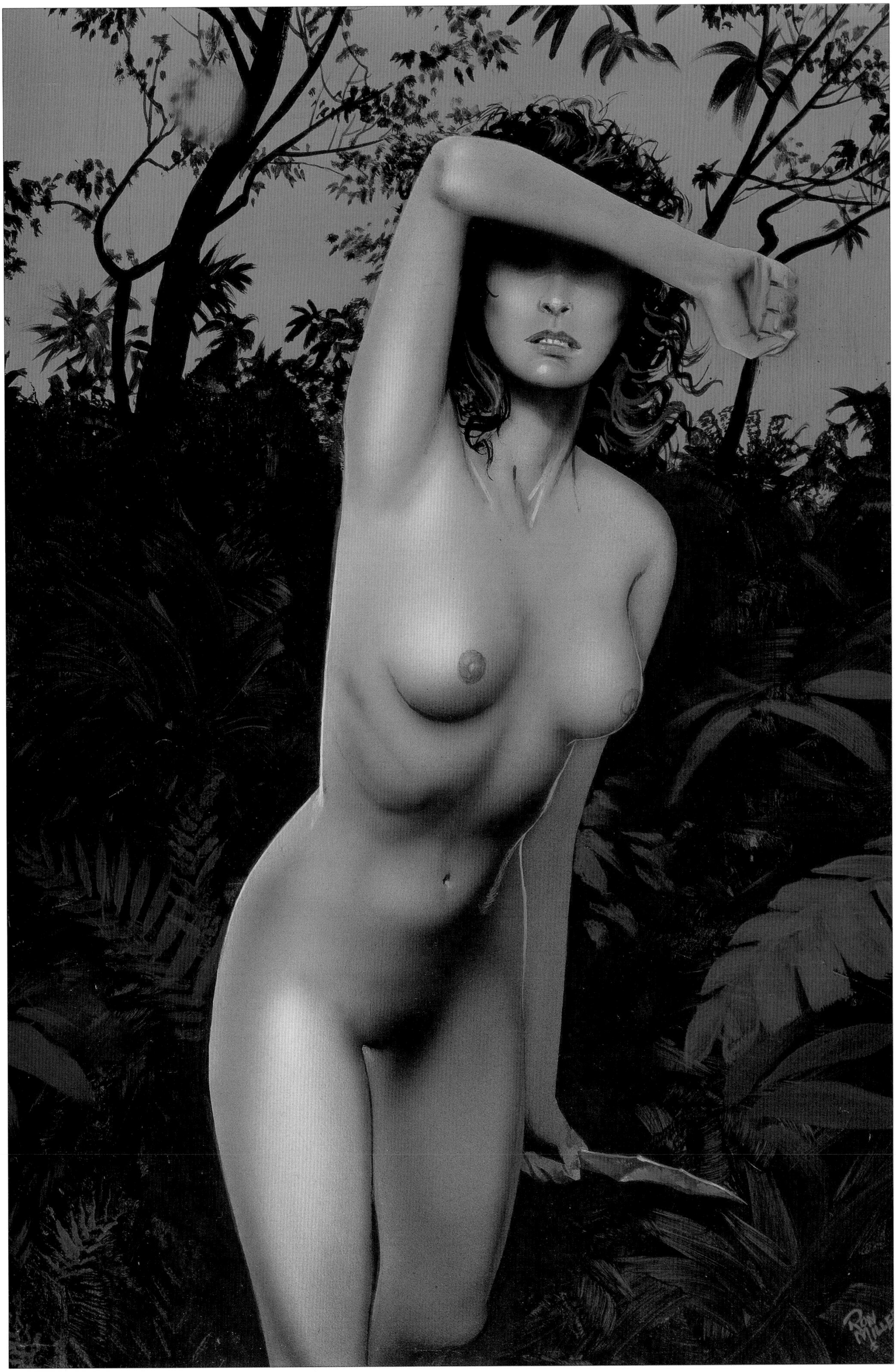

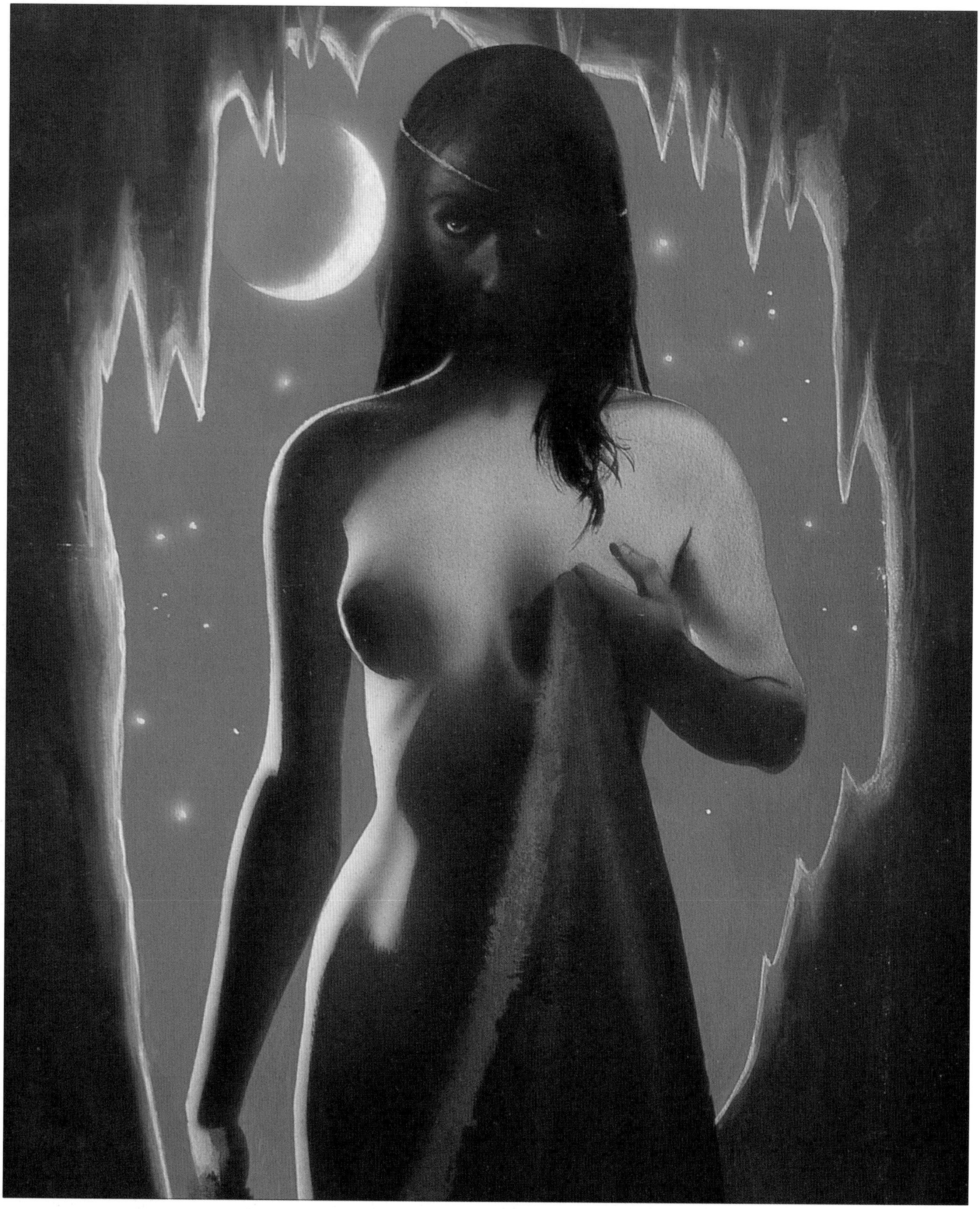

Evalie (above) and **Lur** (opposite)
(*Dwellers in the Mirage*, Abraham Merritt, 1932)
The innocent Evalie and the evil queen Lur represent opposite sides in a war for the domination of the weird extradimensional half-world that is the Mirage. To overcome the sorceress, Evalie must enlist the aid of earthling, Leif Langdon. Lur, on the other hand, believes him to be the reincarnation of Lord Dwayanu, the man she once loved and is now determined to win back.

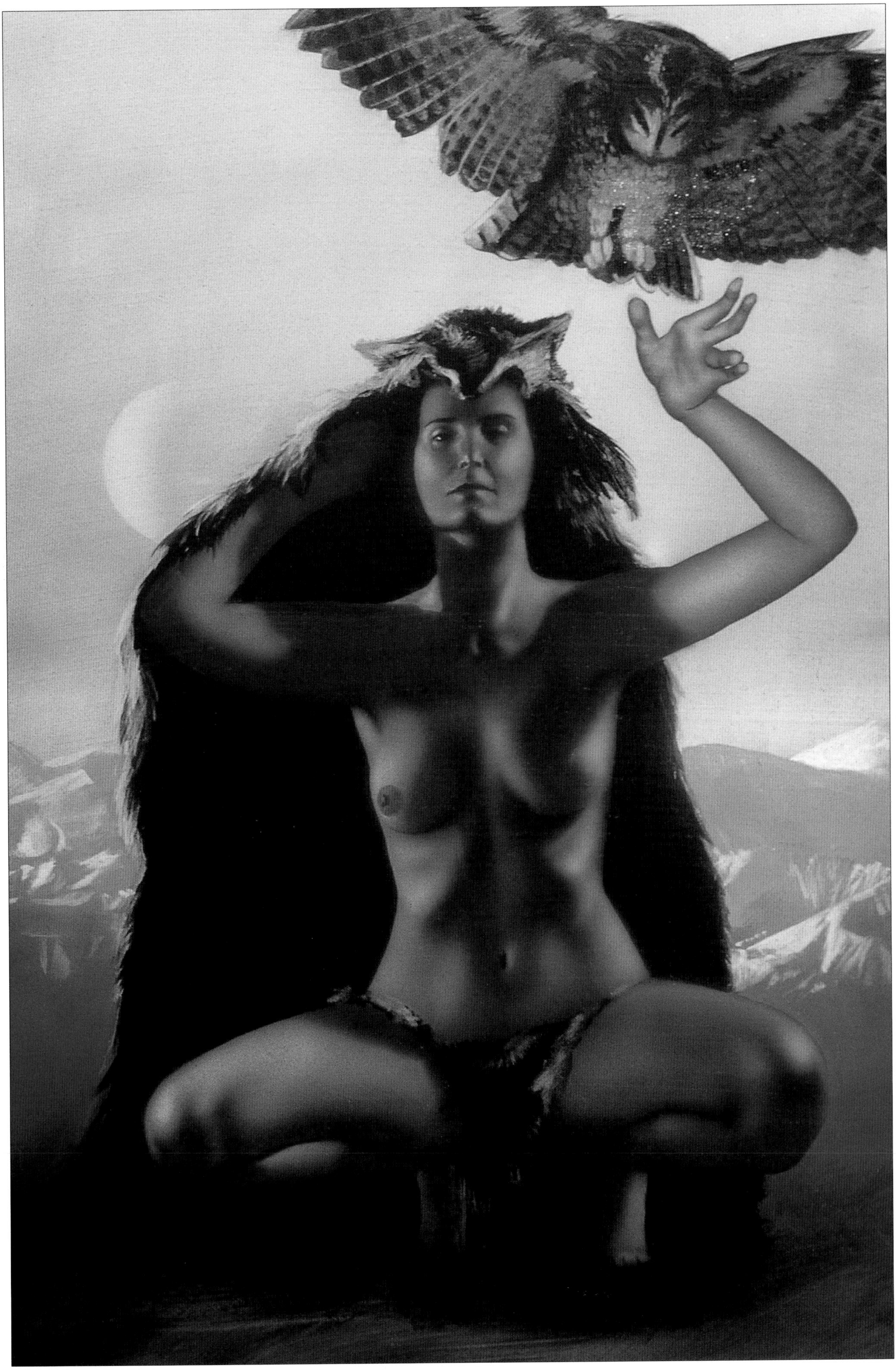

Shambleau (left)
('Shambleau', C. L. Moore, 1933)
The fabulously seductive invader from some unknown planet – she is known only as a Shambleau. She is a species of vampire – or vampires may be a species of Shambleau. Although she has human form, even that may be an illusion. Taking the appearance of human females, they draw nourishment from the life-forces of men, whom they first key up to the highest pitch of emotion. They give 'always, that horrible, foul pleasure as they feed. There are some men who, if they survive the first experience, take to it like a drug . . .'

Meg (left)
('The Priestess Who Rebelled', Nelson Bond, 1939; also 'The Judging of the Priestess', 1940 and 'The Magic City', 1941)
In a matriarchal post-apocalyptic world, Meg is a member of the Jinnia Clan. Her ambition is to become a Clan Mother and to this end she learns to read, write and cypher. She eventually sets off on a pilgrimage to see the Place of the Gods, the 'final secret' of the Clan Mothers to be revealed to her upon her successful return. After numerous adventures, Meg finally arrives at her goal – which proves to be Mt. Rushmore. Realizing that the nonsensical seperation of the sexes is destroying the race, she decides to dedicate herself to a reconciliation.

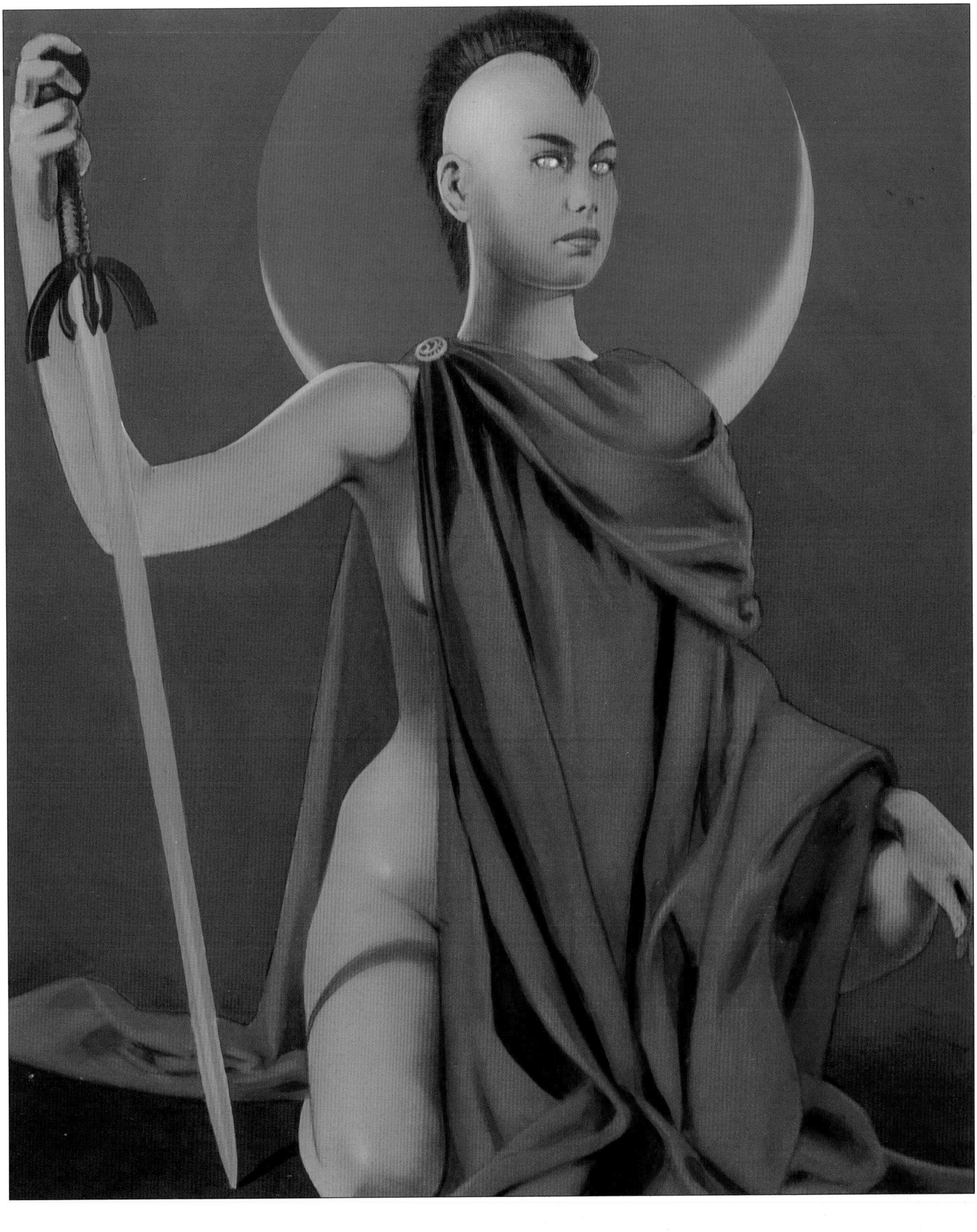

Iroedh (above)
(*Rogue Queen*, L. Sprague de Camp, 1951)
Iroedh is a worker – a neuter female – in the social/sexual culture of her planet – which has an organization not unlike that of the terrestrial honeybee. Against her will, Iroedh – until now a passive dreamer – becomes the 'Rogue Queen' prophesied by the Oracle of Ledhwid. She is told that she must unite her planet by becoming its conqueror.

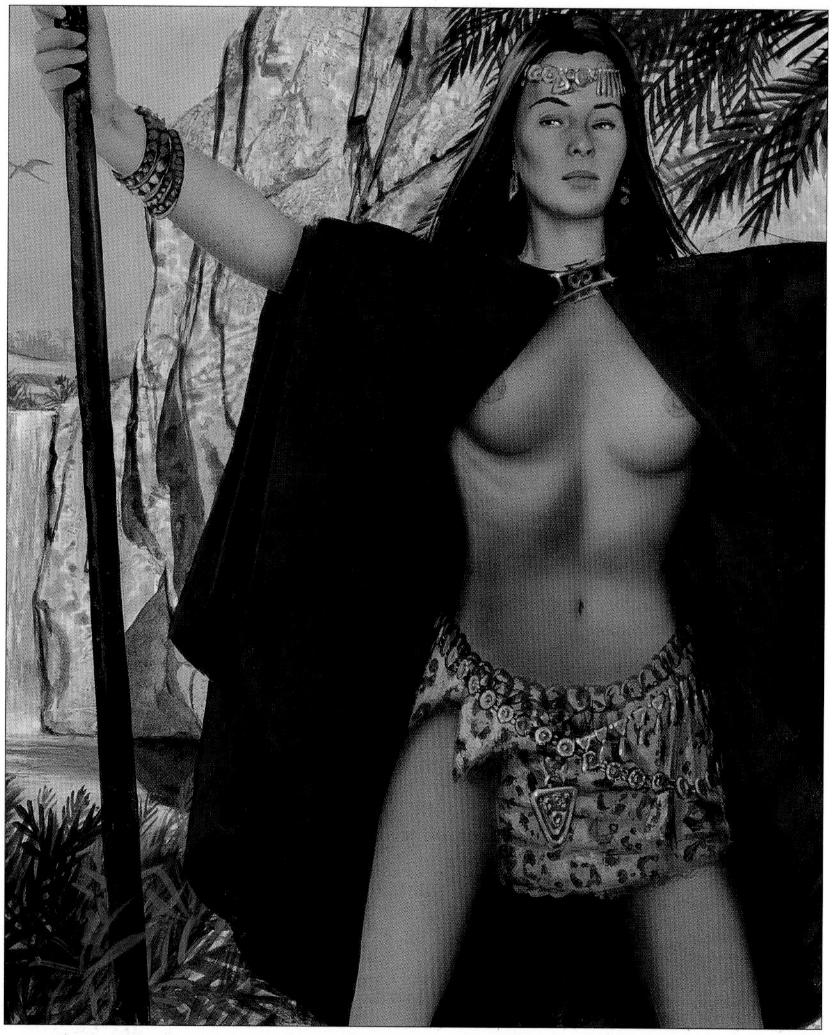

La of Opar (left)
(*The Return of Tarzan*, Edgar Rice Burroughs, 1915)
La is high priestess of the Temple of the Sun in the lost African city of Opar. The colonists are reduced to a small number living in the ruins of the once-mighty city, served by the half-human apes. Indeed, because of human-ape interbreeding, most of the Oparian men have reverted to this semi-animal condition – while the women of Opar have remained human.

Tiger Lily & Tinkerbell (opposite)
(*Peter Pan*, J. M. Barrie, 1904)
Indian princess Tiger Lily leads her tribe of warriors in defence of Peter Pan – and the fairy Tinkerbell – whose envy almost leads Peter to his death – ultimately sacrifices her life to save him.

Rhoda (below)
(*The Moon Maker*, Arthur Train & Robert W. Wood, 1916)
Plucky Professor Rhoda Gibbs is one of the first female astronauts in science fiction history. To the horror of her friends, she insists upon joining the crew of an atomic-powered spaceship and is ultimately instrumental in the success of its mission: diverting an asteroid that is on a collision course with the earth.

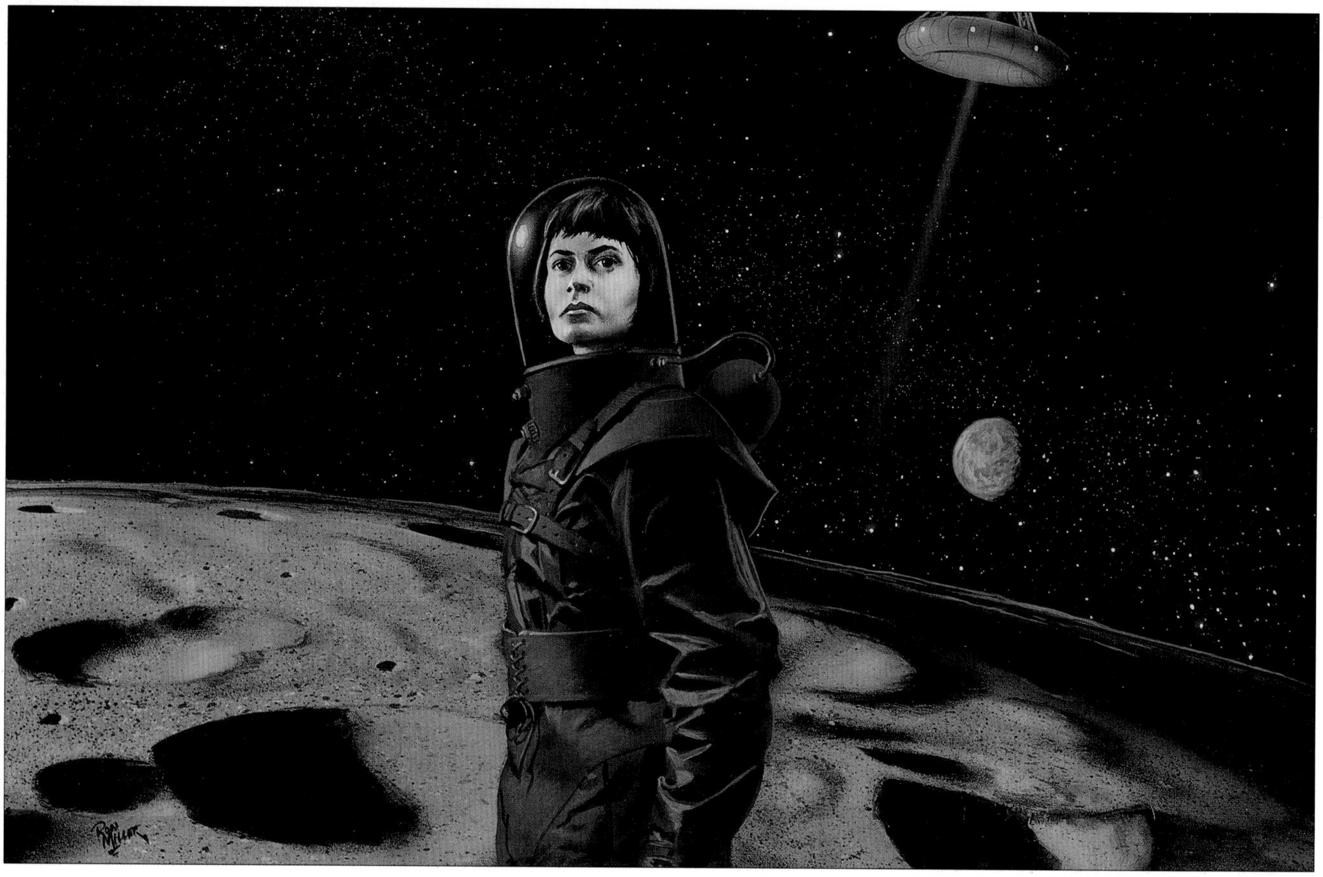

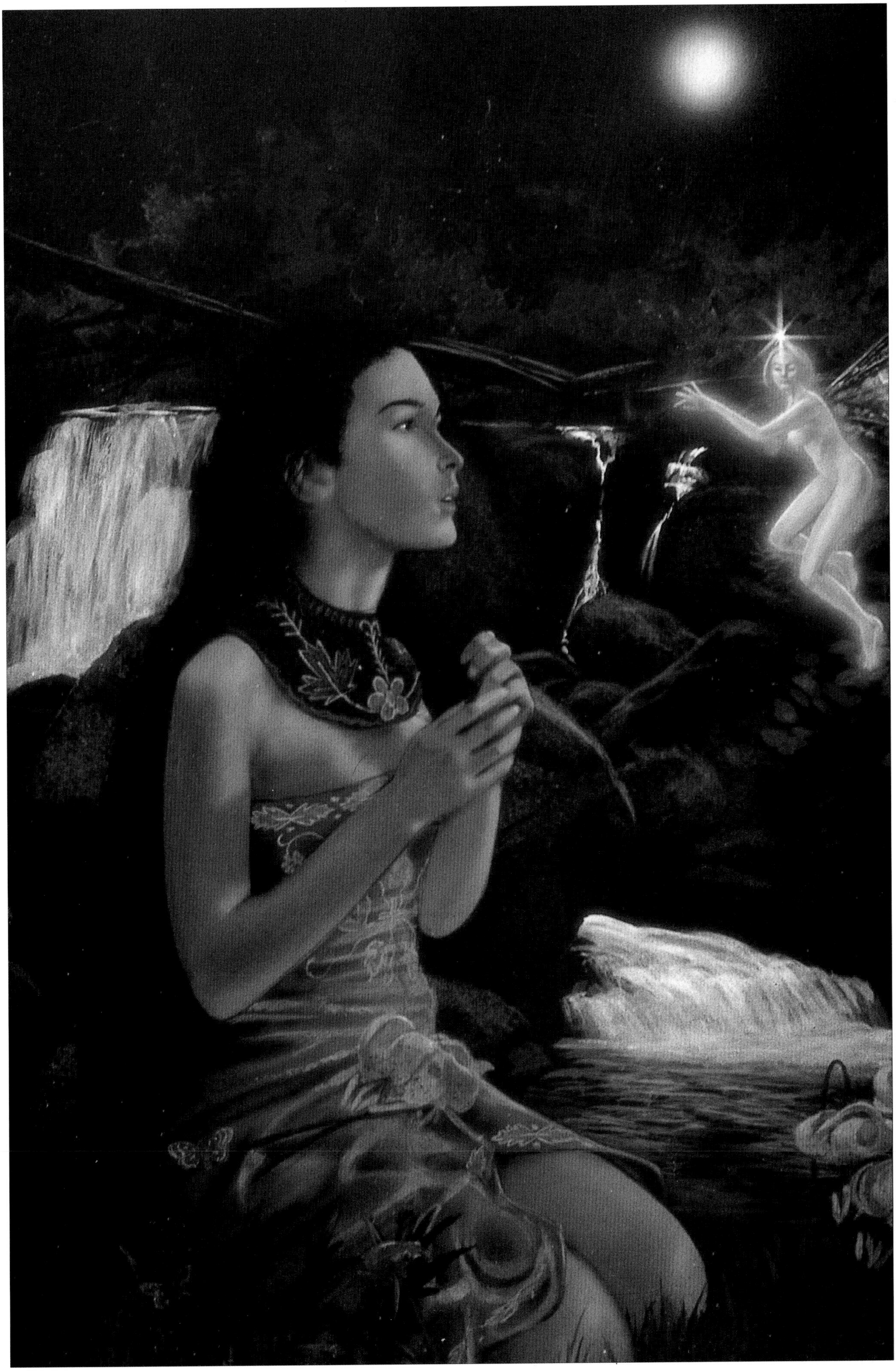

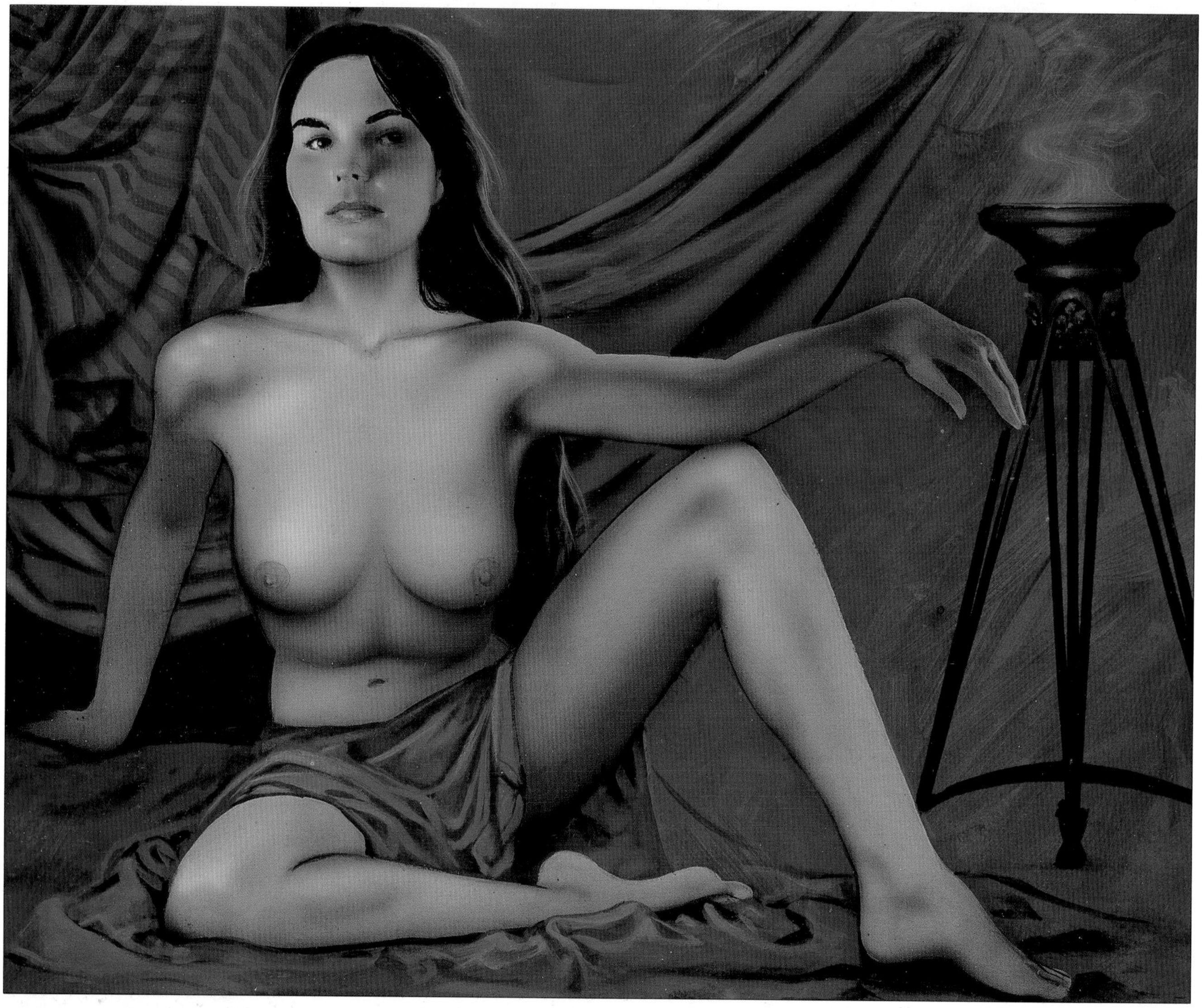

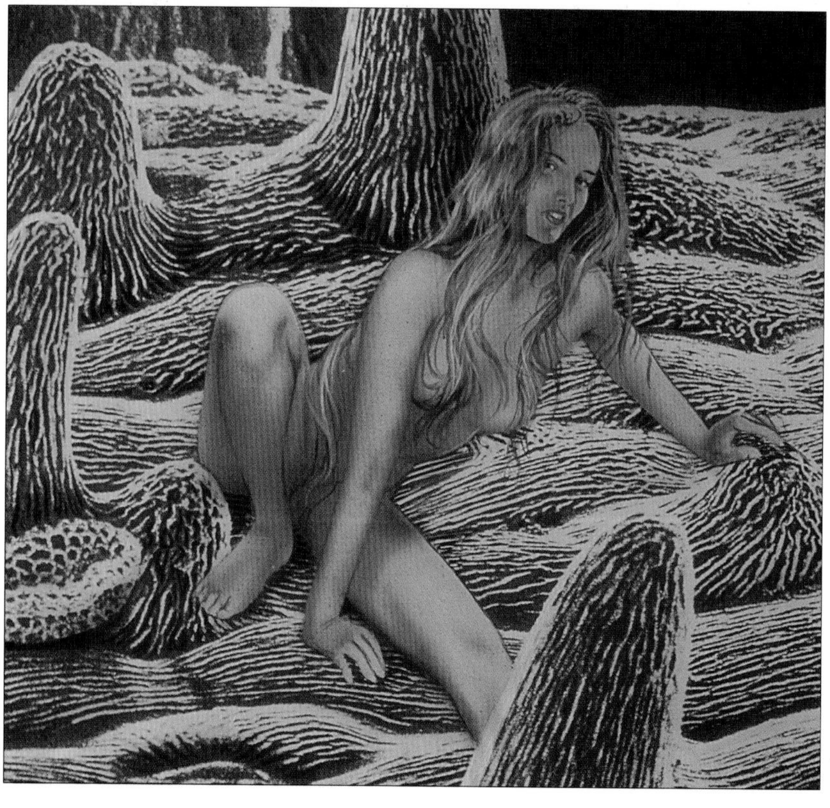

Earani (above)
(*Out of the Silence*, Erle Cox, 1928)

A survivor of the lost continent of Mu, Earani lay in a state of suspended animation, sealed in an enormous metal sphere, for uncounted millennia until she was inadvertently excavated by a pair of modern men. She begins schemes to revive other members of her race, buried in similar time capsules. Equipped with spectacular mental powers and aided by the superscientific devices that had been buried with her, she seems unstoppable.

Lylda (left)
(*The Girl in the Golden Atom*, Ray Cummings, 1919)

Lylda's world consists of the interior of a single atom of gold, visible only by means of a super-microscope invented by the man who falls in love with the sub-atomic princess.

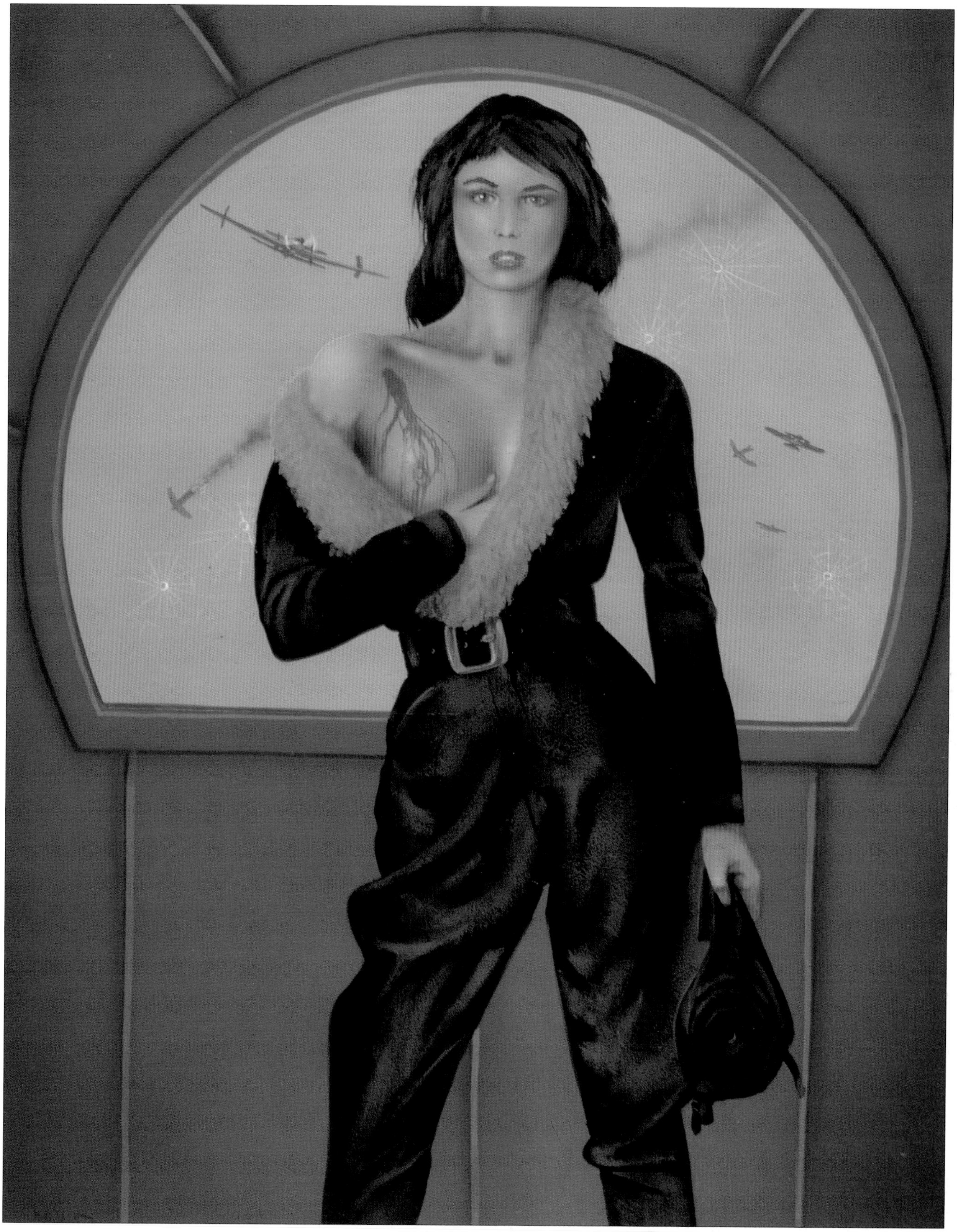

Captain Alden (above)
(*The Flying Legion*, George Allan England, 1920)
Probably the most extraordinary heroine of the early decades of this century, 'Captain Alfred Alden' takes part in an epic Doc Savage-like adventure. and undergoes almost superhuman physical travails, at every turn proving at least the equal of any of her male comrades and the superior of most.

When Captain Alden finally reveals her sex to 'The Master' his first inclination is to drop her from the bomb bay of the giant warplane he and his crew had hijacked. She pleads her case passionately, at the same time speaking eloquently for a great many other equally put-upon adventure heroines.

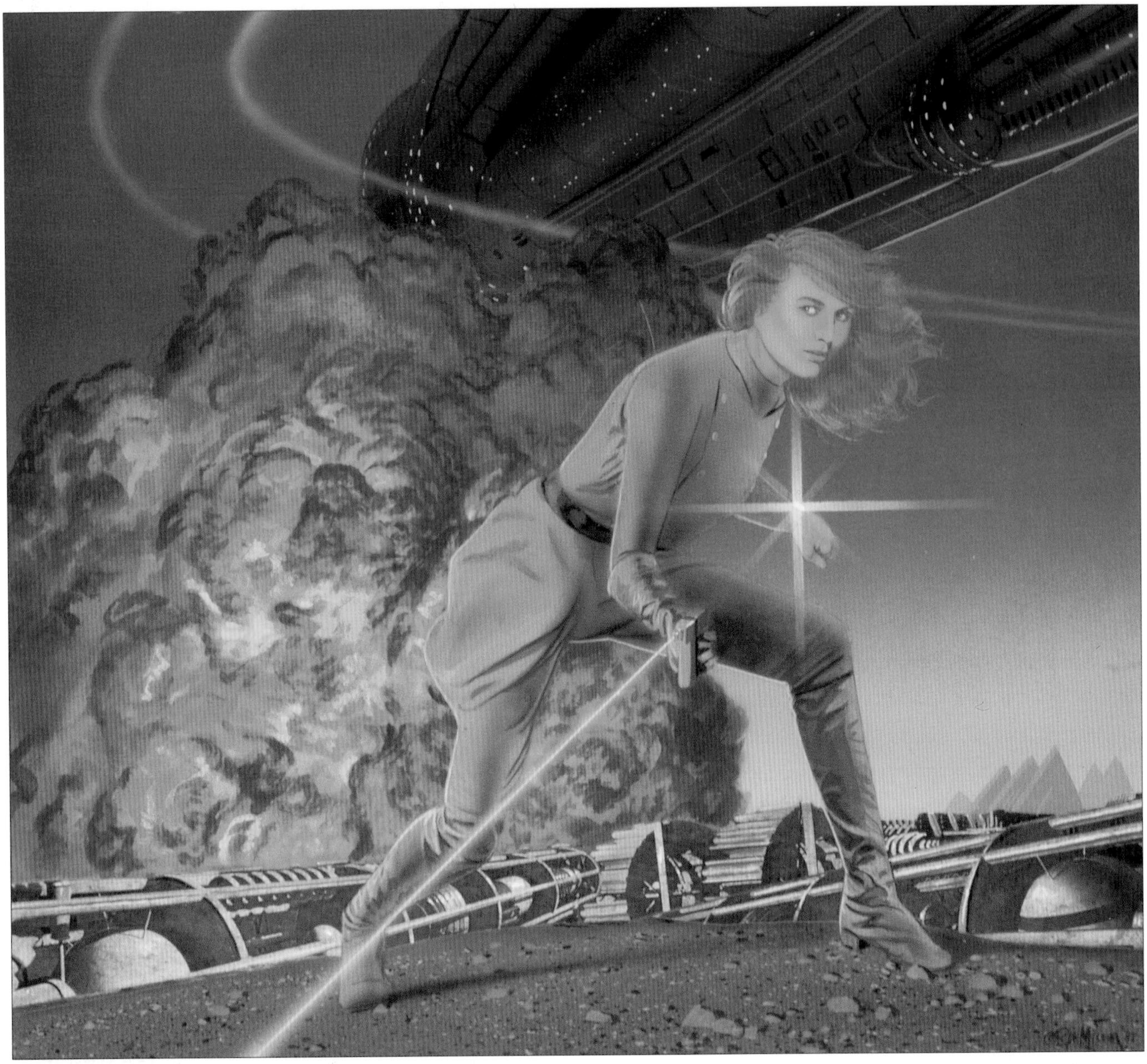

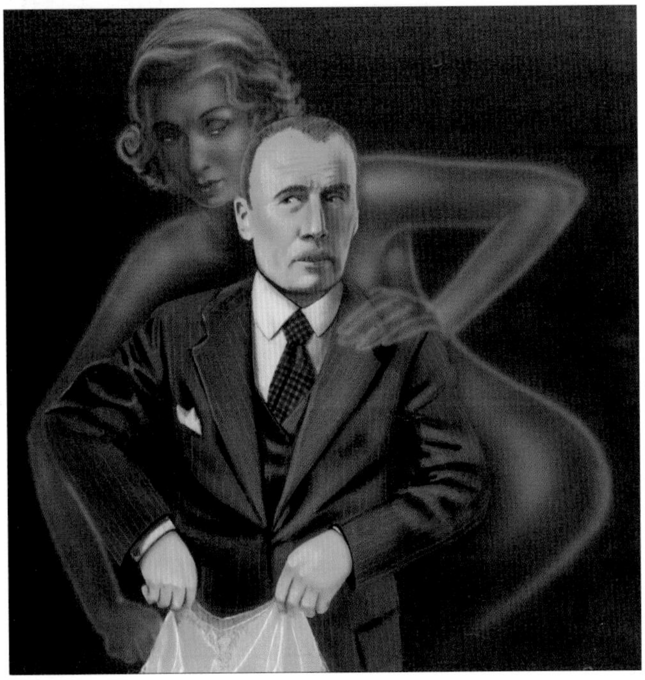

Clarrissa May MacDougall (above)
(*Galactic Patrol, Grey Lensman, Second Stage Lensman, Children of the Lens*, E. E. Smith, PhD, 1937-1947)
The mother of the five Children of the Lens, Clarrissa was a descendant of Phryges of Atlantis, Patroclus the Gladiator and innumerable other heroes and heroines. She was the penultimate goal of the ages-long Arisian breeding programme that culminated in the Children of the Lens. Introduced in the series as a nurse, Clarrissa takes part in a series of astonishing, galaxy-spanning adventures.

Marion Kerby (left)
(*Topper, Topper Takes a Trip*, Thorne Smith, 1926, 1932)
The late Marion Kerby likes gin, nudity and murder. 'I'd like to shoot you,' she tells the horrifed Cosmo Topper, the staid, middle-aged banker she has fallen hopelessly in love with. It is the only way she can think of to keep him with her forever.

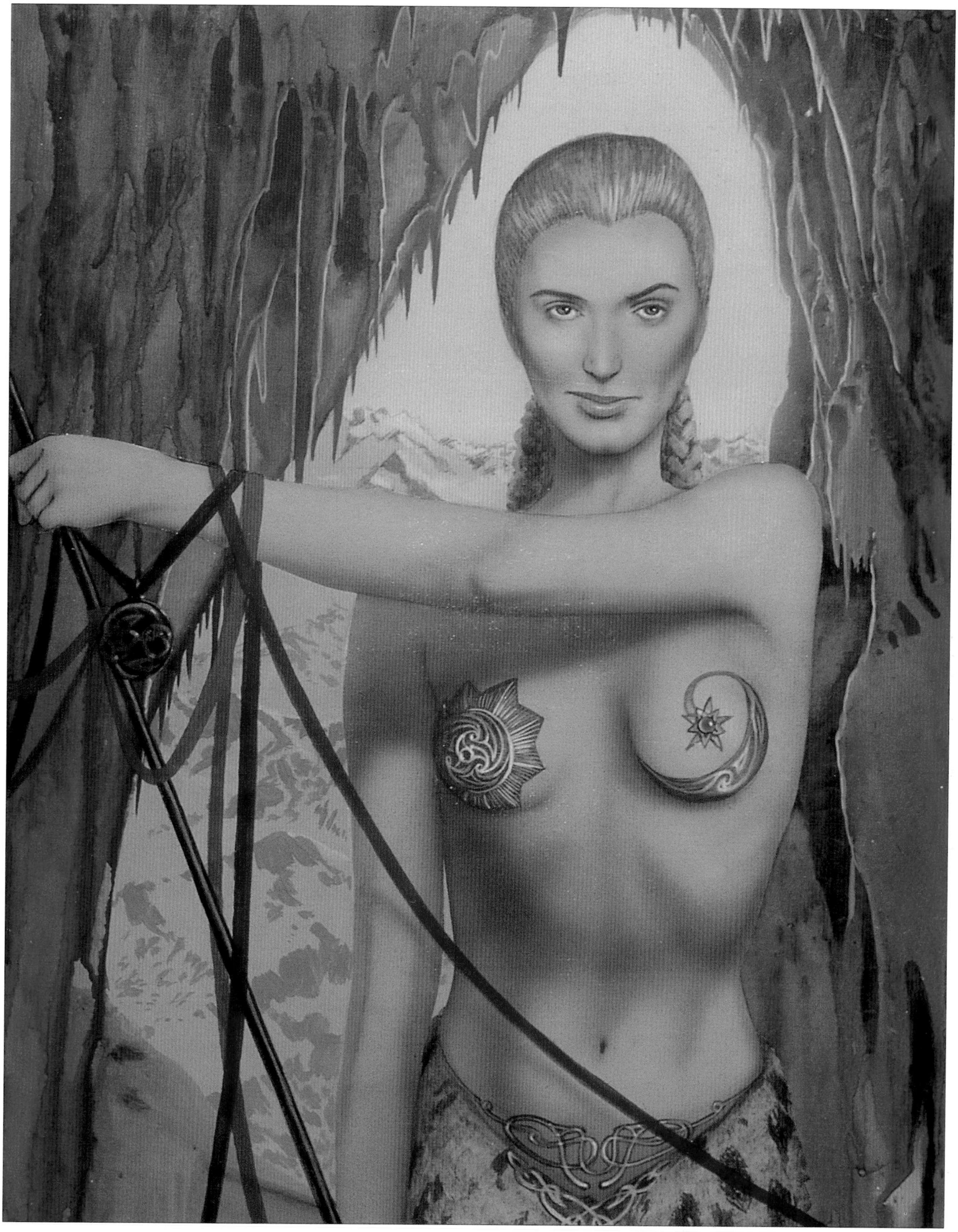

Dian (above)
(*Dian of the Lost Land*, Edison Marshall, 1930)
Princess of a lost race descended from Cro-Magnons who fled Antartica to escape the bloodthirsty, ogreish Neanderthals, Dian now faces an even greater threat: the invasion of the 20th-century world.

Chapter 2
The 1940s to 1950s

IN SPITE OF the ascendancy of a more realistic kind of science fiction, the tradition of pulp adventure did not disappear. It survived throughout the Forties and Fifties in works by Jack Williamson, Leigh Brackett, Edmond Hamilton, E. E. Smith, Arthur K. Barnes and Wallace West, to name only a few writers of space opera. This tradition still thrives today in such popular entertainments as the Star Wars series and in the works of numerous writers. But a more realistic approach to stories was moving to the centre of the genre and would soon come to dominate serious science fiction.

Leigh Brackett, who was known and loved for her colourful adventure fiction, featured males, among them her popular hero Eric John Stark, as the protagonists of her stories but she also created some memorable, if often villainous, female characters. One striking Brackett character is Ciaran, in 'The Black Amazon of Mars' (1951), a woman who can impersonate a man. A quite different Brackett character is Laura Darrow of 'The Halfling' (1943), a Cat-woman of Callisto who has been physically altered to resemble a human woman; Laura is seductive and a trained assassin. In 'The Lake of the Gone Forever' (1949), beautiful and brave Ciel guides Earthman Rand Conway on his quest to find out the cause of his father's suicide; in common with other Brackett heroines, Ciel is strong and competent, even if ultimately subordinate to the hero. 'The Woman from Altair' (1951) offers several female characters: Marthe Walters, a reporter, whose tough exterior resembles that of the women in the films of Howard Hawks (Brackett wrote screenplays for Hawks during the Forties and Fifties), Bet McQuarrie, kid sister of the story's hero, and the alluring Ahrian, seemingly delicate but secretly determined to have revenge on the Earthman who has taken her away from her own people of Altair.

Jean Meredith
(opposite)
(*The Fox Woman*, Abraham Merritt, 1946 [completed by Hannes Bok])
Raised by a mysterious fox-worshipping Tibetan cult when her parents are murdered by her uncle, Jean Meredith returns to the United States on a mission of occult vengeance.

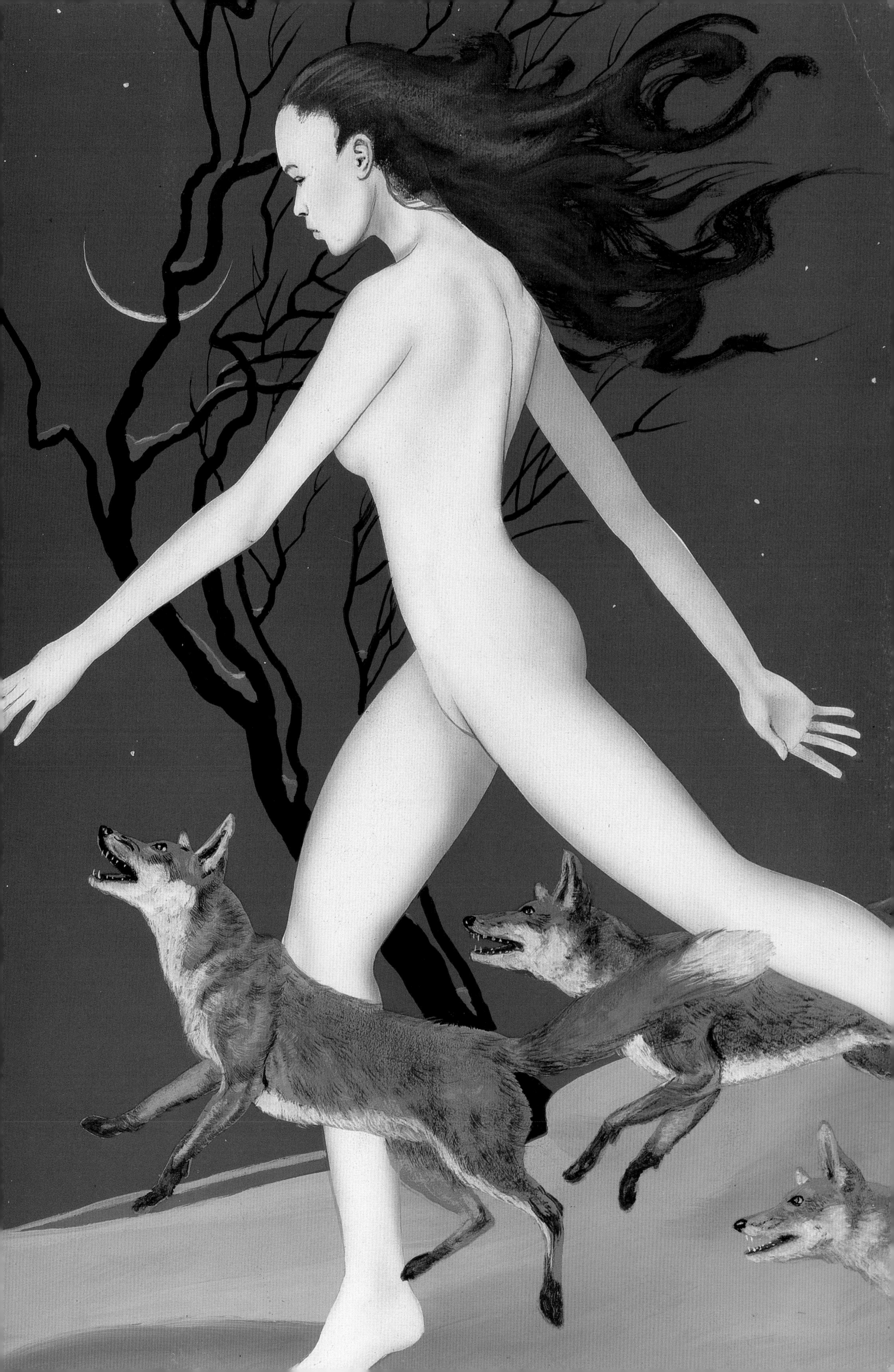

Plaxy Trelone (right)
(*Sirius*, Olaf Stapledon, 1944)
'I congratulate you, Mr. Sirius, on your bride.'

Plaxy is more than the owner, protector and trainer of Sirius, a genetically-altered dog possessing an intelligence equal to and perhaps greater than a human's – she is his lover as well.

Brackett's vivid blend of science fiction and fantasy was to influence many of the writers who followed her, among them Marion Zimmer Bradley, Anne McCaffrey and C. J. Cherryh.

Heroic characters on a mythic scale continued to appear in the works of other writers of the Forties, even as science fiction was changing. Certainly one of the most striking was the Empress Innelda in A. E. van Vogt's classic novels *The Weapon Shops of Isher* (1941) and *The Weapon Makers* (1943). Robert Hedrock, the central character of *The Weapon Makers*, has this impression of Innelda: 'The tigress had shown her claws, and they were made of steel and quiescent violence.' Innelda, the ruler of the vast Isher Empire, is in fact the most powerful human being in the universe and more than a match for her antagonist Hedrock.

Some writers of earlier pulp adventures moved toward more realism in their fiction. C.L. Moore, creator of the warrior Jirel of Joiry, went on to write the classic story of a female cyborg, Dierdre, in 'No Woman Born' (1944). Dierdre's body has been destroyed in a fire and her brain transplanted into a metal body. She is a cyborg, a person who is partly or mostly machine. The men responsible for her transformation begin to fear at first that she is deluding herself by believing that she can continue her career as a dancer and later that she may lose her humanity; Dierdre herself seems to welcome her new body. Vivid as Moore's Jirel is, Dierdre is a more complex character, a woman whose femininity survives even in her artificial body and who suggests through her behaviour that beauty and femininity may be no more than cultural constructs.

A more domestically inclined female protagonist appeared in 'That Only a Mother' (1948), a story by Judith Merril, who was later to have much influence on science fiction as an editor with her series of best-of-the-year anthologies published in the Fifties and early Sixties.

Siren (opposite)
('Cage of a Thousand Wings', Algis Budrys, 1955)
'Somewhere out in those stars,' he said clearly, 'there are witches.' And these words of the Mars-bound astronaut prove to be more accurate than he realizes as he is lured towards the Red Planet by the siren call of a strange and lonely entity.

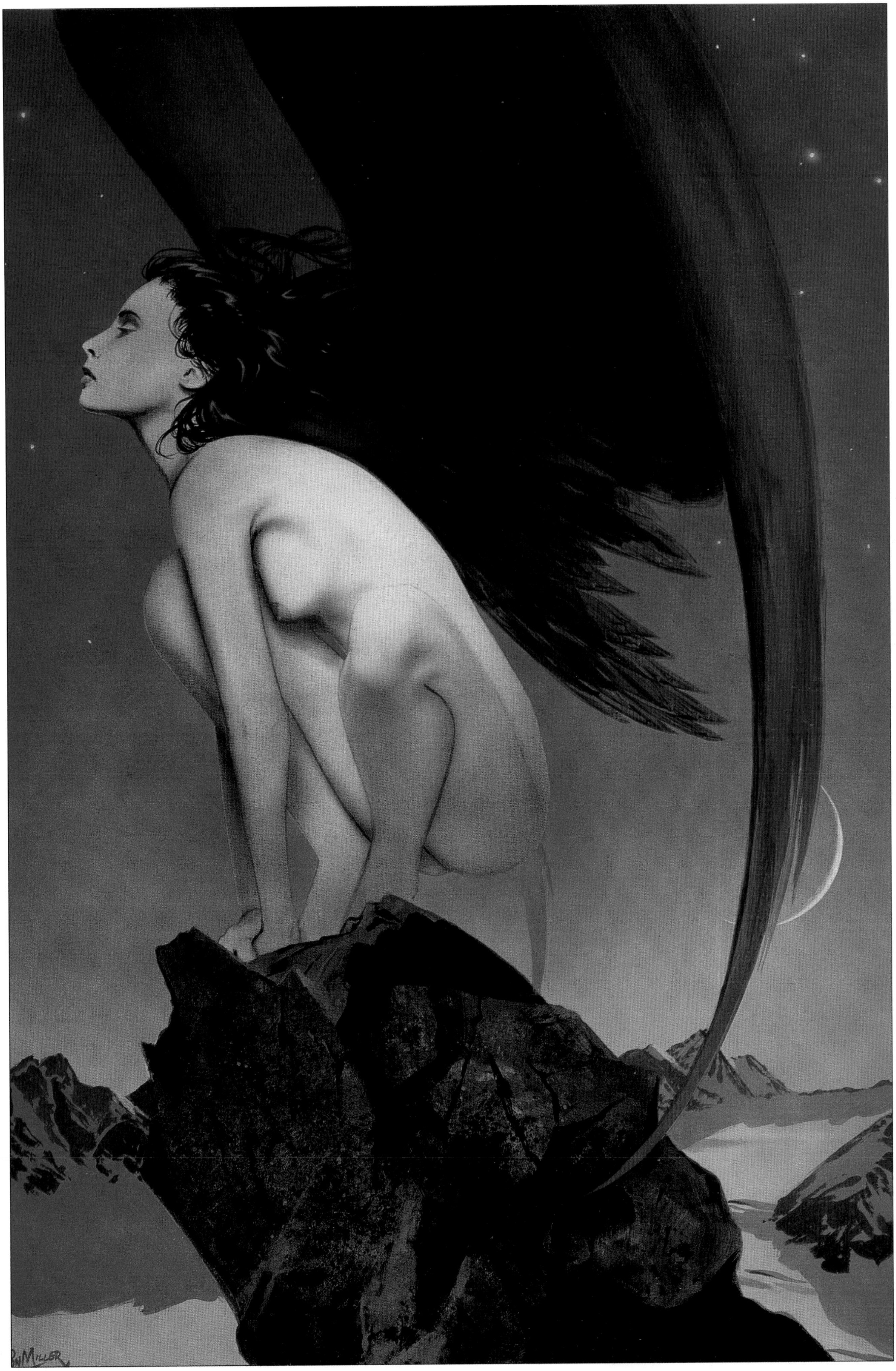

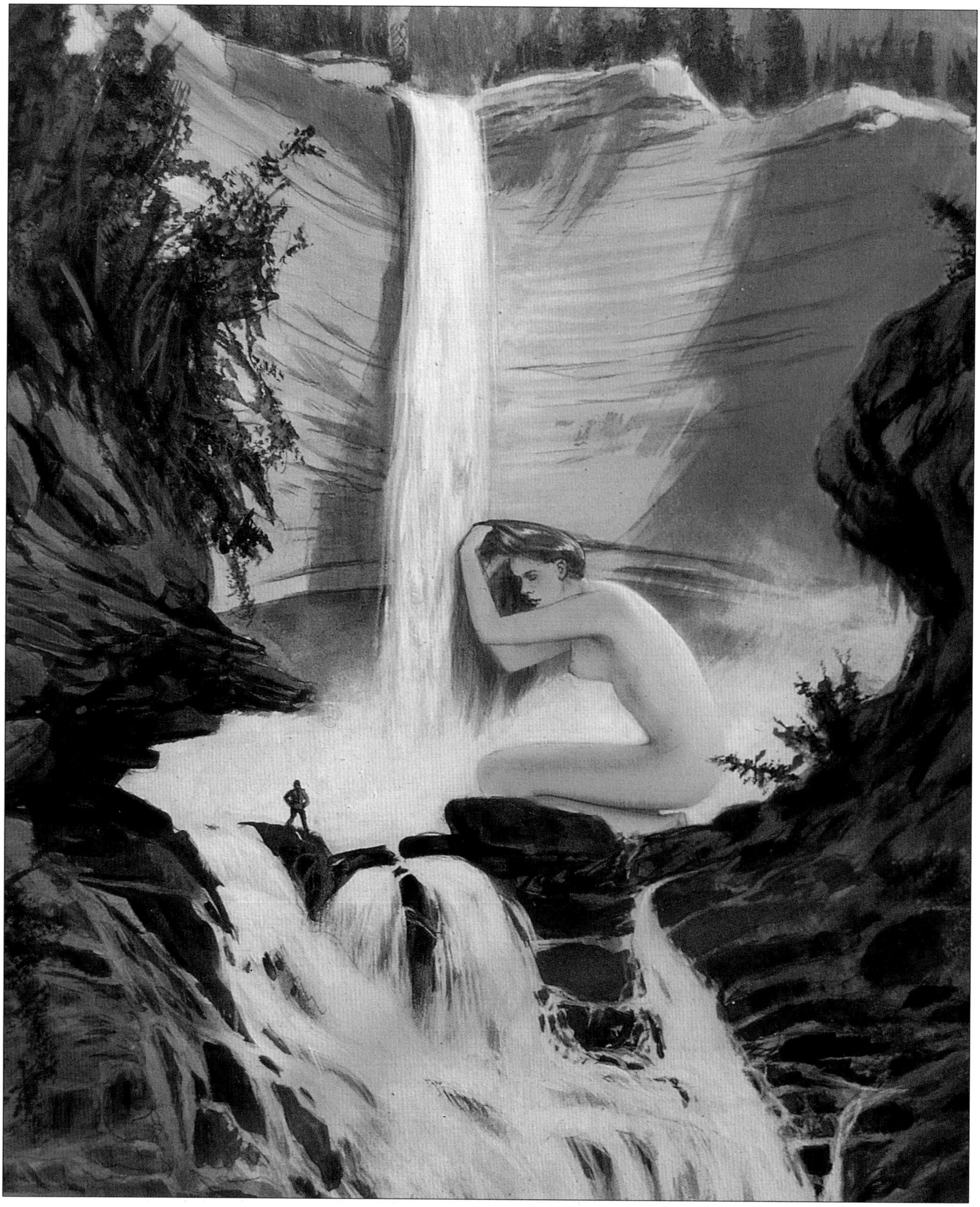

Aurore (above)
('Witch of the Andes', Richard Shaver, 1947)
The product of a kind of genetic engineering, Aurore is a 15-foot giantess created from a vat of primordial soup. It is only by means of her courage and scientific genius that the earth is saved from genetic catastrophe and slavery under a vast, artificially-created brain.

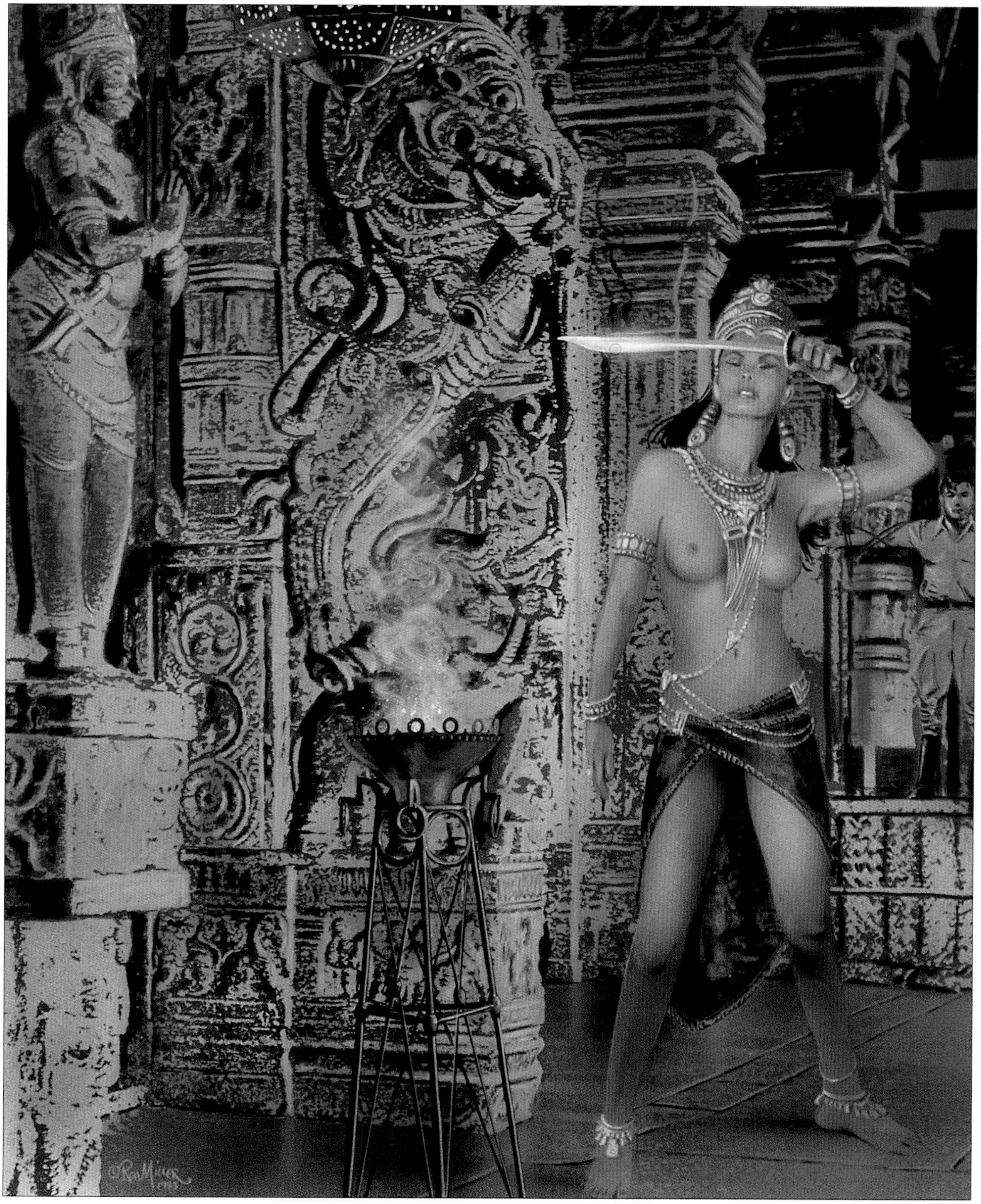

Fah Lo Suee (above)
(*The Daughter of Fu Manchu*, Sax Rohmer, 1931)
The subject of her own series of books, Fah Lo Suee did all that she could to live up to her infamous heritage. After capturing her father's indefatigable nemesis, Wayland Smith, in her first novel, she appeared to taunt him while costumed as the bloodthirsty Indian goddess, Kali.

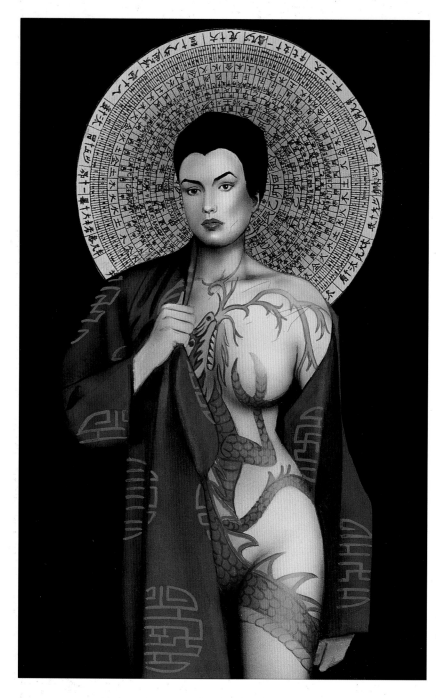

Sumuru (left)
(**Nude in Mink**, Sax Rohmer, 1950)
*The creator of the insidious Fu Manchu
introduces that villain's female counterpart: Sumuru, whose goal is the subjuga-
tion of the earth itself. She was featured
in a number books after her first
appearance in 1950.*

roles, or at least more conventional ones. If the societies in
which science fiction writers
lived offered few exceptional or
unconventional women as models, writers working in the realistic mode could conclude that
women in their imagined future
worlds would lead conventional
lives too. Science fiction often
prides itself on inventive speculation about possible futures but it
is also affected by the culture in
which its writers exist.

In the aftermath of World
War II, women who had worked
in factories in the US or who had
served in the British armed
forces were encouraged to
return to more traditional pursuits. As Judith Merril put it in her
collection *Survival Ship and Other
Stories* (1974): 'The wonderful
working-mothers' day-care cen-
tres all closed down, and from
every side the news was shout-
ed that Woman's Place was after
all in the home.' In her first novel,
Shadow on the Hearth (1950), Merril writes a
tale of the days immediately after a nuclear
attack on the United States. Most of the novel
takes place entirely within the suburban home
of a housewife trying to survive and protect
her family in the absence of her husband.
Conventional as the main character's role is,
she is a heroine all the same.

Margaret Marvell, the central character of 'That
Only a Mother', lives in a world at war, in which
nuclear weapons have been used and popula-
tions exposed to radiation. She gives birth to a
mutant but cannot perceive her child's defor-
mities; it is implied that other women have
given birth to such children and that the babies
have been killed by their fathers. This frightening story uses a woman in a traditional role,
caring for her child and waiting for her husband
to get leave, to issue a warning about the possible consequences of nuclear warfare.

It may seem as though the demands for
more realism and plausibility in science fiction
would consign most female characters to lesser

Laura Darrow (opposite)
('The Halfling', Leigh Brackett, 1943)
*'Laura Darrow' is a species of humanoid cat who joins an
interplanetary circus as an exotic dancer in order to
avenge the honour of her tribe.*

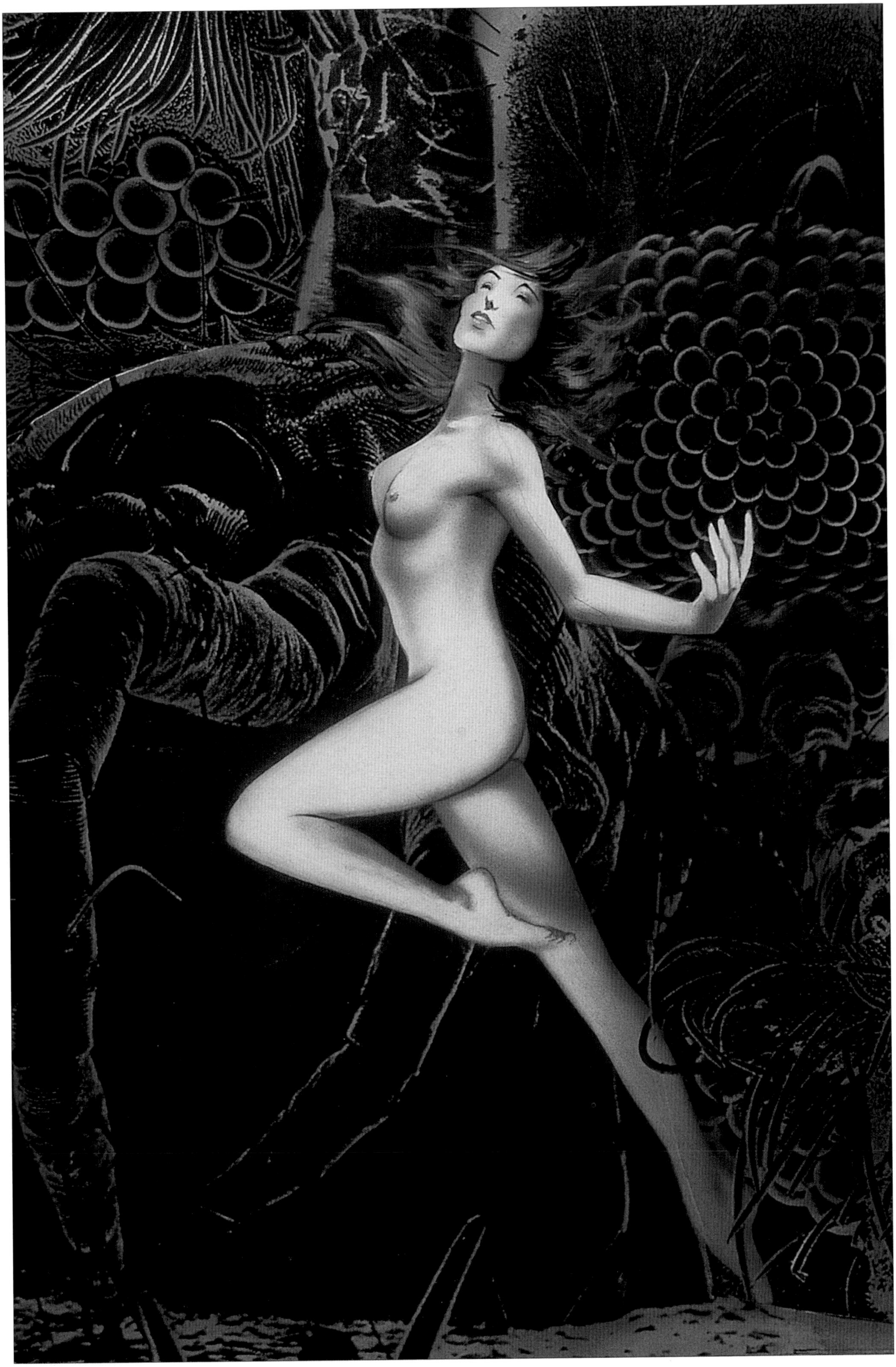

Empress Innelda (above)
(*The Weapon Shops of Isher, The Weapon Makers,*
A. E. Van Vogt, 1942, 1943)
Ruler of the Isher empire, the Empress Innelda holds more
power than any other human being. Her power is threat-
ened only by the mysterious and invulnerable Weapon
Shops which can appear anywhere and will sell weapons
to anyone.

Luria (above)
(*Queen of the Panther World*, Berkeley Livingston,
1948)
Even the superhuman strength of Queen Luria and
her retinue of black panthers would not be equal to
the great cunning of the evil Loko and his following of
lizard men – unless Luria could capture the enchanted
Groana bird.

Other science fiction writers who wrote of female characters in traditional roles during the Fifties were Mildred Clingerman, Zenna Henderson, Kit Reed, Pauline Ashwell and Rosel George Brown; two women writers who achieved later prominence, Kate Wilhelm and Carol Emshwiller, also began publishing at this time. Much of the writing of these authors (although not all of it) centred around the hearth and home, leading to the impression in some quarters that there was a distinct sub-genre of women's science fiction, referred to by disparaging critics as 'wet-diaper' science fiction. But Zenna Henderson achieved a

devoted following with her stories of The People, humanoid extraterrestrials with psychic powers who must survive on Earth, while Kit Reed often hinted at the horror that can underlie normality, notably in her story 'The Wait' (1958), when a mother and her daughter learn of a small town's frightening ancient custom. Carol Emshwiller would eventually become one of the most literary writers of science fiction, using the devices of the genre to write of human estrangement.

A novel that speculates on what might happen if women and men inhabited separate worlds is Philip Wylie's *The disappearance*

Bêlit (above)
('Queen of the Black Coast', Robert E. Howard, 1934)

Pirate queen Bêlit falls in love with arch-barbarian Conan and is both astonished and pleased to meet a man who is her superior at swordplay. She swears that should she be the first to die she would return from the gates of Hell to assist Conan should he ever need her. And she does.

Ciaran (above)
(*The Black Amazon of Mars*, Leigh Brackett, 1951; also *People of the Talisman*, 1964)

Ciaran is a warrioress so ferocious that she is able to successfully masquerade as a man, dominate and become the leader of a vast army of mercenaries. The goals of this army, however, are personal vengeance and self-aggrandizement.

(1951). Suddenly, both women and men on Earth disappear from each other's world. We see the world of the women through Paula Gaunt and the men's world through the eyes of her husband, Bill Gaunt. The women, in the absence of men, must struggle to master the skills they need to survive, including hunting and repairing machines; the men give in to violence. *The Disappearance* ends with the reuniting of women with men and the hope that future generations will allow each person, regardless of gender, full equality.

A classic tale of an all-female society is John Wyndham's *Consider Her Ways* (1956). Jane, a

twentieth-century woman, suddenly finds herself in a monstrous, ungainly body and learns that she is in a future world of women and that men died out long ago. The women have developed a society modelled on that of insects; Jane, in this world, is a Mother, her only duty to gestate and give birth to her young. Jane is horrified at this society, but the women of the future consider those of Jane's time little more than the slaves of men. Jane eventually returns to her own time, determined to prevent the future she has glimpsed, although it is unclear whether or not she will succeed. Isaac Asimov and Robert A. Heinlein, who

Gerry Carlyle (above)
(*Interplanetary Hunter*, Arthur K. Barnes, 1956)
*First introduced in 1937, Gerry Carlyle was the subject of
a long-running and popular series of stories. Dedicated to
finding and trapping bizarre and exotic extraterrestrial
animals for earthly zoos, 'Catch them alive' Carlyle is the
captain of the spaceship Ark.*

were publishing their early work in the Forties,
were destined to become two of science fiction's most influential writers. Both wrote in
the realistic vein, both worked with the influential editor John W. Campbell and it is clear
that science fiction would have developed
quite differently without them. *The
Encyclopedia of Science Fiction* (edited by John
Clute and Peter Nicholls, 1993) says about
Heinlein that he 'may have been the all-time
most important writer of genre SF ... his pre-
eminence from 1940 to 1960 was both earned
and unassailable. For half a century he was the
father – loved, resisted, emulated – of the
dominant U.S. form of the genre.' Writer and
critic James Gunn, writing in the *St James Guide
to Science Fiction Writers*, describes Asimov this
way: 'More than any other writer, Asimov
became the symbol for SF's' Golden Age. He

was the supreme rationalist, valuing clear thinking and cool logic above all else.' Although it
has not generally been acknowledged, both of
these writers also had a pronounced effect on
the development of female characters in more
realistic science fiction.

Isaac Asimov is not known for creating
memorable women in his work, yet he was
responsible for one of the most beloved
female characters in science fiction – the
'robopsychologist' Dr Susan Calvin. In 'Liar'
(1941), the third story in Asimov's Robot
series and the first to feature Susan Calvin, the
robotics expert shows her human vulnerability
when she comes to believe – mistakenly, as it

Alianora (opposite)
(*Three Hearts & Three Lions*, Poul Anderson,
1953)
*'The swan stopped, poised, spread its wings wide and
stood on tiptoe. Its body lengthened, the neck shrank, the
wings narrowed – "Jesu Kristu!" yelled Holger and crossed
himself.*
   "No, a girl."
   *Alianora, the swan-may, is instrumental in helping
Holger Carlsen in combating trolls, giants, nixies and dragons in their struggle to help the forces of Law defeat
those of Chaos for control of the world.*

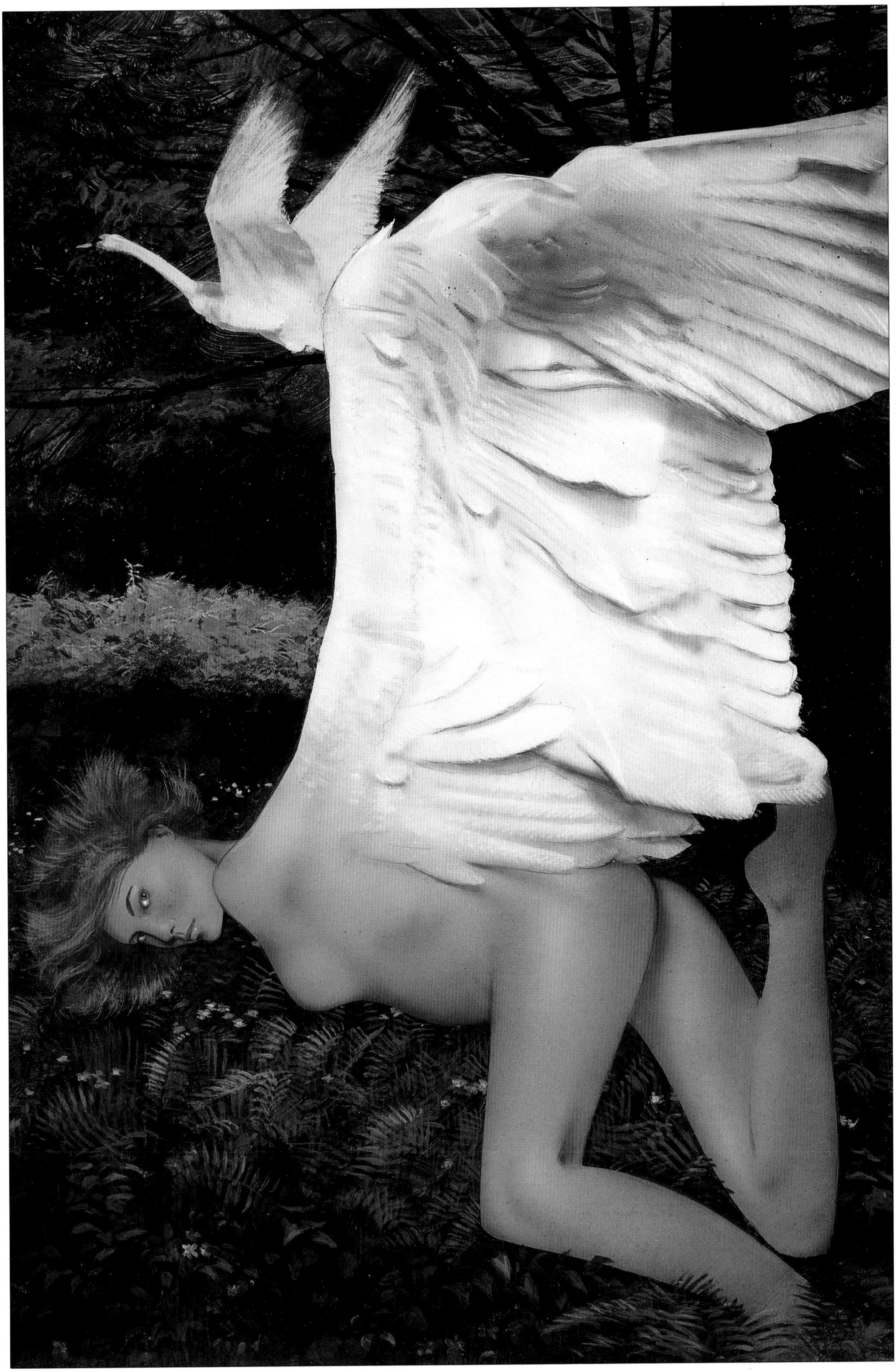

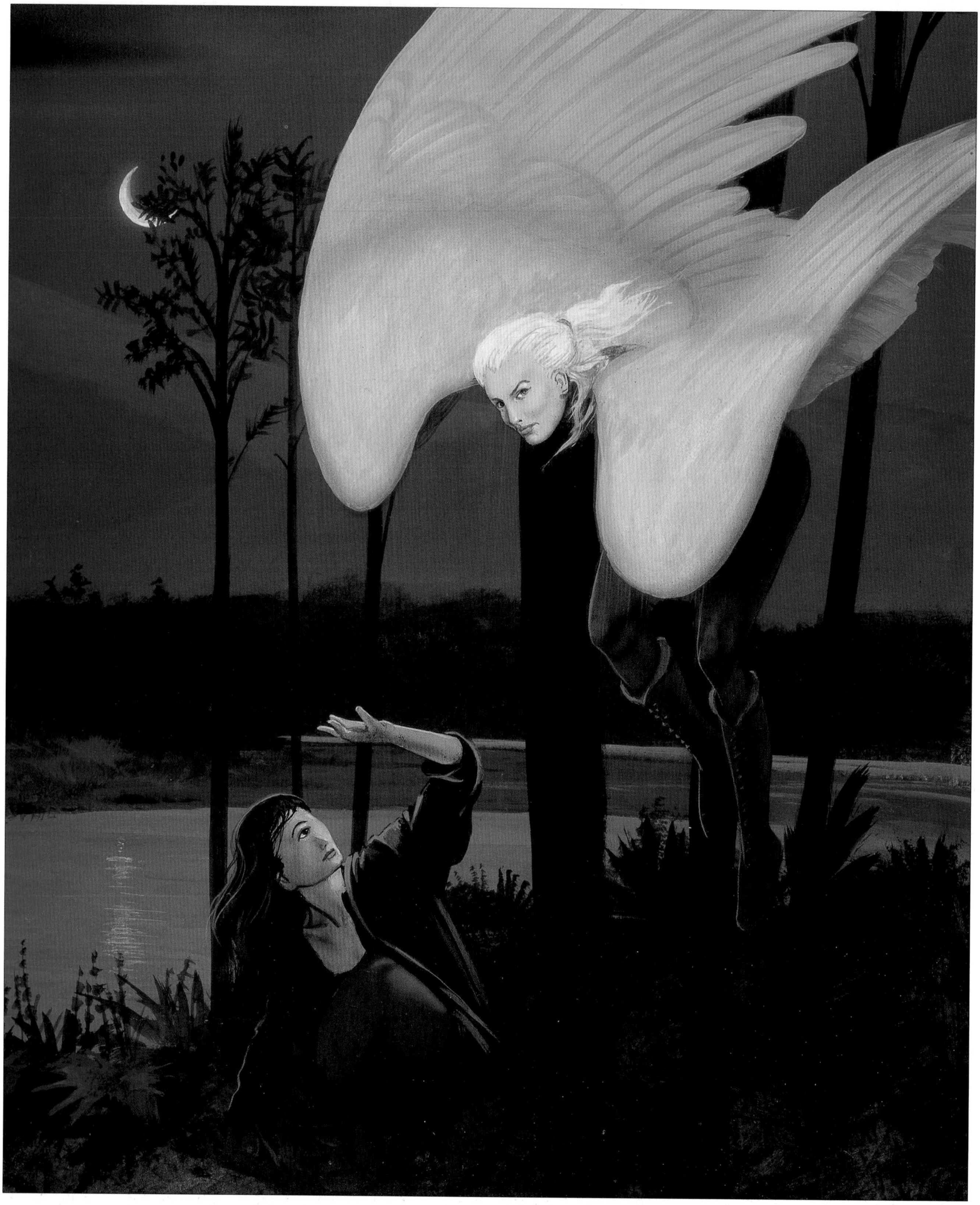

Kua and Elja (above)
('The Way of the Gods', Henry Kuttner, 1947)
Post-nuclear-war mutants – such as winged Elja and cyclopean Kua – must band together in order to survive the deadly witchhunt against them by the self-proclaimed 'normal' humans – who don't realize that the mutants hold the key to the survival of all humans.

The Green Lady of Perelandra (opposite)
(*Perelandra*, C. S. Lewis, 1944)
She is the Eve of the watery world of Venus, the world known to her as Perelandra, where Man has not yet fallen and Sin is unknown. When the earthlings invade her world and begin to struggle for control of it, she opens a veritable Pandora's Box of perils and terror.

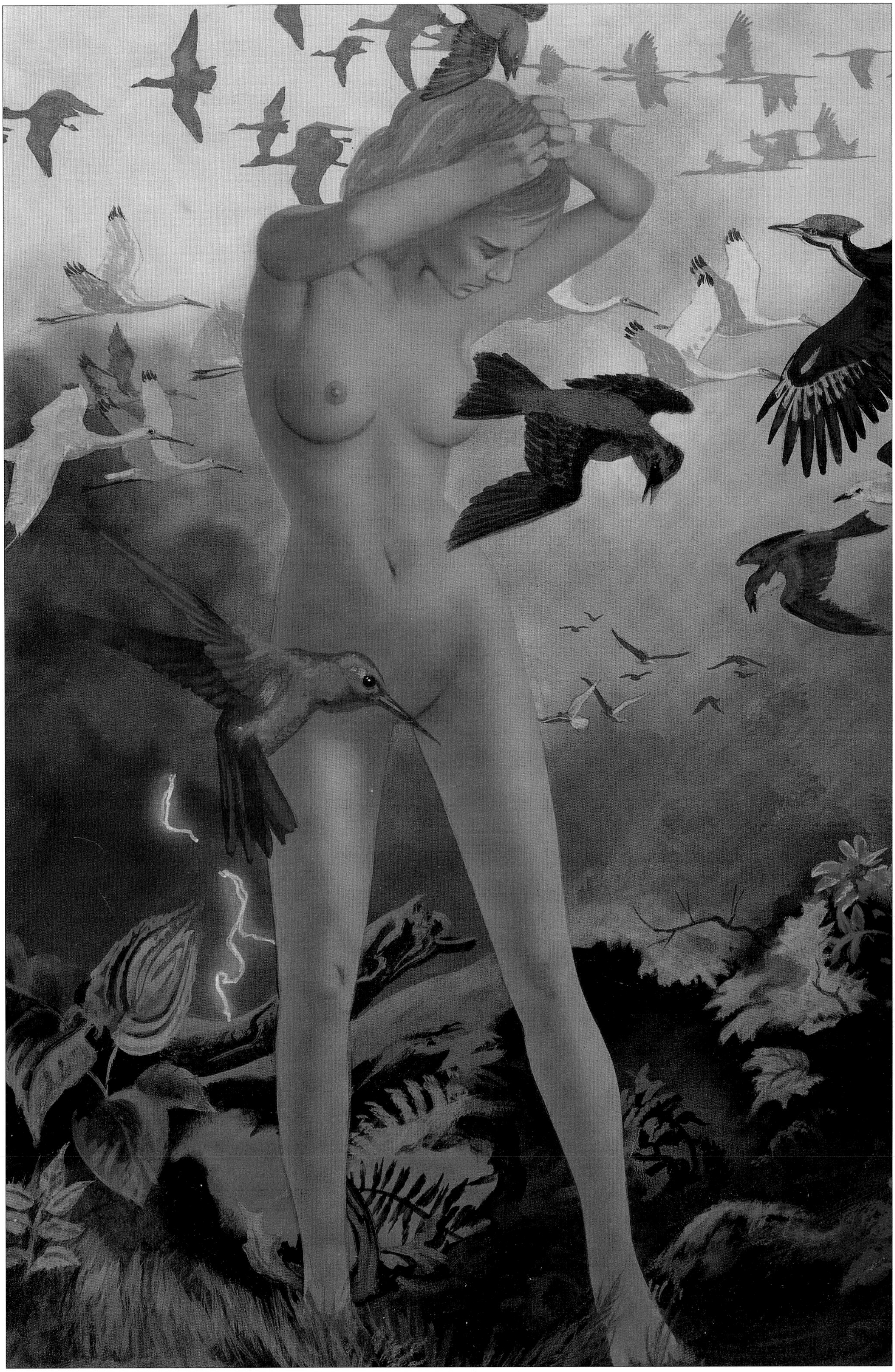

Pentizel (above)
(*'Special Feature'*, Charles De Vet, 1958)
*Cat woman Pentizel is truly a stranger in a strange land:
marooned in an earth city when her spaceship crashes
and sinks in a river, she must survive solely by her wits
and strength.*

happens – that a man she secretly loves is in love with her. In other stories, collected in one volume as *The Complete Robot* (1982), her emotional armour is harder and thicker and it is obvious that she prefers robots to people. (This seems logical in the context of the stories; Asimov's rational and endearing robots do seem to be better than most people.) The narrator of *I, Robot* describes Susan Calvin as 'a frosty girl, plain and colorless, who protected herself against a world she disliked by a mask-like expression and a hypertrophy of intellect.' Such a description makes her seem yet another example of a familiar female character – the frustrated spinster – but, given the cultural context of these stories, one cannot call this portrayal of Susan Calvin unrealistic. Asimov wrote of her at a time when most women in his society had to choose between careers and more traditional pursuits; to his credit, he was able to evoke in his readers both respect for Susan Calvin's intelligence and affection for her as a character.

Robert A. Heinlein was a writer rooted in plausibility and realism, who had both a didactic streak and the aim of writing about future societies that could actually come about. He was able to see that these future societies might not resemble his own and that they might also allow more of a range of activities for women. Heinlein has often been criticized

April Bell (opposite)
(*Darker Than You Think*, Jack Williamson, 1940)
*Changeling, witch, werewolf, April Bell is homo-lycanthro-
pus, a throwback to a time when the bloodstrain of were-
wolfism flowed more strongly in human veins.*

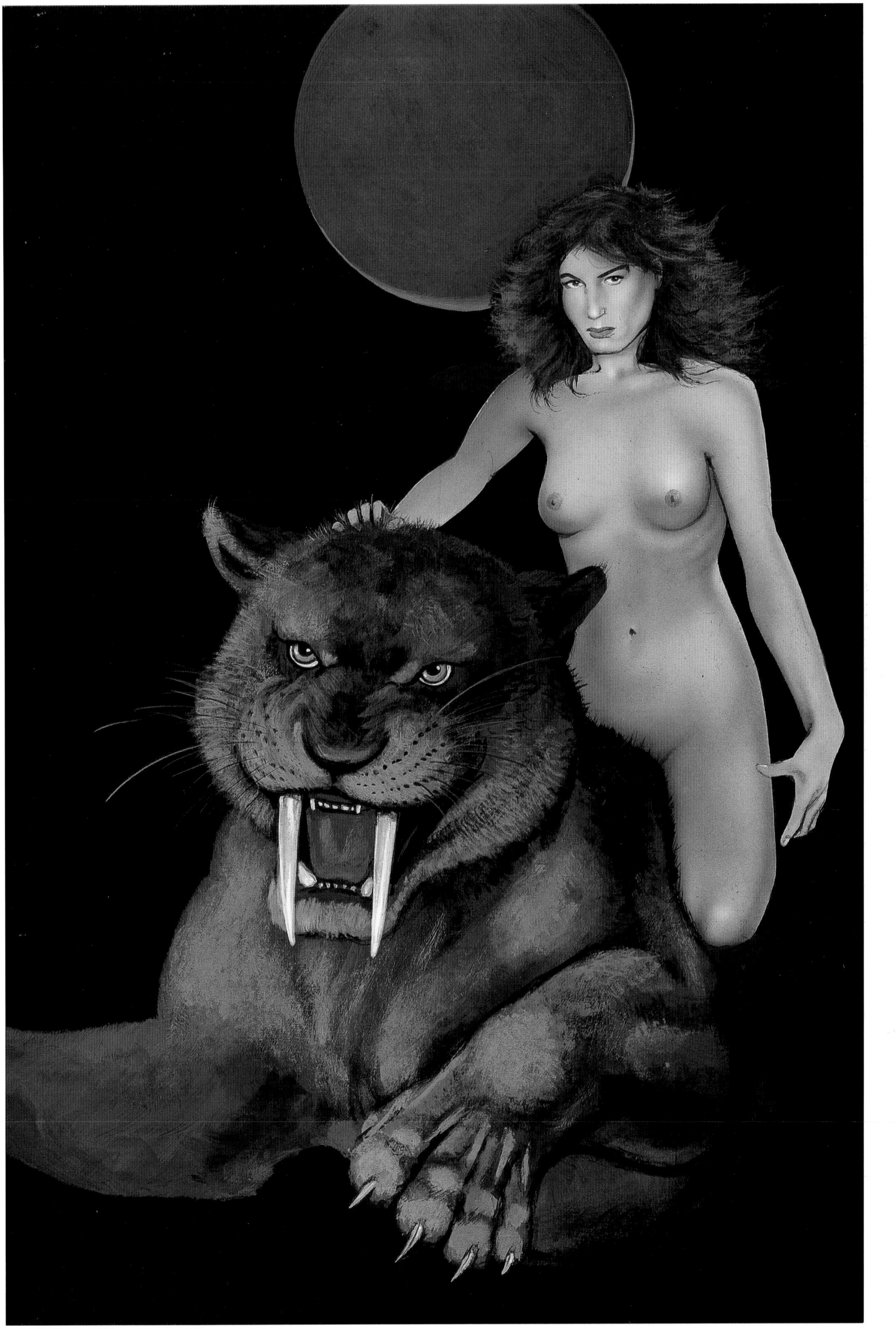

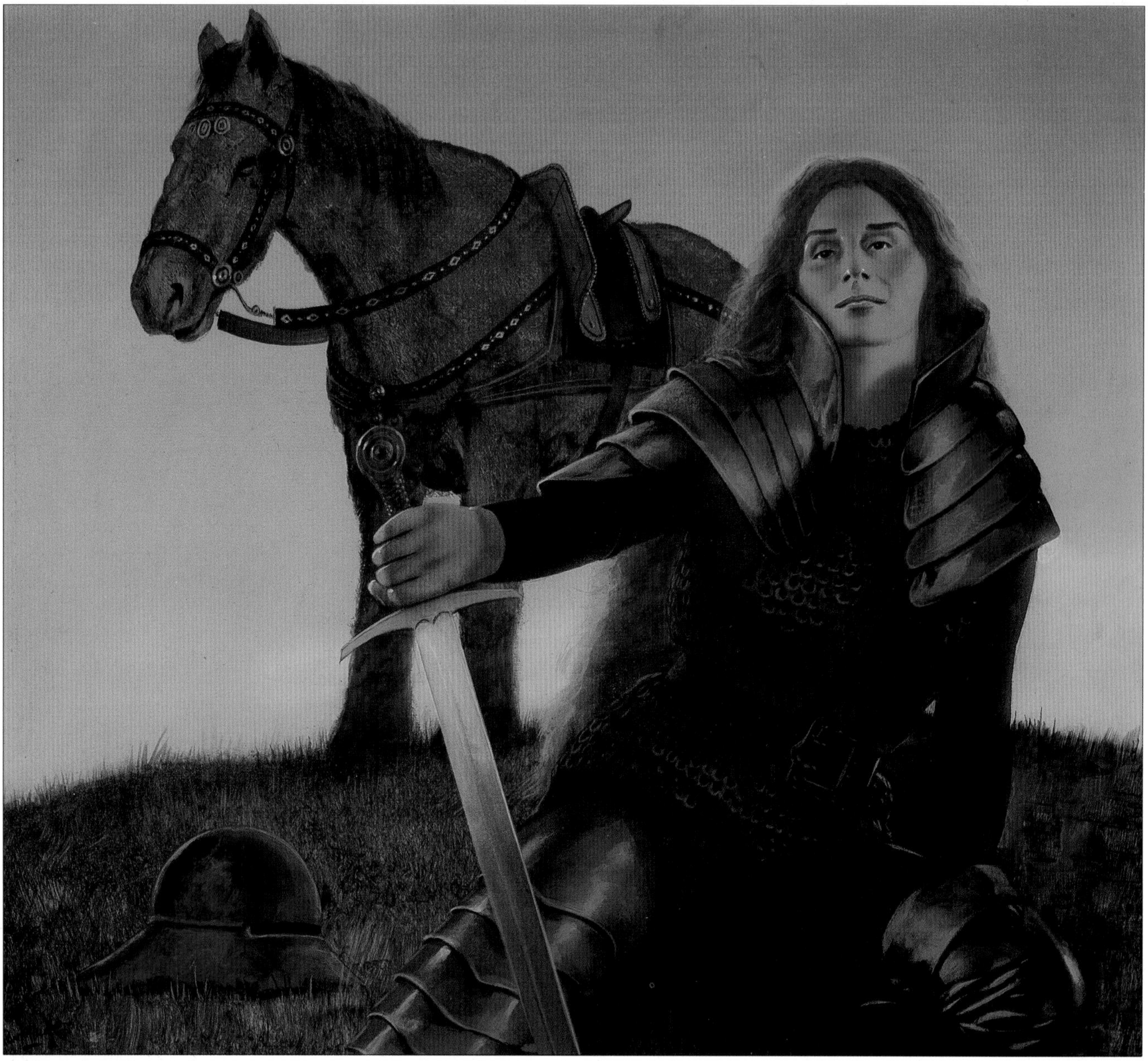

for his depictions of female characters and some of them do seem excessively preoccupied with flirting and finding good husbands, but many of them also follow occupations that are extremely untraditional.

As early as 1941, in a speech entitled 'The Discovery of the Future', Heinlein spoke of using the scientific method in dealing with people and went on to say: 'You can't be a woman-hater, not if you use the scientific method, you can't possibly – you don't know all women . . . you don't even know a large enough percentage of the group to be able to form an opinion on what the whole group may be!' Heinlein's novels are filled with female characters who join the armed services, are engineers and doctors, who pilot spaceships

Éowyn (above)
(*Lord of the Rings*, J. R. R. Tolkien, 1965)
Éowyn – the 'Lady of the Shield-arm' – had a skill with horse and blade that matches any Rider of the Mark. She was determined to find an honourable death as a 'shield-maiden' on the battlefield.

C'Mell (opposite)
('The Ballad of Lost C'Mell', Cordwainer Smith, 1962)
C'Mell is a cat-derived parahuman. Like her fellow creatures – whatever animal may have been their genetic origin – she is considered to be little more than furniture and no less disposable. Although little more than a mere 'girly girl' a kind of sub-human geisha – C'Mell is instrumental in attaining full human status for her kind.

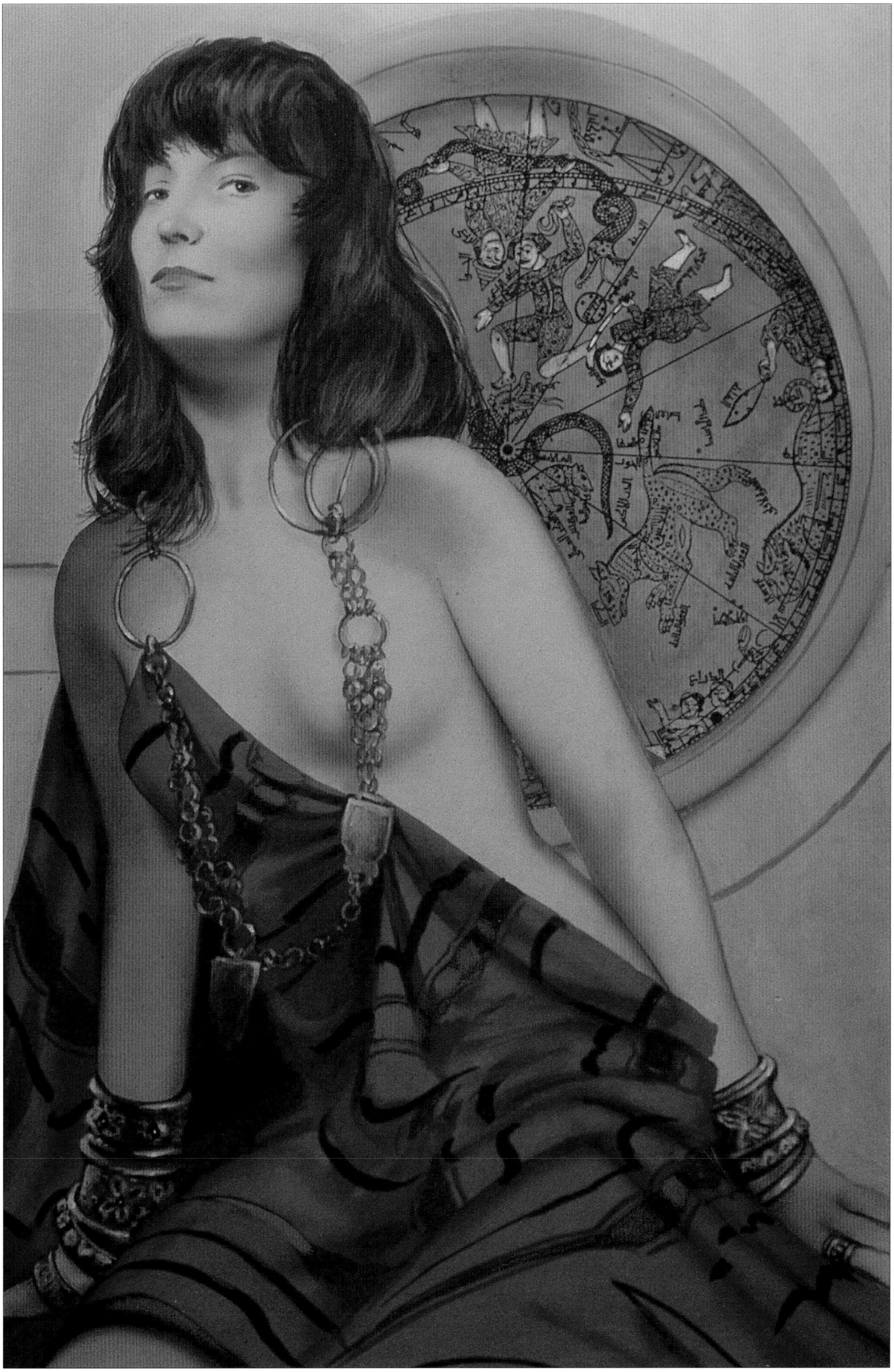

Aubretia (right)
(*World Without Men*, Charles Eric Maine, 1958)
Aubretia is a citizen of a world 5000 years in the future. Because all reproduction is carried out through partheno-genesis – and everyone is a virtual mirror image of everyone else – there are no longer any male humans. When the body of a man is discovered frozen in arctic ice, Aubretia discovers the true nature of the censorious, repressive, dictatorial society that she had hitherto so blithely accepted – and she becomes the spearhead of the movement to destroy that society.

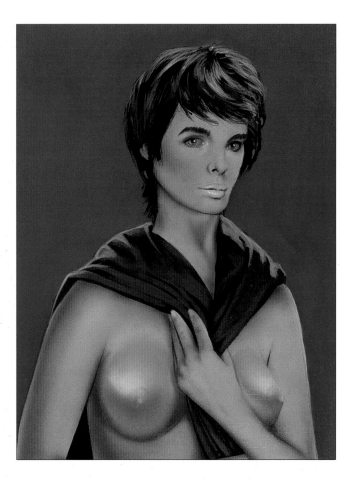

and are familiar with higher mathematics. Yet it is also true that some of them are, in the end, content to be subordinate to men and to choose more conventional roles.

In his novel *Have Spacesuit, Will Travel* (1958), Heinlein gives his boy hero, young Kip, an even younger sidekick, a little girl called Peewee who proves to be every bit as intelligent and brave as Kip. *The Star Beast* (1954) features a young female character who has divorced her parents and, in *Tunnel in the Sky* (1955), the protagonist's older sister is a sergeant in the armed forces. With other female characters, Heinlein reflects more ambivalence about what their proper roles should be. In *The Puppet Masters* (1951), Heinlein's protagonist, Sam, battles against

alien invaders with the aid of Mary, who eventually becomes his wife; the novel ends with both leaving on a ship heading to the home planet of the aliens, but it is Sam who is in command of this expedition. *Podkayne of Mars* (1963) has as its central figure an intelligent and lively teenaged girl. Podkayne wants to be a starship captain, but she also knows that she can get further with men by concealing her intelligence and using her 'feminine wiles'. By the end of the novel she has decided that raising children and becoming a paediatrician are more exciting pursuits than piloting spaceships.

In a later novel, *Friday* (1982), Heinlein seems to be answering those who criticized his earlier portrayals of women. (Indeed, the novel was dedicated to a long list of women associated with science fiction, as well as to Heinlein's wife, Virginia.) Friday Jones is an

Mary Winston (left)
(*The Woman in Skin 13*, Gerald Vance, 1952)
In order to infiltrate their secret base Special Agent Mary volunteers to be transmuted into the semblance of one of the aliens who have invaded the earth – but her transmutation is far more successful than either she or her superiors ever suspected it would be.

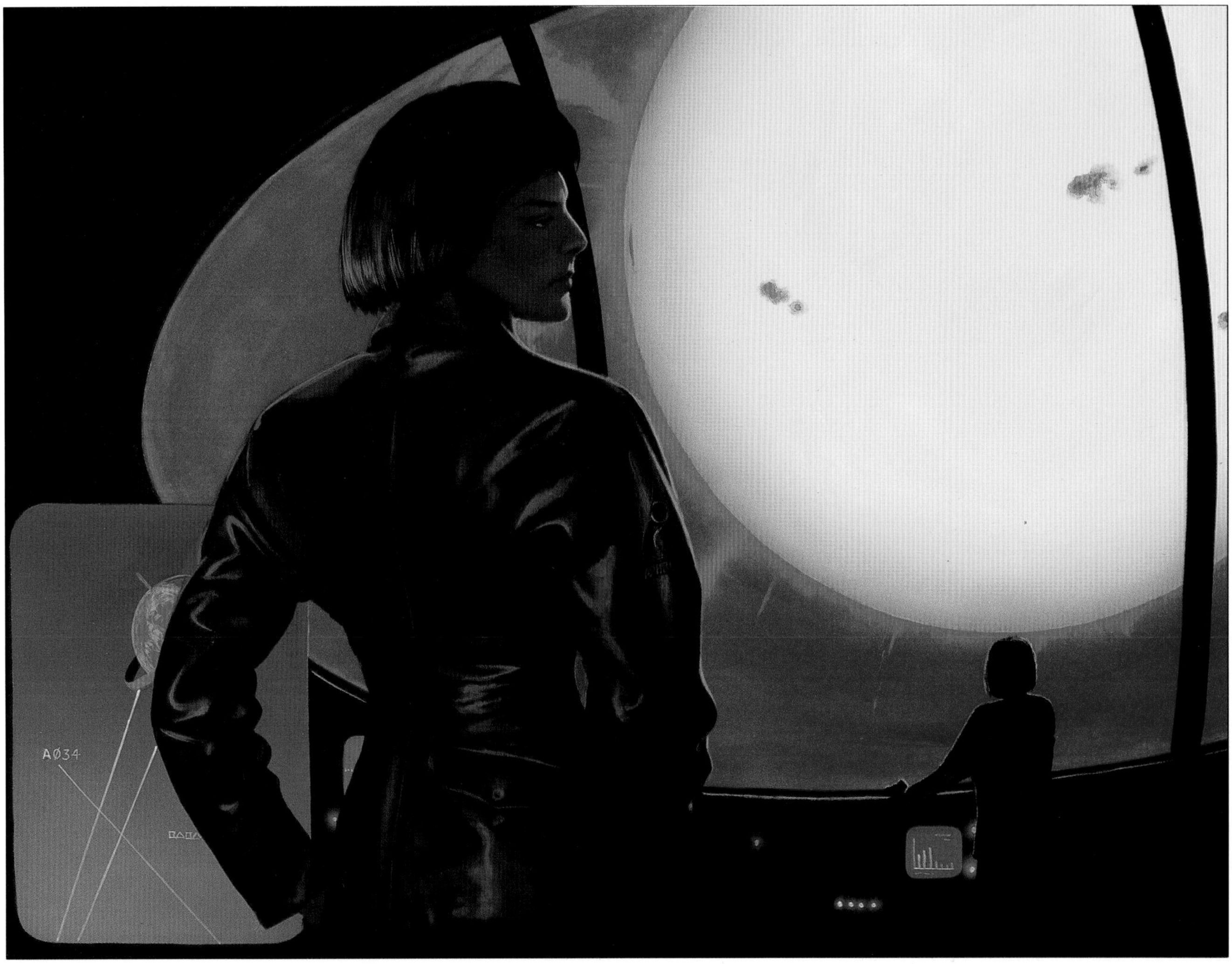
AØ34

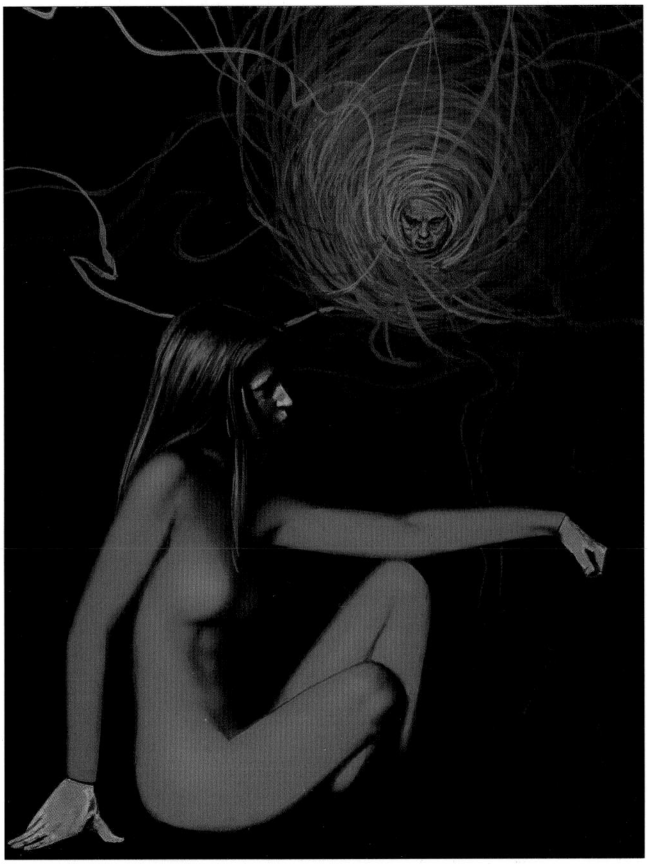

Lieutenant Ivy Hendricks (above)
('Jinx Ship to the Rescue', Alfred Coppel, Jr., 1948)
Lieutenant Ivy Hendricks, of the T.R.S. Aphrodite, is at the helm when her spaceship has to drop into the photosphere of the sun in order to save two sister ships and their crews. It is only through the use of a device of her own invention that the mission succeeds.

Nona & Anti (left)
('Accidental Flight', F. L. Wallace, 1952; also as *Address: Centauri*, 1955)
Nona and Anti are perhaps the strangest heroine team in science fiction history. They are inhabitants of a kind of orbiting 'hospital' – in truth a ghetto – where all of the world's biological misfits are sequestered by a society that has achieved physical perfection, and is too embarrassed to admit the existence of creatures like Nona, Anti and their shipmates. Nona is a beautiful autistic, with an extraordinary empathy for machines. Anti is a woman so grossly obese that she must live in an acid bath to keep her ever-increasing flesh from overwhelming her. During the rare moments she is free, she must keep herself wrapped in acid-soaked bandages. Together, they are instrumental in a revolt that succeeds in turning the space station into in interplanetary ship destined to make the first human trip to the stars.

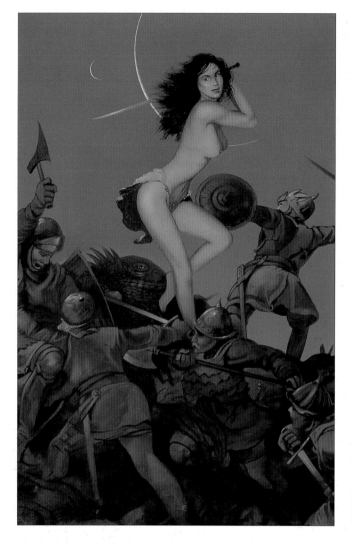

Iskra (above)
(*The Dark Tower*, 1951; also as The Memory Bank, Wallace West, 1961)
A representative example of the science fiction heroine of the late 1940s – most particularly the subtype of the wildly seductive and powerful warrior queen/sorceress of a lost race or civilization.

Lady Fand (above)
(*The Beast-Jewel of Mars*, Leigh Brackett, 1948)
Lady Fand of Mars possesses the technology – and inclination – to turn men into beasts.

operative who is also an 'artificial person', a test-tube baby who has been genetically engineered. She is tough, resourceful and highly intelligent. Even so, her strongest motivation is to 'belong' – to find human beings who will love and accept her as being fully human – and it is motherhood that finally makes Friday feel complete.

It is important to note here that Heinlein's heroines generally choose roles as wives or mothers and are not following the dictates of their societies passively. It is also crucial to point out that his female characters value these traditional roles and are also often involved in innovative domestic arrangements,

the group marriages of Friday and the intergenerational line marriages in his novel *The Moon is a Harsh Mistress* (1966) being only two examples. Women in many of his works also have little compunction about using technology in reproduction. In *Podkayne of Mars*, Podkayne's mother has, like most women in her society, given birth to infants in her youth, then has had the babies frozen cryogenically, to be brought up later when both the parents are older and have established themselves in their careers.

Heinlein's accomplishment, whatever his failings, should not be underestimated here. Earlier science fiction may have offered some

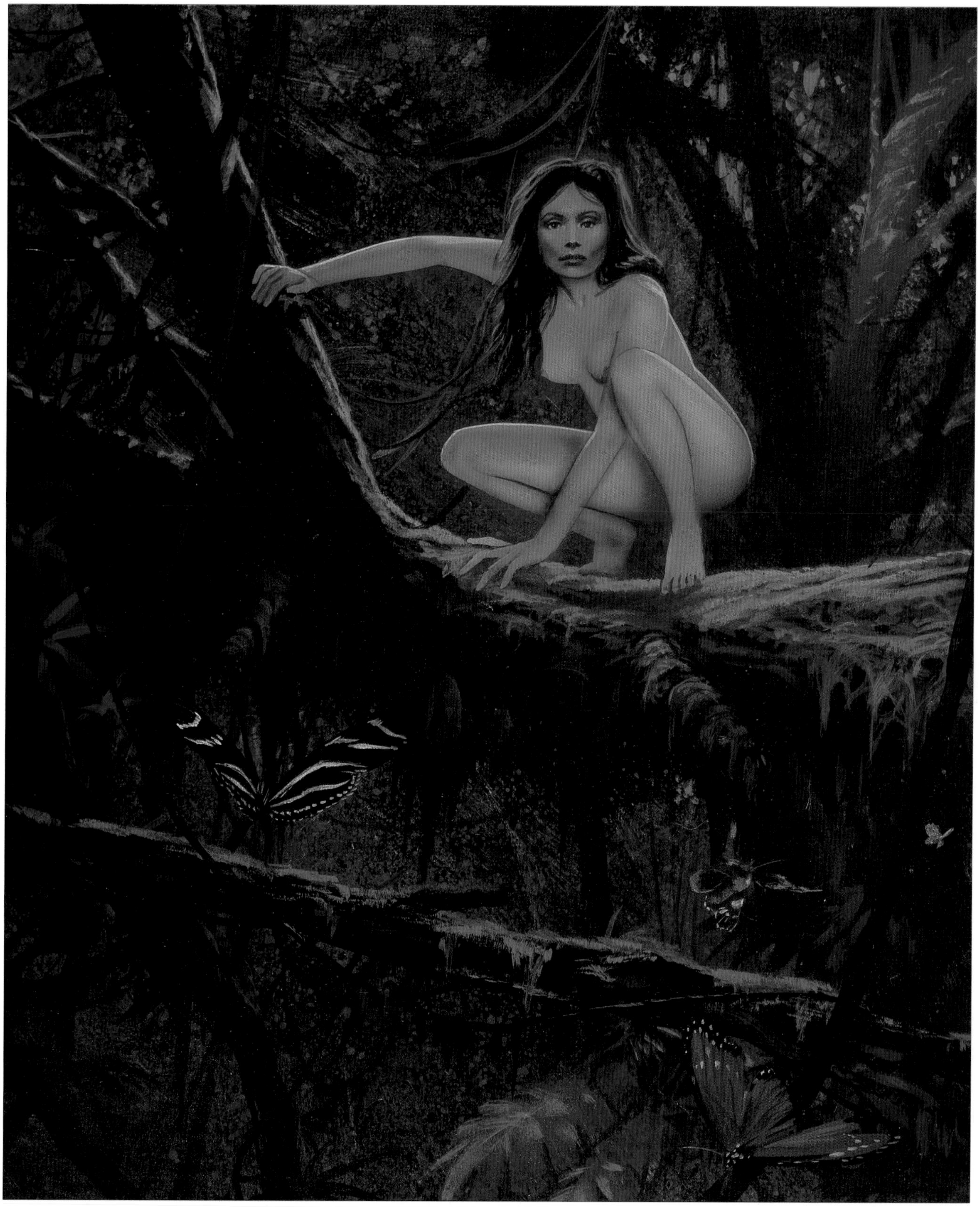

Kratas (above)
('Black Butterflies', Elmer Brown Mason, 1916)
'Such things can't be – but there she was, before our eyes!' Kratas is the mysterious, seductive guardian of a fabulous, terrible secret deep within the jungles of Borneo.

Bhetiru (above)
(*The Continent Makers*, L. Sprague de Camp, 1951)
Jeru-Bhetiru, native of the planet Krishna, is instrumental in helping save the earth from those who planned to destroy its continents in the creation of new ones.

strong female characters, but many of them were archetypal figures in fantastic tales. Heinlein, aiming at plausibility, was in effect saying that women could in fact become the kinds of people he depicted in his books and that the actual future being created was potentially as open to women as to men.

Another way for writers to work their way around the restrictions of realism while still presenting memorable female characters was to write about alien yet humanlike females. The assumption that some alien societies might be made up of beings much like ourselves was both plausible and a staple of past science fiction; perhaps for some writers it was also easier to assume that alien females could play roles that Earthly women could not.

Sometimes these roles were of a traditional self-sacrificing variety. In Philip José Farmer's

The Lovers (1952), a female of the alien Lalitha is able to take on human form in order to attract males and reproduce her kind. An Earthman on her planet, Hal Yarrow, falls in love with her. When Jeannette (as he knows her) becomes pregnant, Yarrow learns — too late — that her children (and his) can only be born by eating their way out of her body. The story won a Hugo Award and was notable for its treatment of sexuality, a subject most science fiction writers avoided until the Sixties. Critic Eric S. Rabkin, in his essay 'Science Fiction Women Before Liberation' (1981, in *Future Females: A Critical Anthology*, edited by Marleen S. Barr), wrote that if Jeannette is viewed through the lens of feminism, 'we may well read Farmer's Jeannette as a neurotic projection of a belief in female hostility toward men; but if we read *The Lovers* as a racial allegory of the Fifties, we find that the narrow stereotypes of the times serve to fashion a story that tries to promote not only the presumably feminine virtue of selflessness but the unsexed virtue of tolerance.'

L. Sprague de Camp offered both inventive speculation and a satirical look at our human

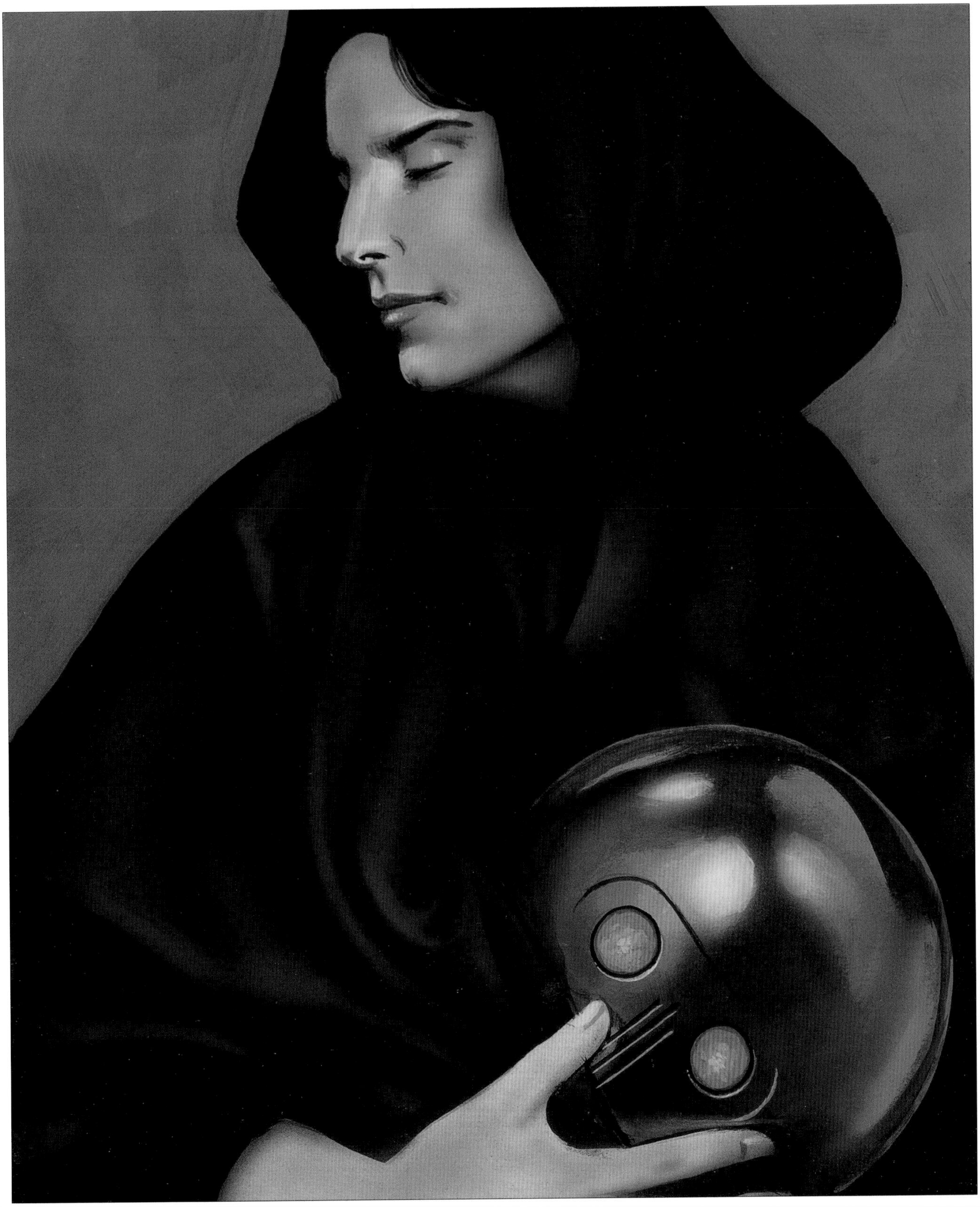

Dr. Susan Calvin (above)
('Liar', Isaac Asimov, 1941; also *I, Robot*, 1950)
The emotionless robo-psychologist, Susan Calvin, is told by the mind-reading robot named Herbie that the man she secretly loves is also in love with her. The tragedy is that Herbie, in attempting to obey the First Law of Robotics, which forbids a robot to harm a human being, has tried to avoid hurting Dr Calvin by lying to her..

Gyda (above)
(*The Skraeling*, R. Milnikov, 1958)

Ewayea is an American Indian princess who was captured by Vikings after one of their abortive invasions of Labrador, 500 years before Columbus. She is taken back to Norway, given the name Gyda and eventually proves herself so impressively that she is taken on a raid of Ireland. Escaping there in a stolen Viking boat, she and two or three others make their way back to the New World – unfortunately, far south of her planned destination. After enormous travails, she remains the sole survivor, marooned at the mouth of the Amazon River. Making her way upstream, she ultimately reaches the headwaters of the great river where, meeting the great Manco Capac, joins him in founding the first Incan Empire.

Earth people to help her save her friend; in the process, she learns about Earth's customs. Along the way, de Camp pokes fun at some of our notions of romantic love.

In spite of the appearance of strong female characters in notable works of science fiction, imagined futures were still seen largely through the eyes of men. Stories of adventure and realistically worked-out tales, usually narrated in a straightforward fashion, continued to comprise most of the works published. But the Sixties would provide a dramatic change in science fiction's status quo.

ways in his novel *Rogue Queen* (1951). The novel is one of the few earlier works of science fiction that has a female as its protagonist. Iroedh is a member of a humanoid, matriarchal society with a social structure similar to that of the bee; when an expedition from Earth arrives on her planet, the ways of Iroedh's people are threatened. In her efforts to save a drone, Antis, who has reached the age where he must be killed, Iroedh tries to force the

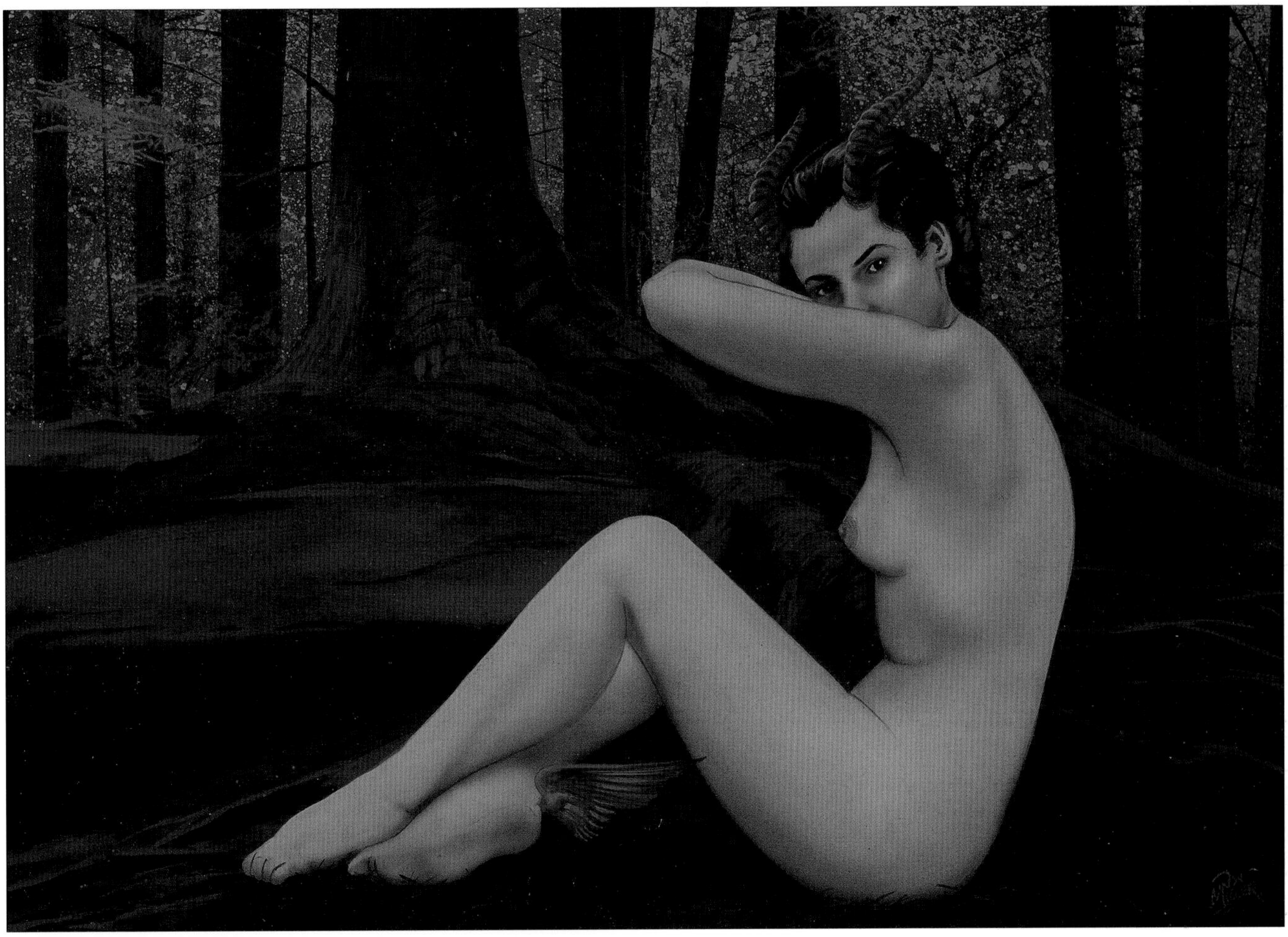

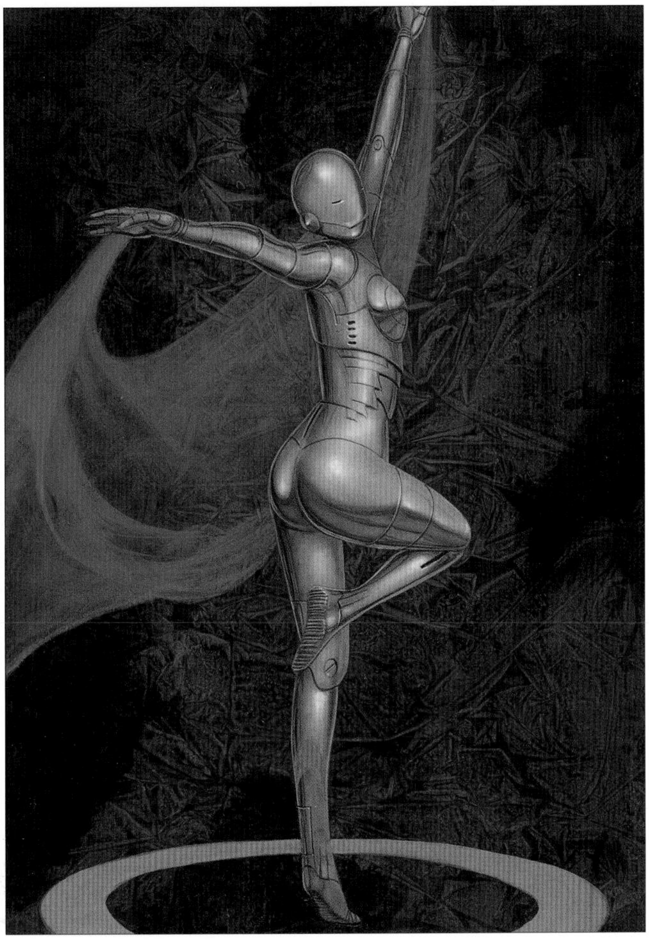

Plura (above)
(*Is This the Way Home?*, Lawrence Chandler, 1952)

When Plura strayed out of the wrong depot of the Planetary Interurban and found herself stranded on a bakward, prudish planet called Earth, she had everything except clothing. She found more friends in the nudist colony than at the dowager's bridge party . . . but how to get back to civilization.

Dierdre (left)
('No Woman Born', C. L. Moore, 1944)

Deirdre, once one of the most beautiful women in the world and a professional dancer, has had her body – destroyed in a fire – replaced by a robotic prosthesis. Indeed, all that remained of her was her brain. Nevertheless, she is still able to stun audiences with her skill and talent.

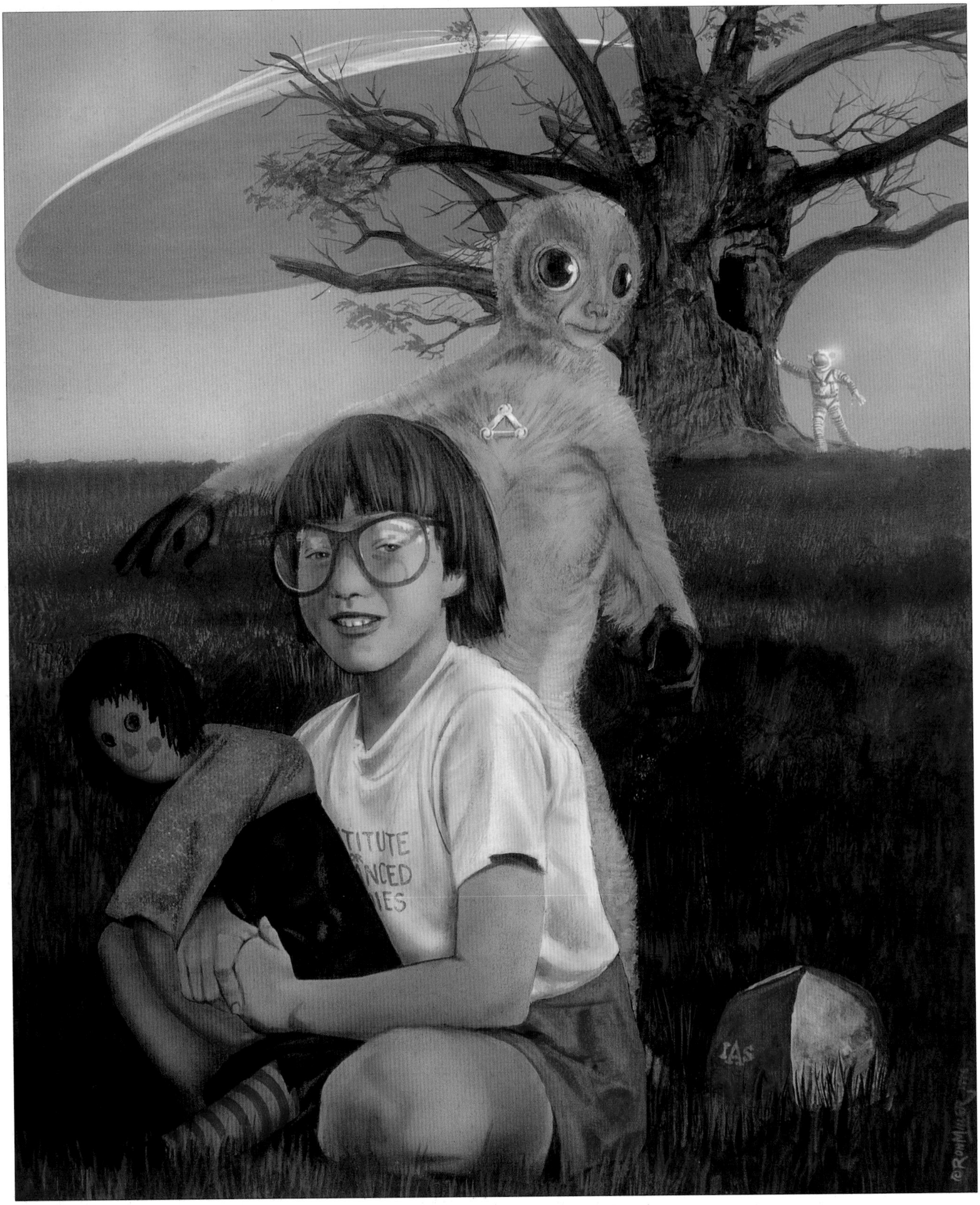

Peewee Reisfeld and the Mother Thing (above)
(*Have Spacesuit Will Travel*, Robert A. Heinlein, 1958)
Super-genius and super-brat Peewee Reisfeld, with the aid of the gentle alien, Mother Thing, manages to save the earth from being obliterated by order of a cosmic court.

Captain Judikah (right)
(*Captain Judikah*, R. Milnikov, 1945)
Notorious space pirate and adventuress, Captain Judikah grew up in the slums that surrounded the greatest spaceport on her planet and fought her way into the coveted ranks of the Space Patrol only to have betrayal force her into a career outside the law.

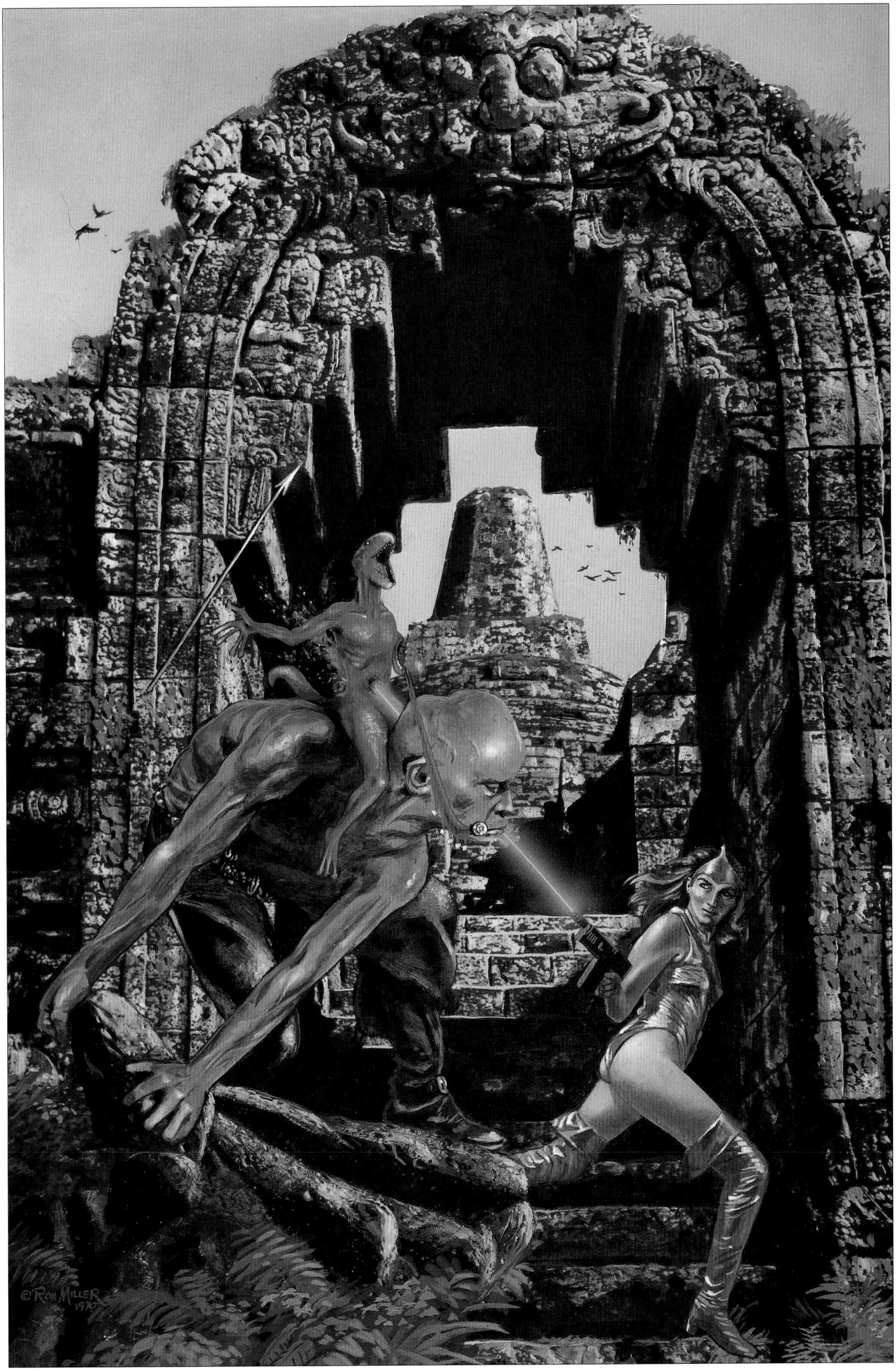
©RON MILLER
1979

Chapter 3
The 1960s to 1970s

Galadriel (below)
(*Lord of the Rings*, J. R. R. Tolkien, 1965)
Galadriel – the 'Woman of the Trees' – was one of the queens of the Noldorin High-Elves of Eldanar during the Elder Days and was leader of the rebellious Noldor who forsook the Blessed Realm at the end of the First Age in order to make war on Morgoth the Enemy in Middle-earth. She was the mightiest of the remaining Eldar.

DURING THE Sixties, several writers, readers and editors began to re-examine the assumptions and style of science fiction; perhaps not coincidentally, more women writers entered the field. This movement, known as the New Wave, was described by writer and critic Brian Stableford in the third edition of *Anatomy of Wonder* (edited by Neil Barron, 1987):

'The first major propagandist for the SF New Wave was Michael Moorcock, who acquired his platform in 1964 when he became editor of the British magazine *New Worlds*. Moorcock thought that the future was not really to be found in the visions of galactic empire and technological triumph seen in so much SF, but in apocalyptic possibilities with which the present was already pregnant. Other British writers, including J. G. Ballard and Brian Aldiss, had already begun moving in the same direction, more interested in the "inner space" of human perceptions and psychological reactions to hypothetical situations than in the "outer space" of colourful futuristic adventure stories.'

American writers associated with this new approach included Harlan Ellison (who was to edit the influential anthology *Dangerous Visions* in 1967), Norman Spinrad, Samuel R. Delany and Roger Zelazny. For them, science fiction had become too predictable and hidebound and was ripe for change.

Tigerishka
(opposite)
(*The Wanderer*, Fritz Leiber, 1965)
Tigerishka is the commander of a planet-sized spaceship that parks itself in earth orbit, causing disastrous tidal cataclysms on our planet in the process. While making some attempt to rectify the havoc she has caused, Tigerishka must also deal with a 'police' planet that is pursuing her.

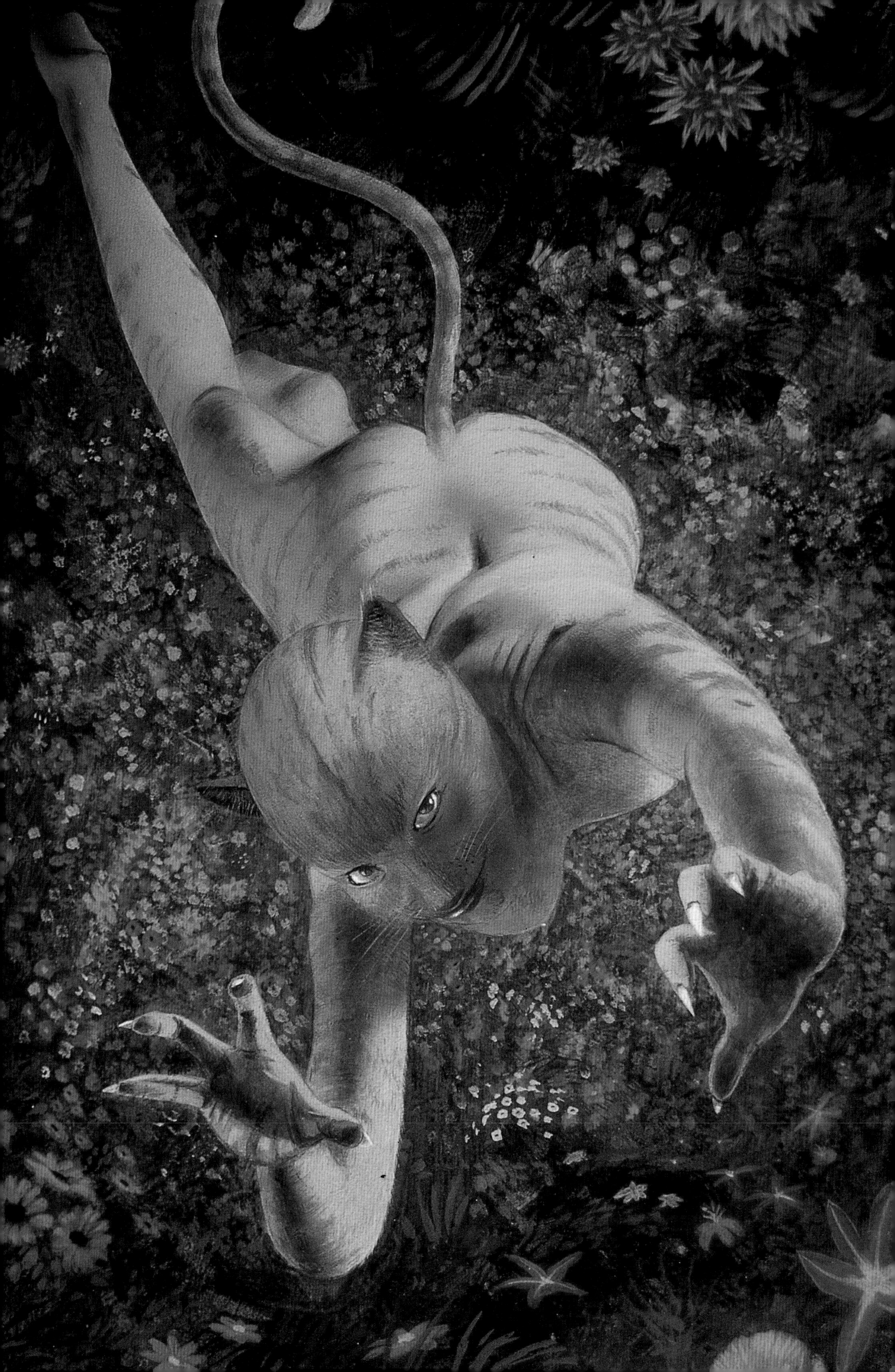

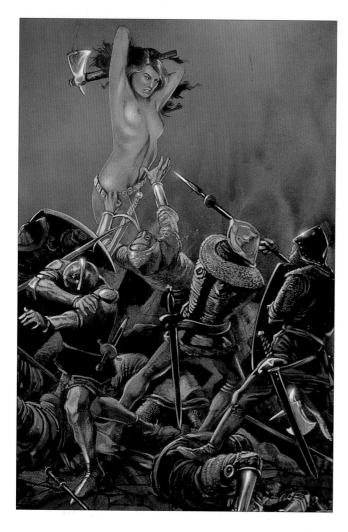

Beudag (above)
(*Lorelei of the Red Mist*, Leigh Brackett and Ray Bradbury, 1946)
A ferocious barbarian warrioress, she is instrumental in overthrowing an insidious evil that threatens to overrun her home planet.

R'Li (left)
(*Dare*, Philip José Farmer, 1965)
The planet Dare – the second of the star, Ceti – is 'colonized' by Earthlings kidnapped and transported in the late 16th century. The humans flourish for four centuries – in spite of an uneasy relationship with the planet's native inhabitants: the horstels of which R'Li is the bravest

Science fiction writers, usually reticent about dealing with sex, now began to write more frankly about sexual matters. For some writers, this simply meant that the role of woman as sex object could be added to the traditional ones of housewife, child rearer, scientist's daughter, love interest and damsel in distress. Other writers seized the opportunity to write about fully realized female characters who could also be allowed a sex life.

Several entertaining and influential science fiction novels of the sixties had women at the centre of the story. Rosel George Brown's *Sibyl Sue Blue* (1968) follows a future police sergeant as she travels to the planet of Radix to solve a mystery involving the murders of several young women. *The Universe Against Her* (1964) by James H. Schmitz brought together several stories featuring Telzey Amberdon, a teenaged telepath who is recruited as an agent. Schmitz was atypical in his treatment of female characters; as the *Science Fiction Encyclopedia* notes:

[Schmitz] regularly produced the kind of tale for which he remains most warmly remembered: space opera adventures, several featuring female heroes depicted with minimum recourse to their 'femininity' – they perform their active tasks, and save the Universe when necessary, in a manner almost completely free of sexual role-playing clichés.

In Samuel R. Delany's *Babel-17* (1966), a colourful New Wave work, Rydra Wong, a poet, cryptographer and linguist, must decipher the language of alien invaders. She later leads an expedition to the aliens' planet. *Babel-17* won a Nebula Award which is given annually by the Science Fiction Writers of America and is one of the genre's two highest honours, the

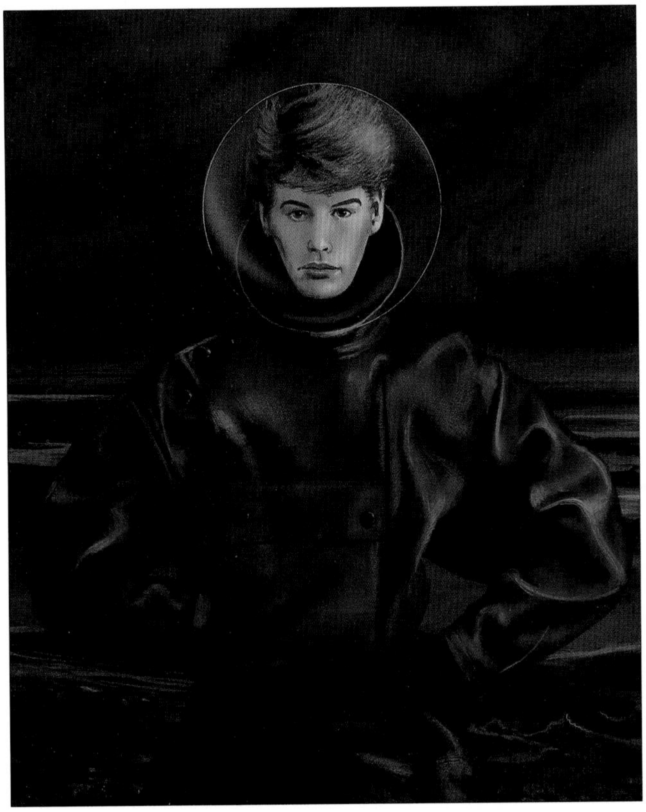

Mary (above)
(*Memoirs of a Spacewoman*, Naomi Mitchison, 1962)
A communications expert specializing in alien lifeforms, Mary's job takes her to many strange environments. Twice she volunteers to have alien lifeforms grafted onto her body in order to better understand them.

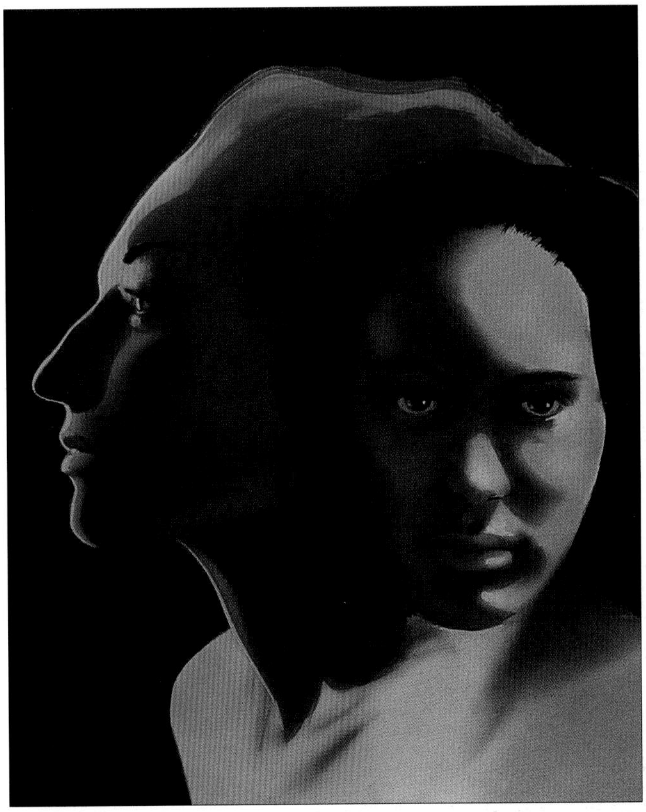

Zelde M'Tana and Rissa Kerguelen (above)
(*Rissa Kerguelen, The Long View, Zelde M'Tana*, F. M. Busby, 1976-1980)
At 17, Rissa finds herself an exile from earth and in a gang of space pirates. Soon she is commanding an armada to invade her home planet. Zelde is scarcely 15, when she, too, swears vengeance and joins the space pirates' rebellion.

other being the Hugo Award given at the annual World Science Fiction Convention. *Rite of Passage* (1968) by Alexei Panshin, another novel honoured with a Nebula Award, follows Mia Havero as she comes of age in a community that lives aboard an asteroid-ship travelling through space. In order to be considered an adult, Mia must travel to a planet of 'Mudeaters'

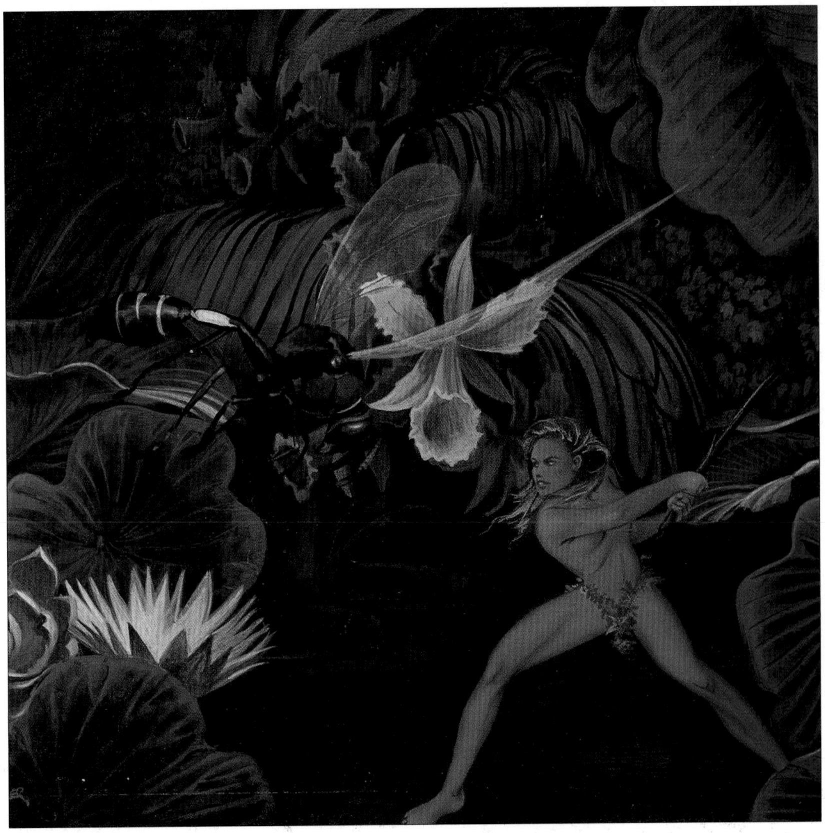

Yattmut (right)
(*Hothouse*, Brian Aldiss, 1962)
In the unimaginably distant future, when the earth steams under a dying sun, the shrunken remnants of mankind – symbiots with intelligent fungi – have to constantly battle sentient plants and enormous carnivorous insects to maintain their precarious existence.

Star (above)
(*Glory Road*, Robert A. Heinlein, 1963)
'Star' is the anglicized version of her real name, which is 'much like' Etarre. She is a niece of the half-legendary Count Cagliostro and the warrior-empress of the Twenty Universes. She must undergo incredible adventures and hardships in her quest to regain the fabulous Egg of the Phoenix.

Estri Hadrath diet Estrazi (above)
(*The High Couch of Silistria, The Golden Sword, Wind from the Abyss, The Carnelian Throne,* Janet E. Morris, 1977-1979)
Estri was high-couch in the greatest house of pleasure in the civilized stars. The most beautiful courtesan in the universe, she was a god and the daughter of light.

(the derogatory term her people use for all those who live on planetary surfaces) and survive. The entire novel, which owes much to Robert A. Heinlein's books for both young readers and adults, is written in the first person from Mia's point of view.

Naomi Mitchison, sister of the biologist J.B.S. Haldane, was already the author of a number of works, including several historical novels, when she published her first science fiction novel, *Memoirs of a Spacewoman*, in 1962. This episodic work is centred around its narrator, Mary, a communications expert exploring alien

intelligences, and is filled with rich speculations about both human and alien biology.

Joanna Russ introduced her memorable character Alyx, a woman of the ancient world who leads the life of a soldier of fortune, in 'The Adventuress' (1967) and soon followed it with other stories, eventually collected in one volume as *The Adventures of Alyx* (1983). Some hailed the appearance of Alyx as something new in science fiction – a swashbuckling heroine in stories written by a woman – but, in fact, C.L. Moore's Jirel had preceded her and Alyx – rationalist, small in stature and often cantan-

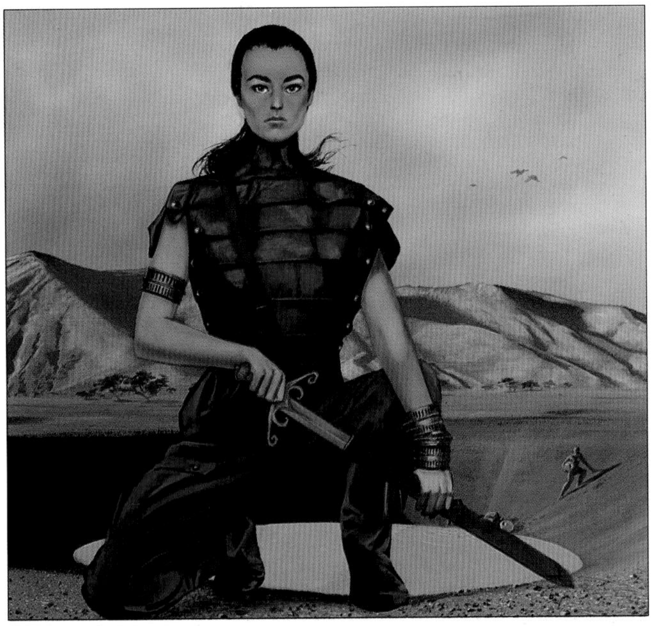

Rifkind (above)
***(Daughter of the Bright Moon* & *The Black Flame*, Lynn Abbey, 1980)**
In a harsh desert world, where most women are bound to the men who rule their clans, Rifkind, a chieftain's daughter, dares to take up a sword and become a warrior.

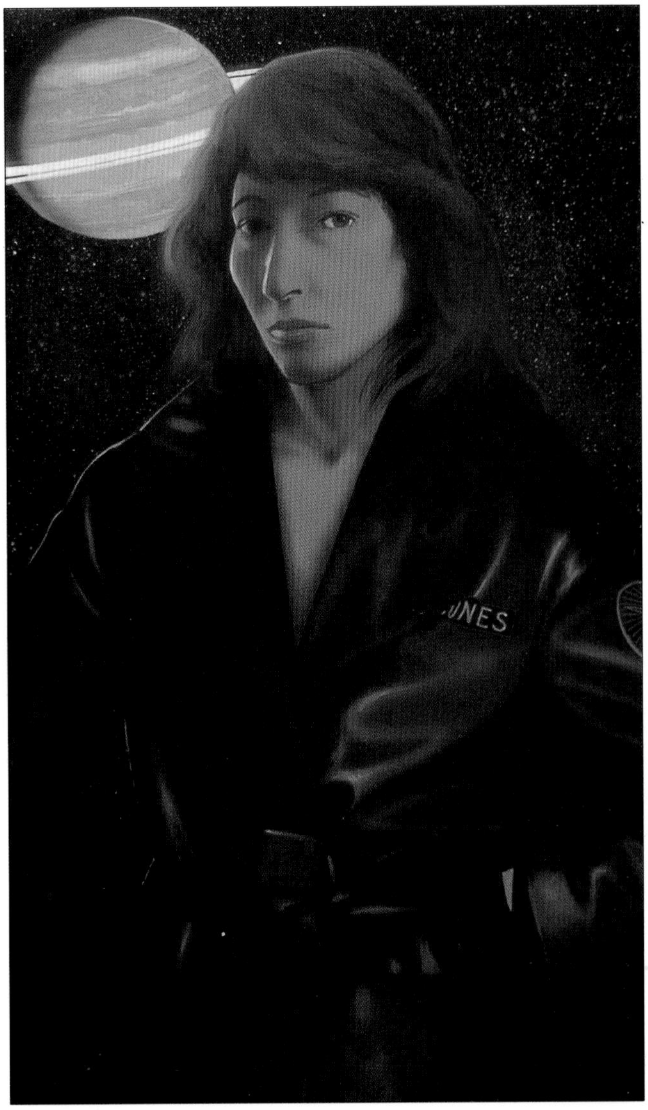

JONES

Captain Cirocco Jones (top right)
(*Titan*, John Varley, 1979; also *Wizard*, 1980, *Demon*, 1984)
Also known as Rocky Jones, she commands the first human expedition to the Saturnian moon Titan, where she discovers an enormous wheel-shaped structure.

kerous – is a character on a more human scale than Jirel. Even so, after the appearance of the Alyx stories, more science fiction writers welcomed the opportunity to cast women in the kind of adventurous roles usually played by men. Russ eventually brought Alyx to the future as a Trans-Temp agent – a kind of time-travelling mercenary – in her novel *Picnic on Paradise* (1968).

Anne McCaffrey, the first woman science fiction writer to be honoured with both the Hugo and Nebula Awards, used female protagonists in both *The Ship Who Sang* (1969)

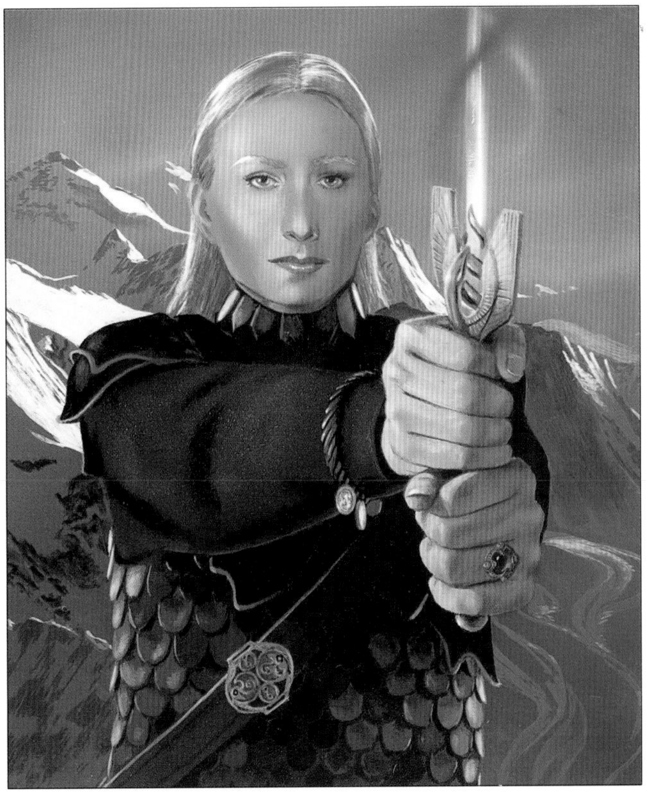

Morgaine Frosthair (bottom right)
(*Gate of Ivrel, Well of Shiuan, Fires of Azeroth*, C. J. Cherryh, 1976-1979, *The Book of Morgaine*, 1979)
Morgaine seeks to close the Gates left by a prior civilization which involved humanity in its time-space collapse: fearing that any Gate misused, could loose the technology elsewhere.

Dragoika (above)
(*Ensign Flandry*, Poul Anderson, 1979)
Dragoika, the Tigery, is second mate of the Sisterhood of Kursoviki merchant ship Archer on Starkad (where most of the ship's officers are female). She saves Ensign Dominic Flandry when he crash-lands on her planet and she proves to be a valuable ally in his secret mission.

Snake (above)
('**Of Mist, and Grass, and Sand**', Vonda N. McIntyre, 1973; also *Dreamsnake*, 1978)
Snake is a healer whose partner in the healing process is the offworld 'dreamsnake', Grass, who has the ability to ease pain. When Grass dies, Snake must make a pilgrimage to her original teachers to tell them of her loss.

and *Dragonflight* (1968). The former is a collection of stories about Helva, a woman horribly deformed since birth who becomes the cyborg guidance system of a spaceship. Helva's relationships with her 'brawns', the pilots who work with her, are an important part of these tales. *Dragonflight*, a novel about a young woman named Lessa, inhabitant of a world of telepathic dragons and their female riders, led to one of the most popular series of science fiction novels ever published, the Dragonriders of Pern series. The popularity of McCaffrey's novels was more evidence that the female audience for science fiction was growing and the realization that there was such an audience led to more works with female protagonists.

As the Sixties drew to a close, the publication of Ursula K. Le Guin's *The Left Hand of Darkness* (1969) marked a turning point in the genre. Here, the planet of Gethen, seen through the eyes of Earthman Genly Ai, is a world of people who are genderless except during their reproductive cycle, when each becomes either male or female without any control over which sex one may become. In a strict sense, there are no female characters in the novel and male pronouns are used in referring to the Gethenians, but every Gethenian character has the potential to become a female. *The Left Hand of Darkness* won both Hugo and Nebula Awards and became one of the most enduring and influential of science fiction works. As Genly Ai notes about his experience: 'When you meet a Gethenian you cannot and must not . . . cast him in the role of Man or Woman, while adopting toward him a corresponding role . . . One is respected and judged only as a human being. It is an appalling experience.'

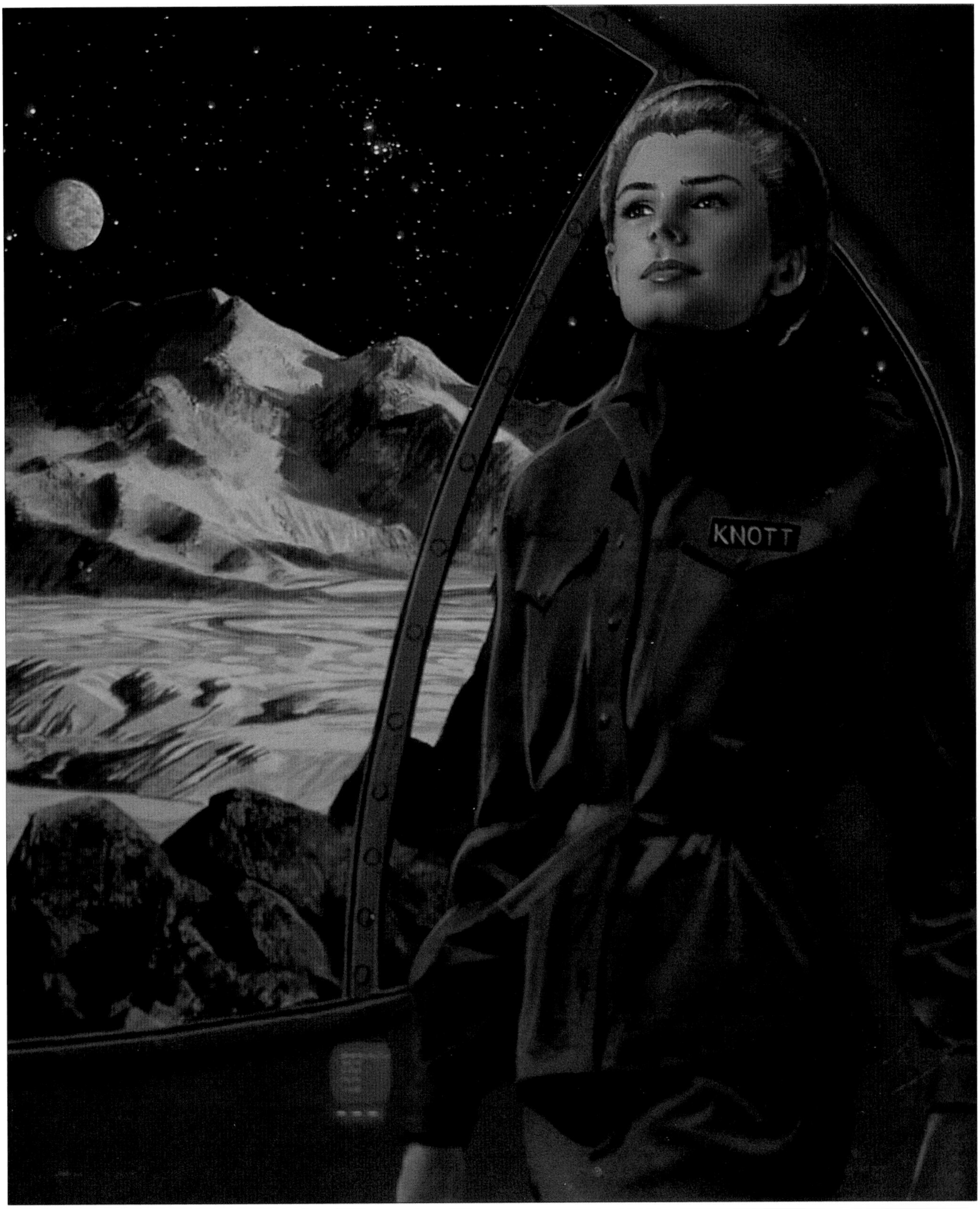
KNOTT

Wyoming Knott (above)
(*The Moon is a Harsh Mistress*, Robert A. Heinlein, 1966)
Although introduced as 'a nice little girl', Wyoming Knott proves – by necessity if no other reason – to be none of these things. She is a prime instigator, mover and participant in the bid and eventual war for independence of the earth's lunar colonies.

Suona of Shalin (above)
('The Silken Dragon,' Stephen Edward McDonald, 1980)
Suona, daughter of the Devil-King Tamien, must battle the evil sorcerer Vardret Kovair with no other defence than the weapon in her hand. Will the dragon, conjured into life from the silken tapestry, come to her aid or her enemy's?

Alyx (above)
(*The Adventures of Alyx*, Joanna Russ, 1976)
'Alyx ... had come to the Coty of Durdh as part of a religious delegation ... In due time the police chased Alyx's co-religionists down the Street of Heaven and Hell and out the swamp gate ... and Alyx — took up a living as a pick-lock.'

Le Guin's novel was published at a time when a resurgent feminist movement was bringing more people, men and women, to question gender roles. Earlier science fiction writers had shown female characters in a variety of roles, but usually in the context of a society where males were still dominant, or in tales of dominant females where the roles were simply reversed. Now more writers were to discover that science fiction was especially suited for imaginatively exploring gender roles; this would have a noticeable effect on how both female and male characters were portrayed.

Science fiction has often been regarded as a thought-experiment of sorts, a way to set up certain imagined conditions and then to see the results. Utopian writers, part of a tradition closely wedded to that of science fiction, had often created what they regarded as ideal societies (or, in dystopian works, their nightmares). During the Seventies, more writers in the mainstream of science fiction, many of them women, drew on both feminism and the Utopian tradition for inspiration. Only science fiction and, in a different way, fantasy, can depict women in entirely new and different surroundings. The genre can explore what women might become if and when present restrictions on their lives vanish, or reveal possible new problems. It can depict the remarkable woman as normal, where past literature has shown her as the exception.

An important writer of science fiction who came to prominence during the seventies was Kate Wilhelm, who had begun publishing stories during the Fifties. Wilhelm's special strength as a writer is showing readers life as it is lived and characters who are much like the

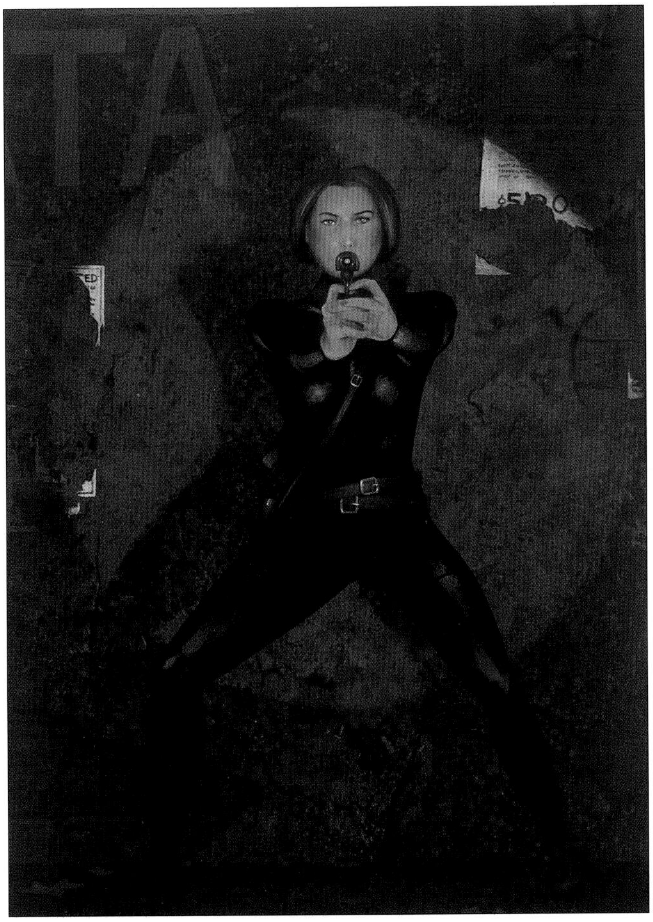

Angelina DiGriz (above)
(*The Stainless Steel Rat*, Harry Harrison, 1961)
'... she was an artist to her fingertips ... temptress, sorceress, murderess ... actress, liar, cheat ...' Even her husband, the amoral supercriminal called 'The Stainless Steel Rat', is hard-put to restrain his bloodthirsty wife.

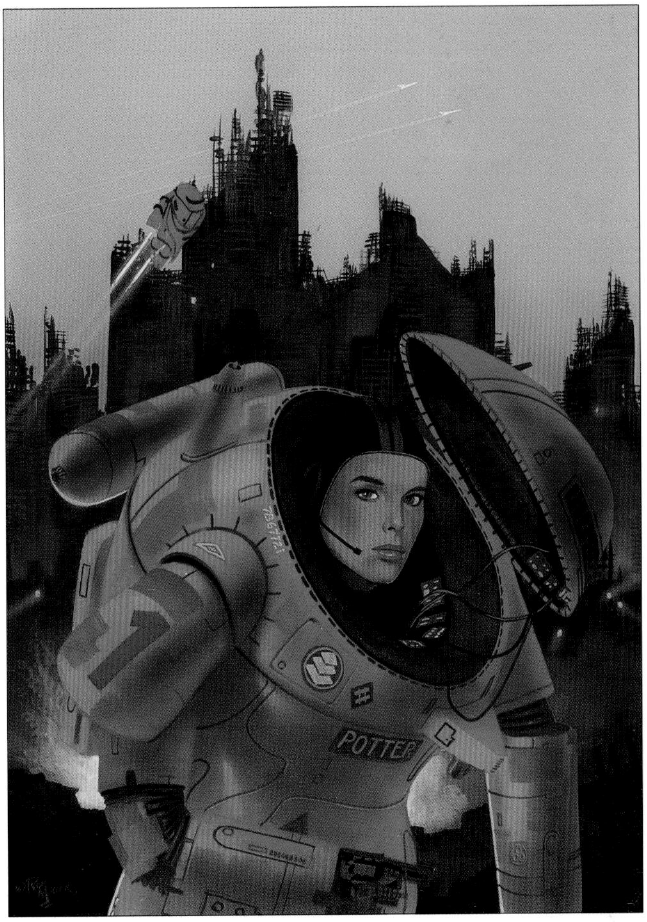
POTTER

Marygay Potter (above)
(*The Forever War*, Joe Haldeman, 1974)
Born in 1977, Marygay Potter spends her military career in fighting the millennium-spanning Forever War which, thanks to the effects of time dilation lasts 1166 years. She must then wait for her mate, William Mandella.

people we might meet in our everyday lives. One of the many memorable women who can be found in the pages of Wilhelm's works is Anne Clewiston, the protagonist of *The Clewiston Test* (1976). Anne, a research scientist, has to struggle against both an oppressive husband and colleagues who suspect that she may have experimented on herself and who eventually come to doubt her sanity.

Marion Zimmer Bradley, already popular for her series of Darkover novels, often has strong women characters in her work. With *The Shattered Chain* (1976), another Darkover novel, she moves a female character, Jaelle n'ha Melora, to the story's centre. Jaelle, rescued from the more restrictive environment of a Drytown, joins the Free Amazons of Darkover, women who live their lives apart from men. Other women in the book are Kindra, a Free Amazon who rescues Jaelle and Magda Lorne, an anthropologist who has come to Darkover. Unlike many earlier works of science fiction, women characters in science fiction of the Seventies often had networks of female friends and relations.

Men writing science fiction were also apparently influenced by the women's movement in their depictions of female characters. Joe Haldeman, himself a veteran of the Vietnam War, wrote a Hugo and Nebula award-winning novel, *The Forever War* (1974), about an interstellar war that lasts over a thousand years. The protagonist of his story is William Mandella, drafted to fight for Earth, but Marygay Potter, another draftee, is nearly as important a character as Mandella. Because of the time dilatation caused by their interstellar jumps to distant worlds to do battle, both soldiers and

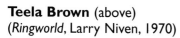

Teela Brown (above)
(*Ringworld*, Larry Niven, 1970)
Recruited as a crew member of the first expedition to the fabulous Ringworld, Teela is chosen for her extraordinary luck – like Gladstone Gander, nothing bad has ever happened to her.

Telzey Amberdon (above)
(The Telzey series, James H. Schmitz, 1971; also *The Telzey Toy*, 1973)
A typical, bright, pretty teenage girl – except that Telzey is a fabulously talented telepath whose abilities are vital to the survival of her world – but at a terrible cost to herself.

their comrades – those who survive – return to an ever-changing Earth from which they become progressively alienated. Haldeman's novel has been seen as a response to Robert A. Heinlein's 1959 novel *Starship Troopers* (in which Heinlein, interestingly, speculated that women might make better starship pilots than men). Haldeman has acknowledged Heinlein's influence on his work but *The Forever War* also reflects his own experience as a draftee fighting a war with unclear or changing objectives and being cynically used by those in command. The equality shown in his novel is one in which female and male soldiers are equally brave – and equally mistreated – and he portrays his characters with remarkable evenhandedness.

Samuel R. Delany, one of the most literary and innovative of science fiction writers, populated his earlier novels with exotic characters – males and females often portrayed in untraditional ways. In *Triton* (1976), the main character, Bron Helstrom, begins life as a man, but lives in a society where sexual orientation and gender are fluid and easily changed; several dif-

ferent genders are recognized. Bron, unlike the other inhabitants of Triton, is convinced that there are inherent differences between men and women; this belief eventually leads him to become a woman, since this is the only way he can express the qualities he sees as female.

Some writers address feminist issues explicitly and sometimes angrily, in their work. In *Walk to the End of the World* (1974), Suzy McKee Charnas gives us Alldera, a woman raised in the Holdfast, where men treat women as beasts of burden and brood mares. Eventually, Alldera escapes to the wilderness. In the sequel, *Motherlines* (1979), Alldera meets the Riding Women, who live entirely apart from men. Although there are many science fiction novels in which women barely exist, or there are no female characters at all, *Motherlines* is one of the few in which there are no male characters.

One of the most honoured writers of the Seventies was the pseudonymous James Tiptree, Jr. In the late Seventies, it was revealed that Tiptree was in fact Alice Sheldon, a retired

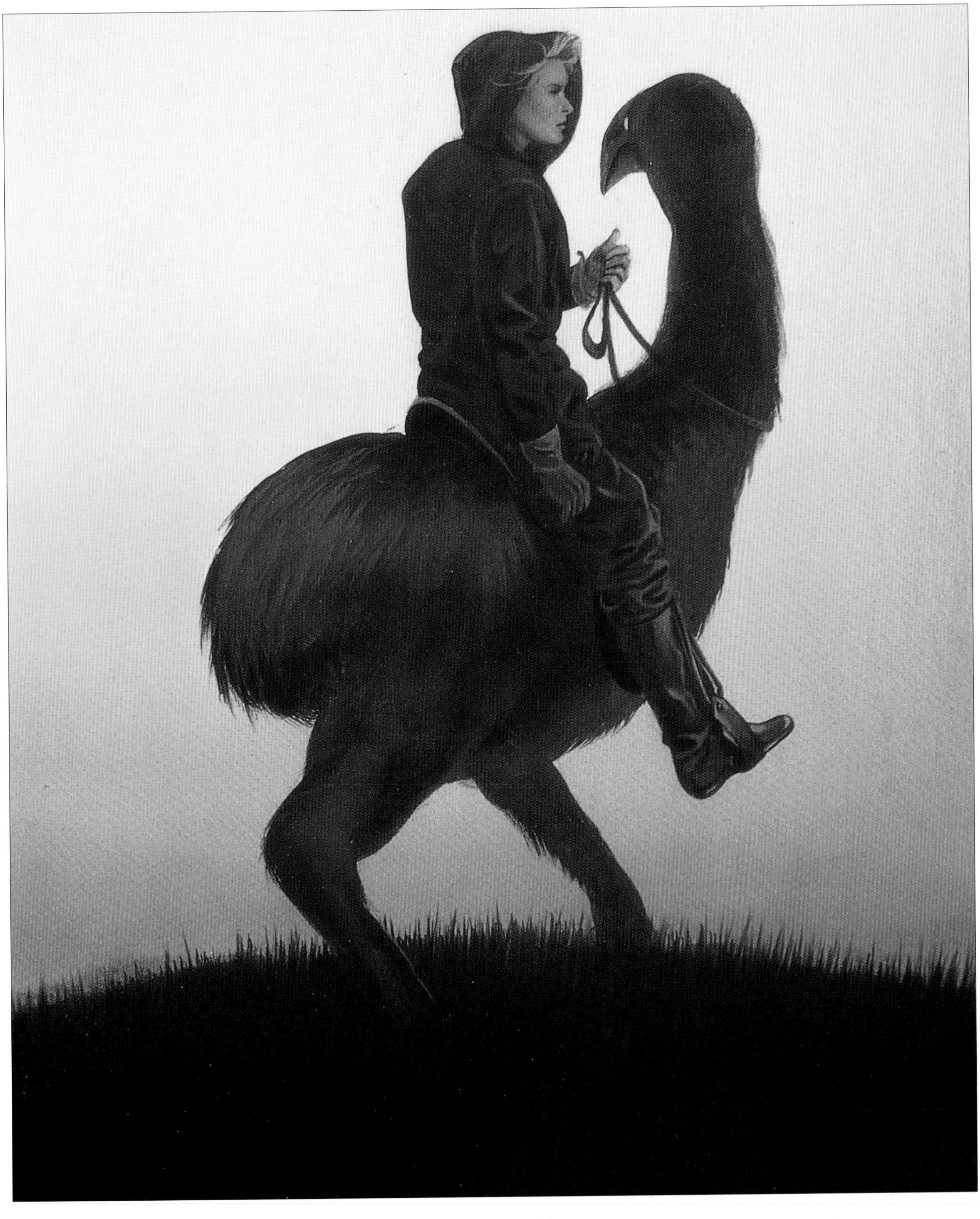

Cija (above)
***(The City, Some Summer Lands, Atlan, The Serpent, The Dragon,* Jane Gaskell, 1965-1977)**
Princess Cija is the daughter of an Atlantean dictatrix who rules a South American kingdom while Atlantis proper has cut itself off from the outside world by a kind of force field. Cija survives war, revolution, oppression, starvation, slavery, beating, rape, wild beasts, mortal foes and deadly plots.

Lessa (above)
(*Dragonflight*, Anne McCaffrey, 1967-1968)
Lessa, a telepath, turns a patriarchal system against itself to contrive the death of her male oppressor and to secure her own freedom.

psychologist who had served in the US Army and had also been an intelligence officer. Two classic Tiptree stories deserve mention here. 'Houston, Houston, Do You Read?' (1976) is the award-winning and highly controversial tale of three American male astronauts who go through a time warp and find themselves on a future Earth populated entirely by women who are female clones. The women decide that they cannot allow these men to survive and the author clearly sympathizes with the women's decision. A quieter, but equally powerful Tiptree story is 'The Women Men Don't See' (1973). The story is told in the first person by a man, Don Fenton, but the central character is Ruth Parsons, travelling in Mexico with her daughter Althea. Don, Ruth and Althea are on a small plane with their pilot, Estéban, when it crashes. Aliens are spotted by the four survivors; Don is stunned when the two women, knowing nothing about these

aliens, choose to leave Earth with them. 'What women do is survive,' Ruth has told Don earlier, 'we live by ones and twos in the chinks of your world-machine.' Ruth leaves with the aliens because, on a male-dominated Earth, she has in effect been living among aliens all her life.

Perhaps the most overtly feminist novel of the Seventies was the powerful, angry and polemical *The Female Man* (1975) by Joanna Russ. In an earlier Nebula award-winning story, 'When It Changed' (1972), Russ introduced Janet, an inhabitant of Whileaway, a planet settled many generations earlier by Earthpeople. Since the death of all of the male settlers long ago in a plague, the women have gotten along quite well by themselves — until four men arrive. The men try to reassure the women that things will be better now; Janet very much doubts this. Janet reappears in *The Female Man* but three other women from alternative worlds share the stage with her: Jeannine, the passive inhabitant of a world in the grip of an economic depression; Joanna, who lives in a world much like ours; and Jael, an assassin from a world where men and women are at war with each other. All four are actually versions of the same woman and we see how different

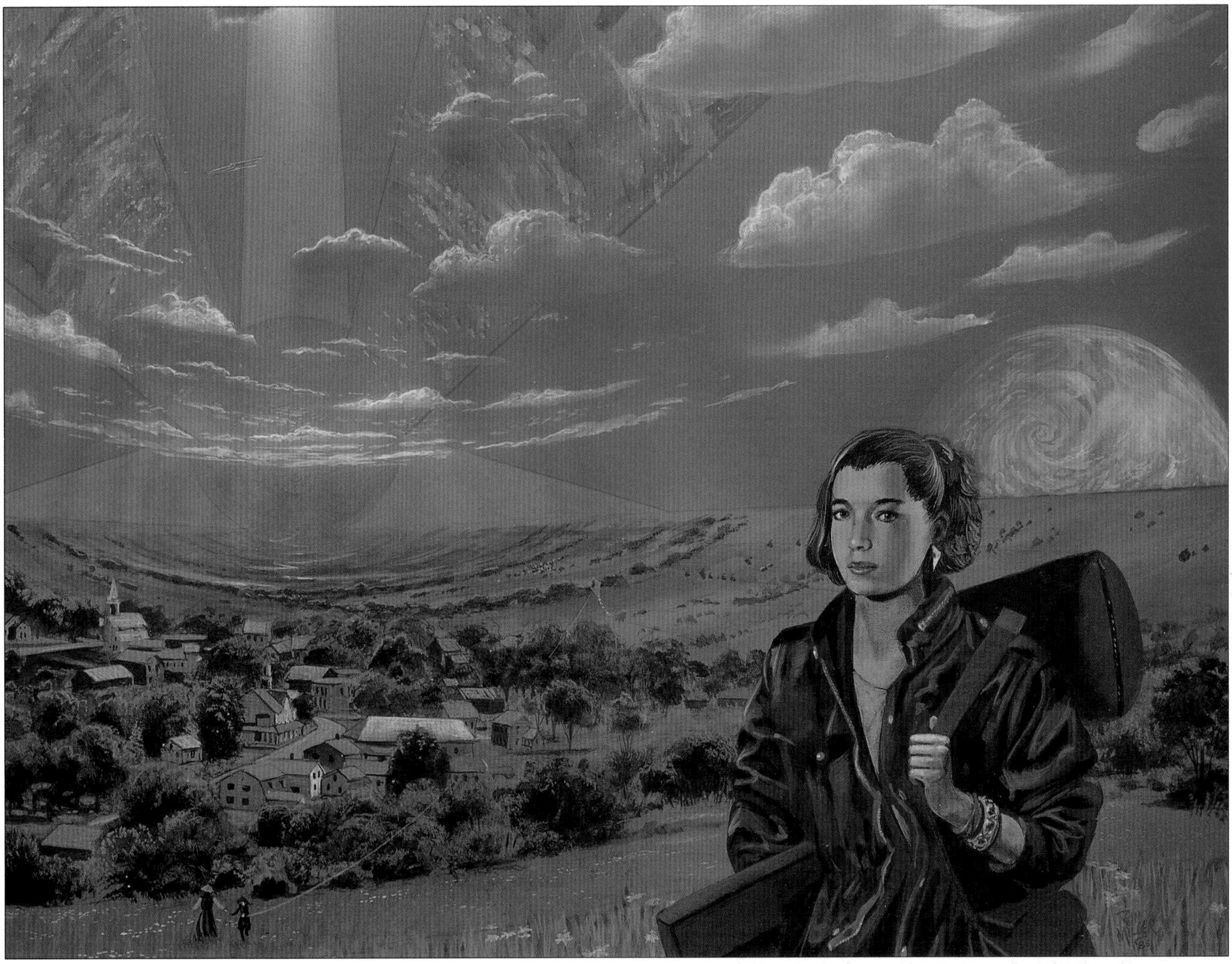

Mia Havero (above)
(*Rite of Passage*, Alexei Panshin, 1968)
Describing herself as 'hell on wheels', Mia lives on an enormous, hollowed-out asteroid. All children in the space colony must endure a 'rite of passage' on reaching the age of 14, when they are left on a planet to survive on their own for 1 month. Mia is prepared to take on an entire alien world as a sort of high school graduation exercise.

Trigger Argee (right)
(*Legacy*, Stanley H. Schmitz, 1962)
Many unscrupulous characters in the Federation wish to obtain a plasmoid, but no one seems really to know what they are, or what they are capable of. Trigger Argee has her hands full trying to second guess the bad guys.

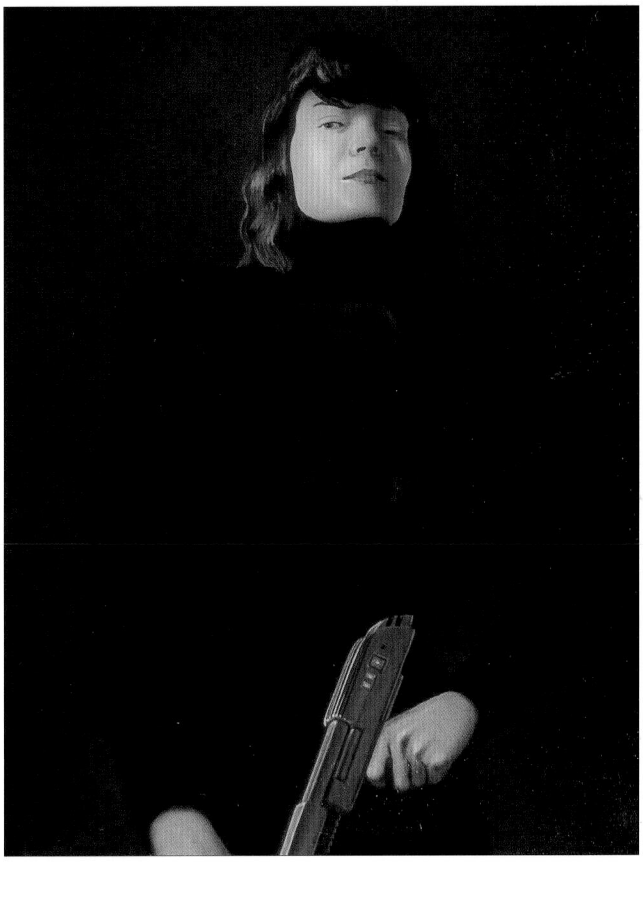

her life would be in each of these worlds. Russ's novel is an excellent example of how the devices of science fiction can be used to address social issues.

Other writers made effective use of female characters in more traditional narratives. Vonda N. McIntyre's novel *Dreamsnake* (1978) is the Nebula and Hugo award-winning story

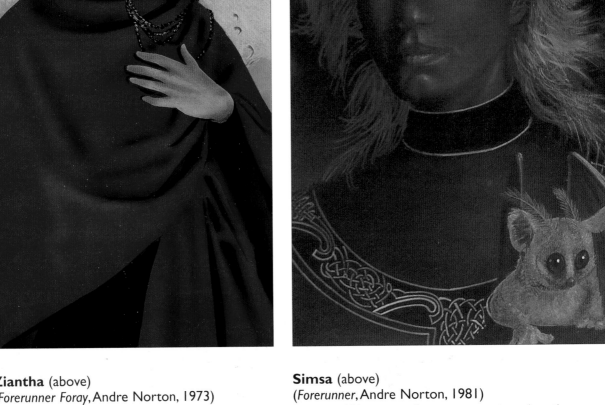

Ziantha (above)
(*Forerunner Foray*, Andre Norton, 1973)
Drawn into the Forerunner worlds in search of the mysterious green stone, skilled and mind-touch-trained psychic agent Ziantha finds herself trapped in an alien alter ego.

Simsa (above)
(*Forerunner*, Andre Norton, 1981)
Simsa would linger near the spaceport, curious about the skymen who had come to her world, not suspecting that her race had also come from the stars, and that her destiny was linked to the ancient race of Forerunners.

Lady Jessica (opposite)
(*Dune*, Frank Herbert, 1965)
Lady Jessica is a member of the Bene Gesserit sisterhood. As part of the Sisterhood's selective breeding programme, she was ordered to bear only daughters to the Duke Leto Atreides. Instead, through her love for Leto, she gave birth to Paul, who would eventually become Emperor of the Universe.

of Snake, a healer living on a future Earth finally recovering from the effects of a long-past nuclear war. Snake leaves her native mountains to go into the desert and loses one of the three metabolically altered snakes she uses in her healing when she tries to help a young boy. Vonda McIntyre makes her feminist points subtly, while showing us the different societies of this world. Desert women can have more than one husband; mountain people are free in offering sexual companionship and are equally accepting of both heterosexuals and homosexuals. Snake is an admirable and also recognizably human character who must regain her self-respect by finding a dreamsnake to replace the one she has lost.

C. J. Cherryh, who was to become a very popular and prolific writer, made her debut in 1976 with her novel *Gate Of Ivrel*, in which she introduced her heroine Morgaine Frosthair. Two more novels, *Well of Shiuan* (1978) and

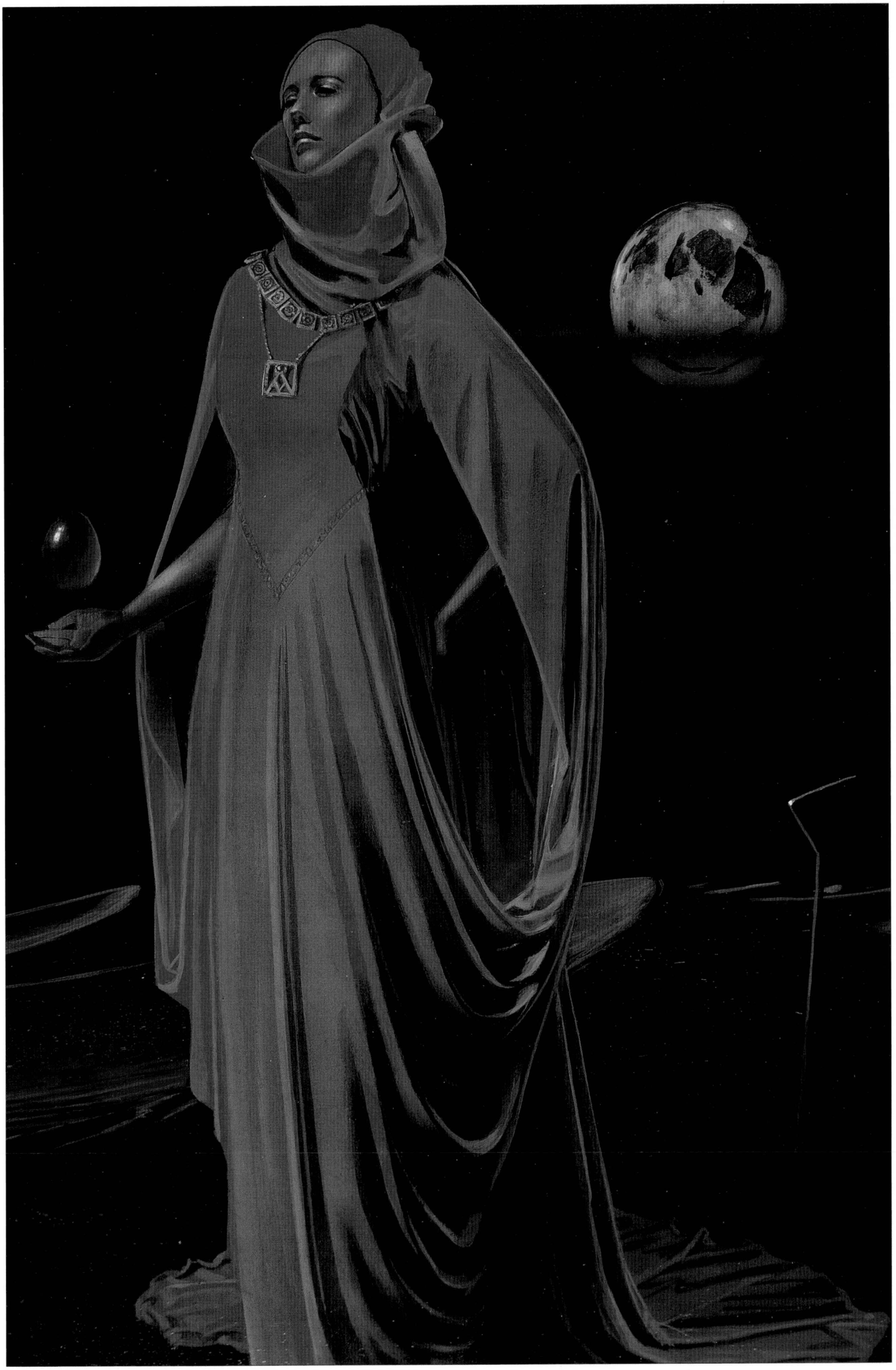

The Crew of the Vortex Blaster (above)
(*The Vortex Blaster*, E. E. Smith, 1960)
Charged with the dangerous task of hunting down and destroying planet-threatening atomic vortices, Neal 'Storm' Cloud's all-but-one female crew consists of pilot Maluleme, the pink Chickladorian; tall, shrouded nurse Nadine; pantherish Vesta the Vegian; and squat, cigar-chewing, muscular Tommy.

Varley's protagonist is Cirocco Jones, also known as 'Rocky', a tough-minded woman who leads a crew on Earth's first space mission in several years. Her ship is destroyed after Rocky and her crew discover a vast, previously unknown structure on Saturn's moon of Titan. Rocky and her crew survive, but eventually she must make a danger-ous journey to the hub of this strange world in her efforts to bring peace to its variety of life-forms. Her crewmate and side-kick, Gaby, is another strong female character who also hap-pens to be in love with Rocky.

Octavia E. Butler's *Kindred*, published in 1979, is a science fic-tion novel that transcends the genre. Butler is, along with Samuel R. Delany, one of the few African-American writers of sci-ence fiction and she brings this cultural background to her work. Dana, a twentieth-century black woman married to a white man, suddenly finds herself a slave on a plantation in Maryland of the 1820s, where she must care for the man who will become one of her ancestors. The experience of slavery is illuminated, nightmarishly, for the reader.

As the Seventies drew to a close, science fic-tion seemed open in ways that it had not been earlier. Both men and women writers were using the genre to explore societies and char-acters that are not limited by our assumptions and this meant more varied roles for their fic-tional females. Writers who preferred to keep to customary social roles for their female char-acters had to find reasons for their existence rather than just simply assume that they would inevitably persist.

Fires of Azeroth (1979), quickly followed; the three were eventually collected as *The Book of Morgaine* (1979). The novels are an intelligent blend of science fiction and fantasy, not unlike some of the earlier works of Leigh Brackett.

John Varley began publishing during the Seventies and soon won a reputation as one of science fiction's most inventive short-story writers. He was especially notable for his mat-ter-of-fact treatment of strong female charac-ters and, indeed, most of the central characters in his novels are women. In *Titan* (1979),

Mavra Chang (opposite)
(Well World series, Jack Chalker, 1977-1980)
'What's it about? An assassination? Smuggling? Something illegal?' asks Mavra Chang, whose strongest trait of character is survival.

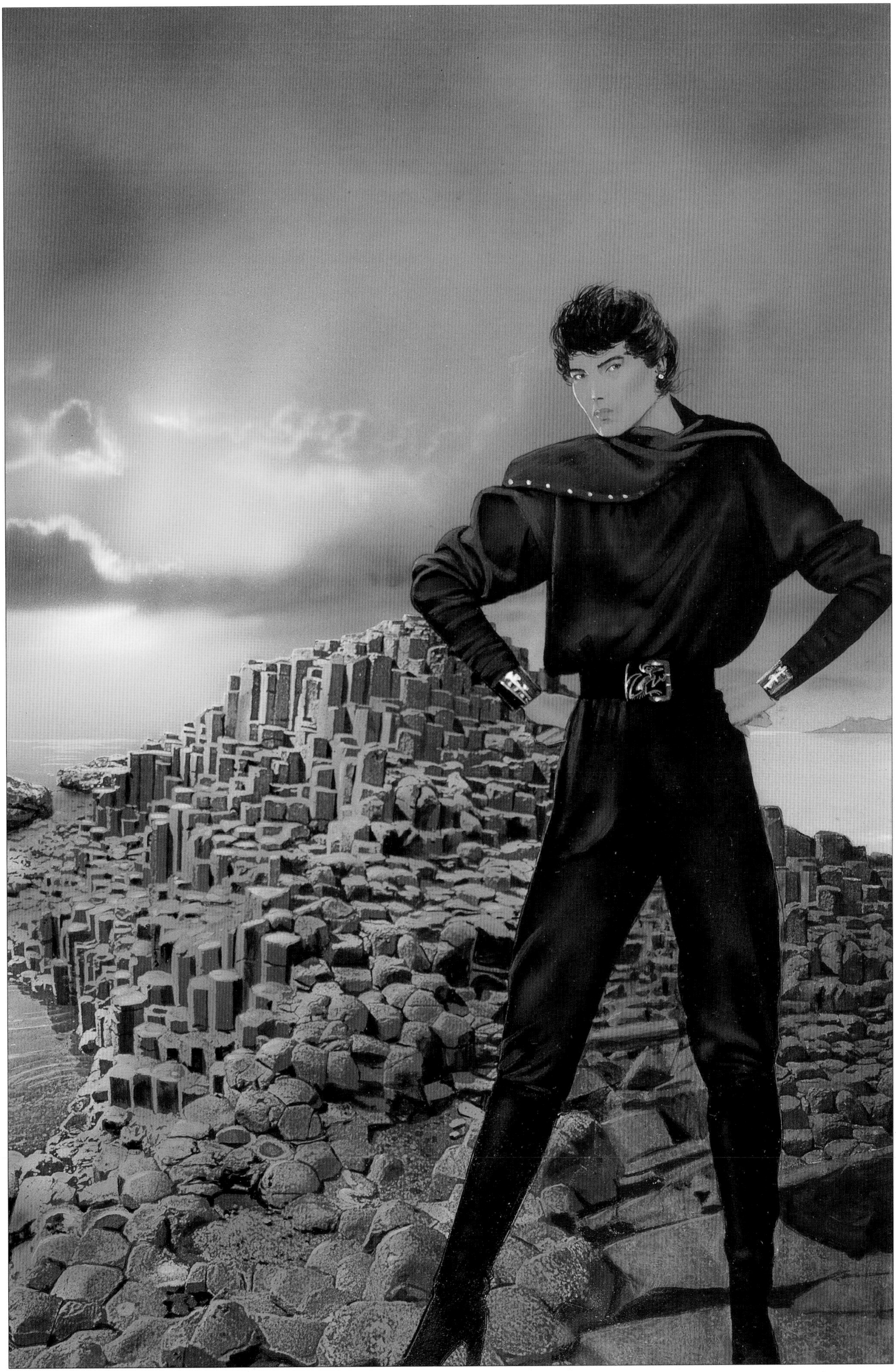

Chapter 4
The 1980s to 1990s

THE EIGHTIES saw the appearance of several important science fiction novels with strong female
characters, although by then the appearance of such
characters was no longer remarkable. John Varley's
Cirocco Jones returned in a sequel to Titan entitled
Wizard (1980). Joan D. Vinge won a Hugo Award for
her novel *The Snow Queen* (1980), an epic story set on
the planet of Tiamat, where the seasons change from
winter to summer once every century. A sibyl, Moon
Dawntreader Summer, gifted with the ability to communicate with beings on other worlds, must contend
with Arienrhod, Tiamat's powerful, ruthless Snow Queen.

In *Wild Seed* (1980), Octavia E. Butler writes about
Anyanwu, an African woman who must struggle with
Doro, a four-thousand-year-old being with supernatural powers who is seeking to breed a superhuman
species. Doro wants Anyanwu as a companion and as
someone with whom to breed children; she hates him
yet cannot free herself from him. Joe Haldeman, in
Worlds (1981), began a trilogy about Marianne O'Hara,
a woman who has grown up on New New York, one
of forty-one 'Worlds', hollowed-out asteroids in orbit
near Earth. When Marianne goes to Earth to study, she
must deal with the ill feeling and suspicion Earth feels
toward the people of the Worlds.

C. J. Cherryh, with her gift for illuminating our human
societies through alien worlds, published *The Pride of
Chanur* (1981), following it with *Chanur's Venture*
(1985) and *Chanur's Homecoming* (1986). Pyanfar
Chanur is an alien feline female who is captain of a
starship, the *Pride of Chanur*. Among her people, the
Hani, the males are considered too unstable to travel
aboard spaceships, but Pyanfar begins to question
some of her culture's assumptions after befriending a
human male, Tully.

Lady Amalthea
(opposite)
(*The Last Unicorn,*
Peter S. Beagle,
1968)
*The unicorn – who
believed herself to be
the last of her kind – is
on a quest to find her
legendary fellows. She is
rescued from certain
death beneath the
hooves of the mon-
strous Red Bull by the
misbegotten magic of
Schmendrick – which
transforms her into a
human being.*

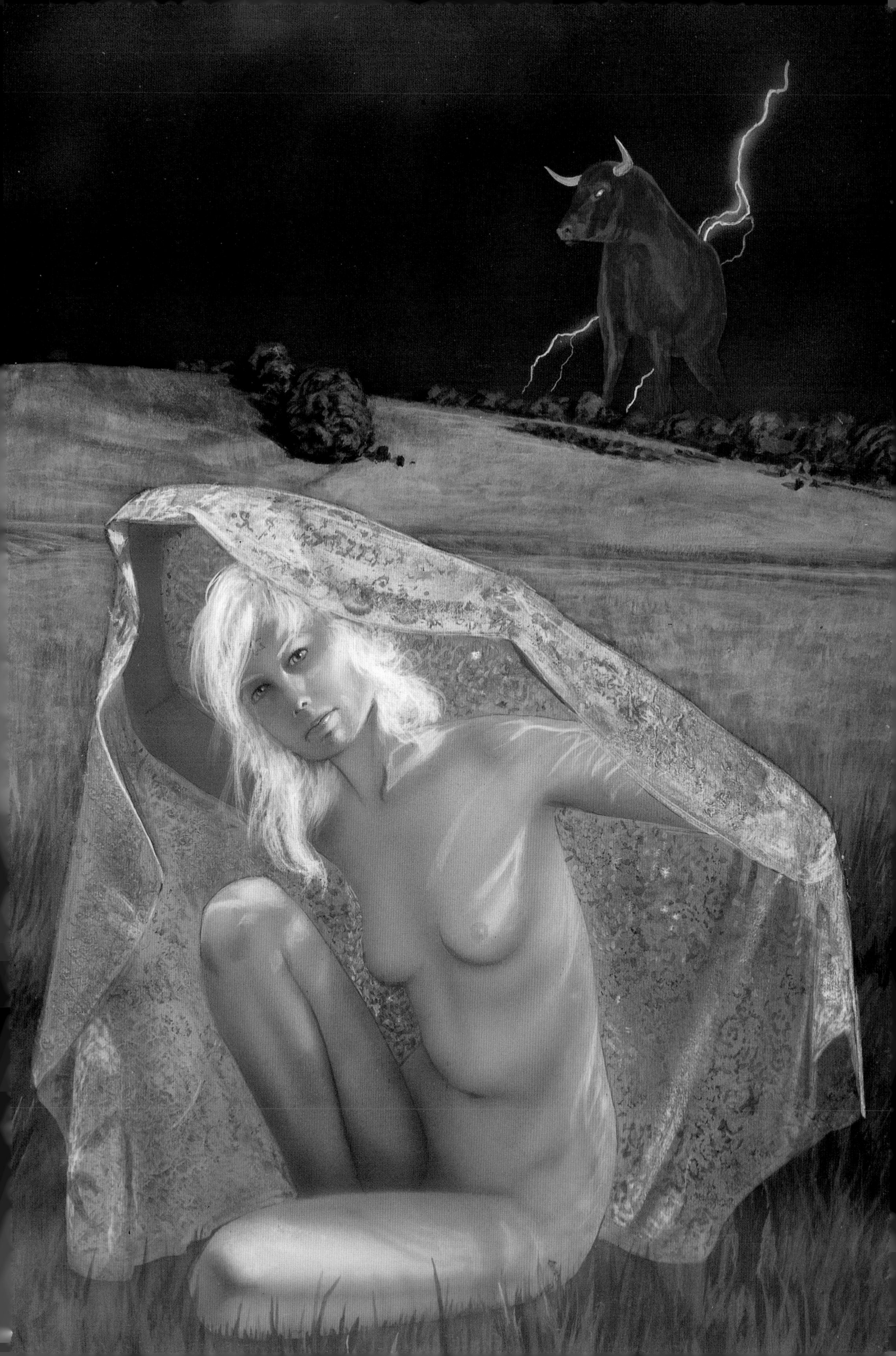

A different heroine is featured in Tanith Lee's *The Silver Metal Lover* (1981). Jane is wealthy, spoiled and discontented; then she falls in love with Silver, a lifelike robot. Silver opens another world to Jane when they are forced to live in the slums of their world; she loses her fear and finds happiness as Jain, Silver's lover. Silver may be a robot but his underlying humanity is never in doubt and Jain's love for him makes her more fully human.

F. M. Busby's 1976 novel *Rissa Kerguelen* is the epic story of a woman on a future Earth who takes her revenge on the man who killed her parents. She later escapes from Earth to become part of a movement to free Earth from the grip of the hated United Energies and Transport. Busby followed that novel with *Zelde M'tana* (1980), a tale of a woman being shipped out from Earth to a brothel. When the crew on board the ship mutinies, Zelde joins with other female prisoners to fight for freedom.

Some of science fiction's most prominent writers – Robert Heinlein, Poul Anderson and Jack Williamson among them – often included interesting and well-portrayed secondary female characters in their earlier works; newer writers such as Gregory Benford and David Brin were giving women more varied roles in their novels. Some writers were undoubtedly moved by their convictions and others by the knowledge that a growing number of readers welcomed stories with female characters and protagonists. That there were more prominent women writers of science fiction and a growing number of female readers had an effect on charac-

Iris Angharads (above)
(*Venus of Dreams, Venus of Shadows*, Pamela Sargent, 1986, 1988)
Daughter of a clan of strong, independent women who live on North America's Great Plains, Iris leaves Earth and becomes instrumental in the physical transformation of an entire world – the terraforming of Venus – albeit at a tremendous personal cost.

George R. R. Martin and Lisa Tuttle combined their talents to write *Windhaven* (1981), set on a planet of the same name. On Windhaven, a world of various islands, flyers – people who use wings that resemble hang-gliders to travel from one island to another – are responsible for communication among the settlements and hold an honoured place in society. The heroine is Maris of Lesser Amberley, who wins a place as a flyer despite the tradition that only the first-born child of a flyer can become one.

Risa Liangharad (opposite)
(*Venus of Dreams, Venus of Shadows*, Pamela Sargent, 1986, 1988)
Iris Angharad's daughter, Risa Liangharad, becomes a powerful leader of the new Venus.

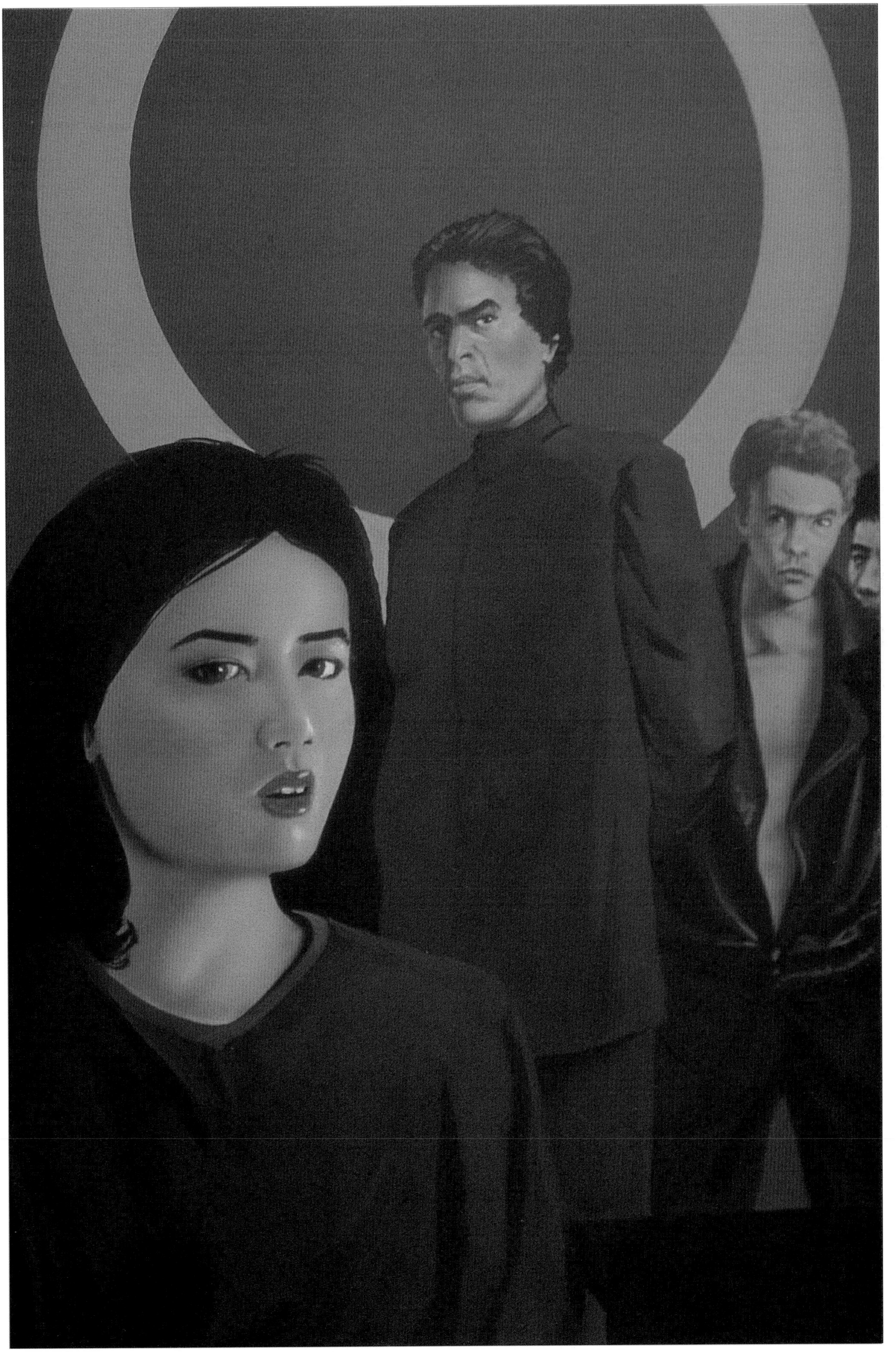

terizations of women as well. By the Eighties, varied roles for female characters were beginning to be taken for granted.

This doesn't mean that most writers of science fiction had become feminists, any more than the appearance of strong women characters in earlier works meant that the authors supported equal rights for women. Overtly feminist science fiction became harder to find during the Eighties, perhaps because of second thoughts about feminism in some quarters.

In spite of these developments, science fiction was still being written in which female characters had a more limited sphere of action, or in which one strong woman might be featured as a token. Old-fashioned 'space opera' had actually been rising in popularity, thanks to the success of the movie *Star Wars* (1977) and its two sequels. People who had little acquaintance with science fiction could be forgiven for thinking that much of it still revolved around male characters and their deeds, because most science fiction on film or television – the media through which most people first encounter the genre – featured men in the most important roles. For every Ripley, the tough-minded survivor of the spaceship crew being preyed upon in *Alien* (1979), there were several characters like Princess Leia of *Star Wars*, who is the only woman among those fighting against the Empire and Darth Vader. The television series *Star Trek* showed women in various capacities but usually centred its dramas around the male characters.

In written science fiction during the Eighties, some light and much heat was generated by an influential and much-hyped movement of writers known as the 'cyberpunks'. Their works are characterized by bleak near-future settings, high-tech details such as vast computer networks, human bodies augmented by machines, minds affected by microchips and biologically engineered drugs and streetwise characters alienated from the rubble-strewn pop-culture worlds in which they live. The movie *Blade Runner* (1982), based on a novel by Philip K. Dick, provides a visual example of this kind of science fiction, while William Gibson's novel *Neuromancer* (1984) was quickly hailed as a template for cyberpunk fiction.

What sorts of female characters were likely to inhabit cyberpunk science fiction? Molly, one of the central characters in *Neuromancer*, offers one example. Molly has silver lenses that resemble mirrored glasses implanted in her face and retractable scalpel blades implanted under her fingernails. She is a 'street samurai', a freelancer who is sent by those she works for to use Case, a matrix cowboy who can link into cyberspace, to steal data. *Neuromancer*, contemporary as it is, also harks back to the works of Raymond Chandler and the film-noir thrillers of the late Forties and Molly to the hardened and dangerous women characters found in those movies and books.

As a group, the cyberpunk writers were interested in the social and technological changes computers, bioengineering and information technology were bringing to the world and in the kinds of futures that might grow out of them; they also tended to look at developments with a radical sensibility, from the vantage points of street people and the dispossessed, rather those that of the powerful.

As for female characters, some saw cyberpunk science fiction as a step backward. Female characters in such works were often cast in secondary roles as whores, leather-clad sex symbols or as victims. The fact that almost all of the prominent cyberpunk writers were men contributed to an impression that cyberpunk writing was basically a hipper form of the kind of technological science fiction designed to appeal primarily to men and boys. Pat Cadigan, the only woman to be included on the list of cyberpunk writers during the Eighties, helped to dispel this impression. In several of her short stories, reworked for her first novel, *Mindplayers* (1987), Cadigan created Allie the Pathosfinder, a woman who is able, with the aid of technology, to heal others by entering the psychodramas playing out in their minds. In other works, including her novels, *Synners* (1991) and *Fools* (1992), Cadigan features women as her protagonists.

A prominent cyberpunk writer, Bruce Sterling, created a memorable female in his near-future thriller, *Islands in the Net* (1988).

Danica (opposite)
('The Borders of Sabazel', Lillian Stewart Carl, 1982)
In order to defend her country, Danica must not only be a brilliant military leader and a ruthless warrior, but a wily politician as well.

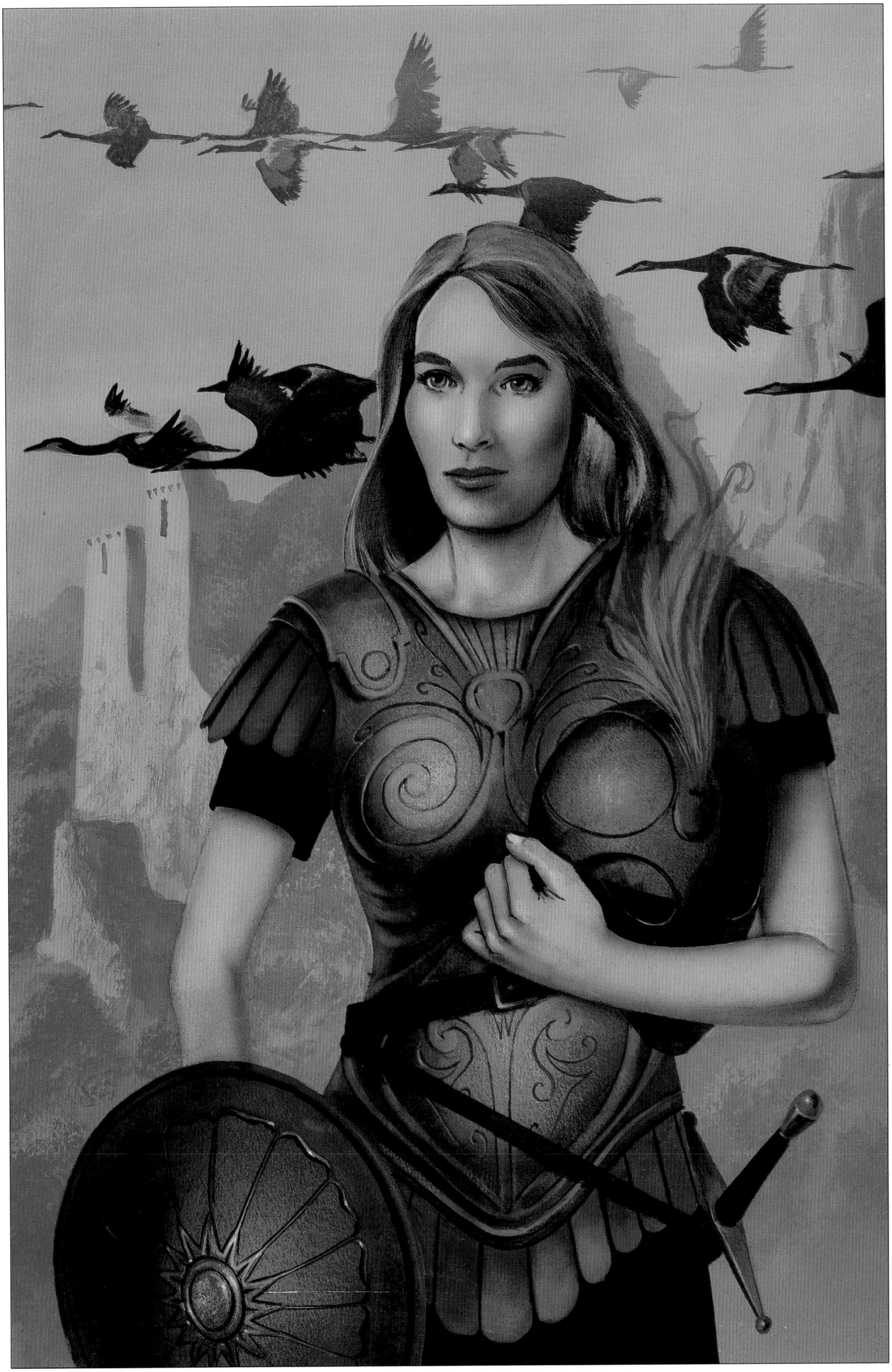

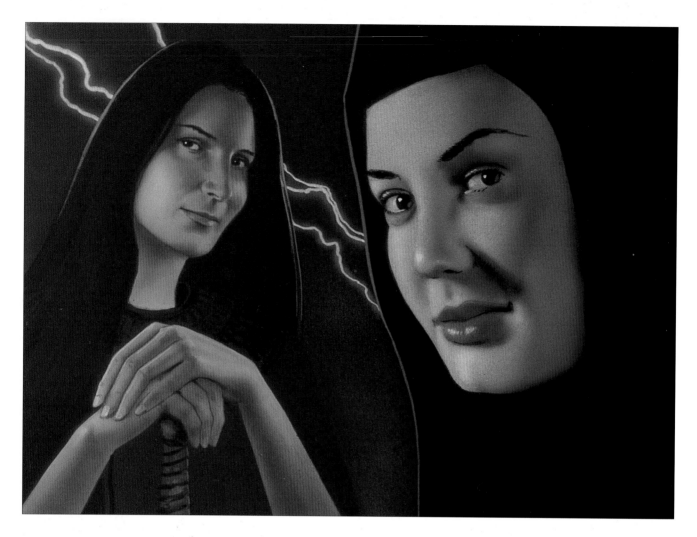

Frostflower and Thorn (above)
(*Frostflower and Thorn*, Phyllis Ann Karr, 1985)
An unlikely duo: pacifist sorceress Frostflower and foul-mouthed, Amazon warrior Thorn. Frostflower wants a child, but losing her virginity would mean losing her powers. Meanwhile, Thorn, reluctantly pregnant, can't afford an abortion, so, Frostflower sorcels the baby from Thorn's womb by speeding up time, in exchange for the child.

Laura Webster, a young executive, lives in a world that resembles the future we may be creating, a world built on information. She, her husband and her baby are caught up in a struggle that threatens her relatively peaceful world.

Despite the attention focused on the cyberpunk form, other kinds of science fiction continued to flourish. Marion Zimmer Bradley, in her novel *Hawkmistress!* (1982), another tale of Darkover, created Romilly, who can communicate telepathically with animals. That year, she had her greatest success so far, *The Mists of Avalon*, in which the Arthurian legend is retold from the point of view of the female characters, among them Guinevere and Morgaine.

Gwyneth Jones, author of several novels for children, published her first science fiction novel for adults, *Divine Endurance*, in 1984. The book is set in a future matriarchy. The protagonist is a female android, Cho (short for Chosen Among the Beautiful), who travels with her intelligent cat, Divine Endurance, from China to the far-future Malaysia where most of the story takes place.

1986 saw the publication of *Shards of Honor*, the first novel by Lois McMaster Bujold, who quickly became one of the most popular writers of science fiction adventure and one with a gift for depicting strong women characters. Cordelia Naismith comes to love Aral Vorkosigan, despite the fact that he is an hereditary member of a warrior class and she

James (opposite)
('Fear of Fly', Lynn Mims, 1980)
Wandering mercenary James, who owes her name to a father who not only had expected but would have preferred a boy, must rescue a prince held captive in a tower protected by an enormous dragonfly.

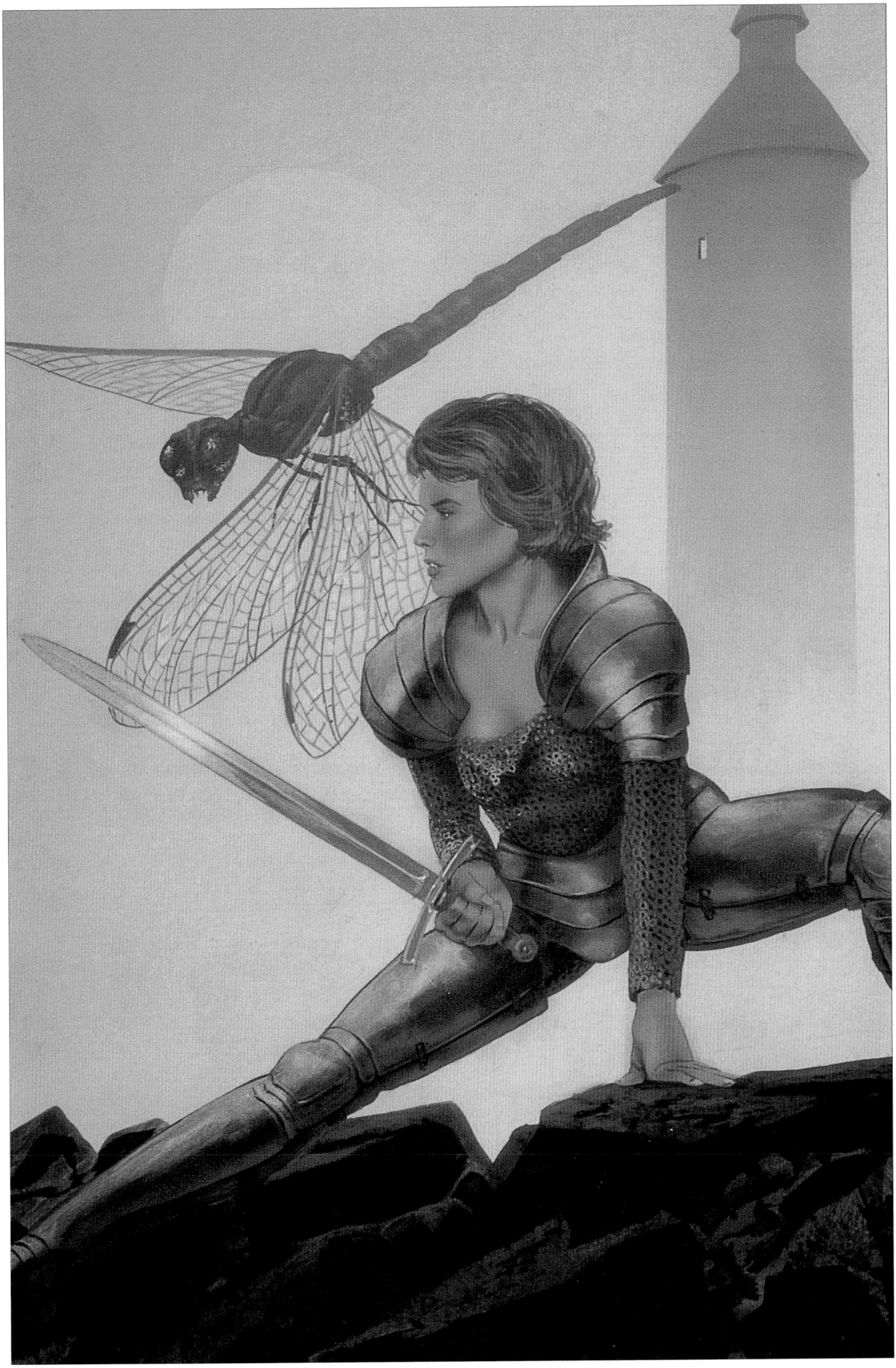

comes from a non-military society. The couple is also featured in Bujold's later novel *Barrayar* (1991) and they are the parents of Bujold's popular hero, Miles Vorkosigan.

Iris Angharads, the protagonist of my own *Venus of Dreams* (1986), is a woman who becomes part of an effort six hundred years from now to terraform Venus – to transform this deadly world into an Earthlike planet. It seemed natural to tell this story using a woman as the central character and to use the opportunities for female imagery that Venus provides.

The Eighties also produced some fine examples of Utopian (and dystopian) science fiction with female protagonists. Because of its author's prominence, Margaret Atwood's *The Handmaid's Tale* (1986), which was also made into a film of the same name, found a wide audience. Atwood's bleak picture of a possible future shows us an American society controlled by religious fundamentalists. We see this society through the eyes of Offred, the Handmaid of the title, who is expected to bear children for her master and his infertile wife. Disturbingly, but realistically, some of the women willingly aid in their own repression. The ending of the novel indicates that Offred's repressive society has been succeeded by a gentler, more egalitarian one, although we cannot be sure of Offred's fate – escape or death.

Joan Slonczewski's *A Door Into Ocean* (1986) is set on the world of Shora, an ocean world of vast floating rafts inhabited by people who are biologically female but socially androgynous. There are no genetically male Shorans; the people of Shora reproduce parthenogenically, using their advanced biological techniques to exchange genetic material. The Shorans are pacifists, but their sophisticated biological science is coveted by the militaristic regime of the planet Valedon. Major characters include Merwen, her mate Usha (who is a lifeshaper or doctor), their daughter Lystra and Berenice, a noblewoman from Valedon who lives among the Shorans as a kind of ambassador. Slonczewski, herself a research biologist, offers a detailed and original portrait of a peaceful, ecologically balanced humanoid society.

Sheri S. Tepper, in the provocative *The Gate to Women's Country* (1988), focuses on Stavia, a young woman of Marthatown. Stavia lives on a future Earth where all technology is in the hands of women and almost all men live outside the settlements of Women's Country in garrisons populated entirely by men. Men are considered too violent to be allowed into the women's settlements except during a yearly festival when sex between men and women is encouraged. Unknown to the men and most of the women, a eugenics programme is attempting to breed violence out of men by insuring that the warriors never sire children; only the servitors, the gentler men who choose to live in Women's Country, father children.

Some have referred to much science fiction of the Eighties and early nineties as 'post-feminist', meaning that, as critic Joan Gordon put it in a recent essay, 'female characters are strong, active, given to non-gender-linked jobs, but although these characters may live as feminists have striven for women to be allowed to live, their right to live that way is not the central issue of the writing.' The genre has become increasingly diverse, encompassing subgenres of literary science fiction, cyberpunk writing, space opera and adventure, realistic depictions of possible futures, stories rooted in scientific speculation and works that owe more to fantasy and magic realism than to past science fiction. This variety of subgenres demonstrates how many different kinds of writing can be found in this often-misunderstood field. However much these subgenres differ, important and imaginative female characters inhabit all of them.

So many memorable women have been created in recent works of science fiction that even to list them all would require a book in itself. As it happens, some of the most important and honoured science fiction novels of the nineties had women as protagonists and casts filled with fascinating females. Among these works are Kim Stanley Robinson's widely

---

Romilly (opposite)
(*Hawkmistress!*, Marion Zimmer Bradley, 1982)
Romilly, daughter of the MacAran Lord, is gifted with the power of telepathic communication with animals and works as a tamer of horses and hawks. She rebels against the limits forced upon her sex. When she is faced with a forced marriage with an elderly man, she disguises herself as a boy and runs away. After many of adventures, she becomes a member of the Sisterhood of the Sword, the ancestors of the Guild of Free Amazons.

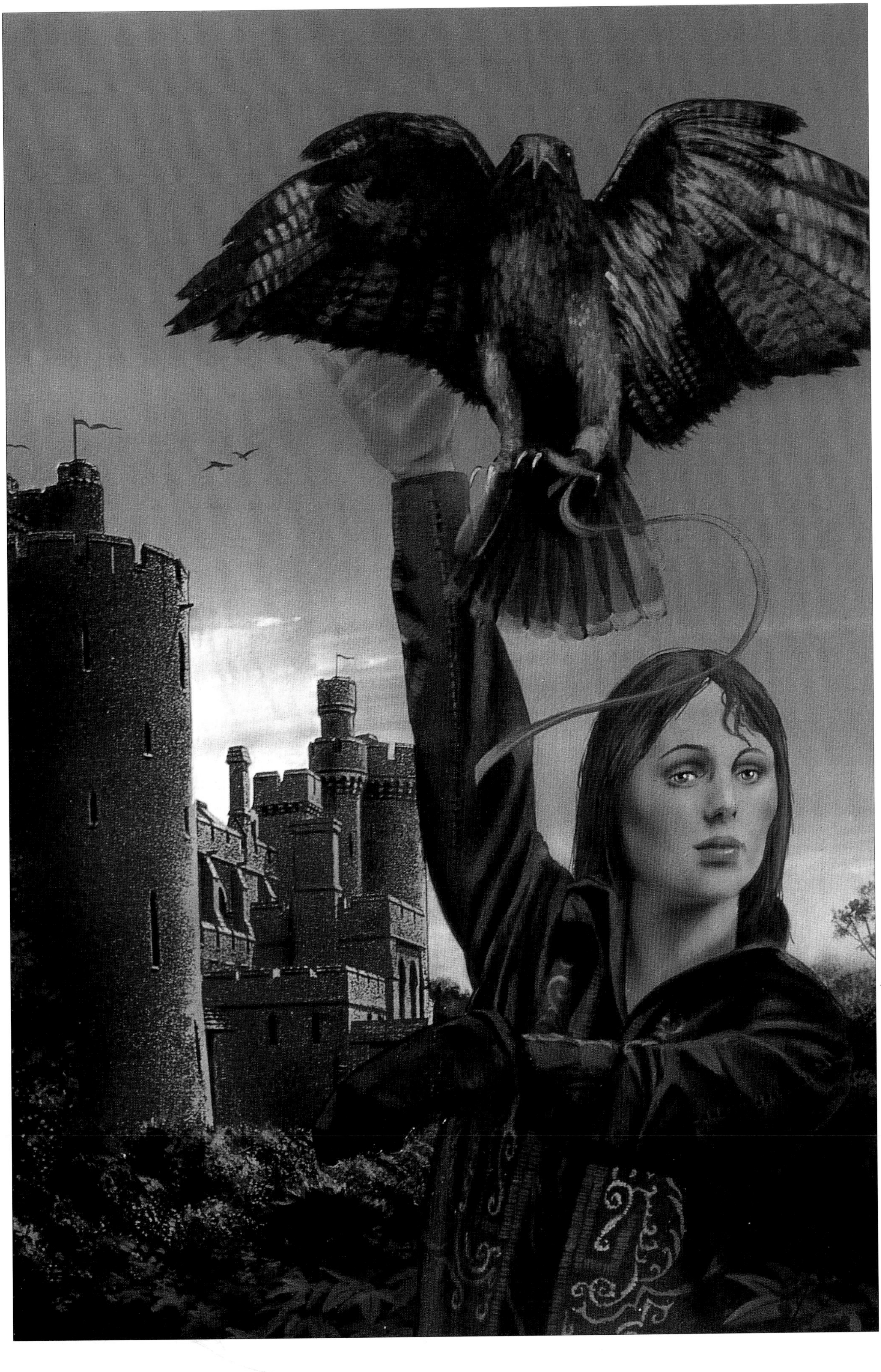

Cordelia Naismith (above)
(*Barrayar*, Lois McMaster Bujold, 1986; also
Shards of Honor, 1991)
*Although a member of a non-militaristic society, Cordelia
comes to love Aml Vorkosigan, a hereditary member of a
warrior class.*

highly entertaining space opera, filled with alien worlds, colourful characters and plenty of adventure. The main character is Tabitha Jute, a tough-minded woman who gets into all kinds of trouble as she travels to different planets in her ship, the *Alice Liddell*.

In 1993, Nancy Kress published her sixth novel, *Beggars in Spain*, developed from her earlier Hugo and Nebula award-winning novella of the same title. Most of Kress's work features women in primary roles; *Beggars in Spain* is the story of Leisha Camden, a young woman who has been genetically modified so that she does not have to sleep. Leisha and those like her must deal with the intolerance of unmodified human beings who fear that they will be supplanted.

Eleanor Arnason, in *A Woman of the Iron People* (1991), writes of Nia, a member of an alien race on the planet of Sigma Draconis II. Nia's people, humanoid and with thick furry pelts, have two sexes but their gender barriers are far more rigid than our own. Women and children live together; men roam in their individual territories outside the villages, lonely and isolated. Men and women come together only during the mating season and are expected to separate after that but Nia has fallen in love with the male who has mated with her. She eventually encounters a team of human anthropologists who have come to Sigma Draconis II to study her people. *A Woman of the Iron People* and Gwyneth Jones's *White Queen* (1991), another novel with a female character at its centre, were honoured

praised and much honoured *Red Mars* (1992), which began a trilogy about the terraforming of Mars, Nicola Griffith's *Ammonite* (1993), about a planet of women, and Nancy Springer's *Larque on the Wing* (1994), in which a middle-aged woman discovers that she prefers life in the body of a young man.

Take Back Plenty (1990) by Colin Greenland was the winner of the Arthur C. Clarke Award, given annually to the best science fiction novel published in Britain. It is an extravagant and

Bronwyn Tedeschiiy (opposite)
(*Palaces & Prisons, Silk & Steel, Hearts & Armor, Mermaids & Meteors*, Ron Miller, 1991-1995)
*Bronwyn, the indomitable Princess of Guesclin, is too
stubborn and too vengeful to know when to quit. Her
adventures take her through lands of kobolds and faeries;
and involve her in swordfights, chases and rocket trips.*

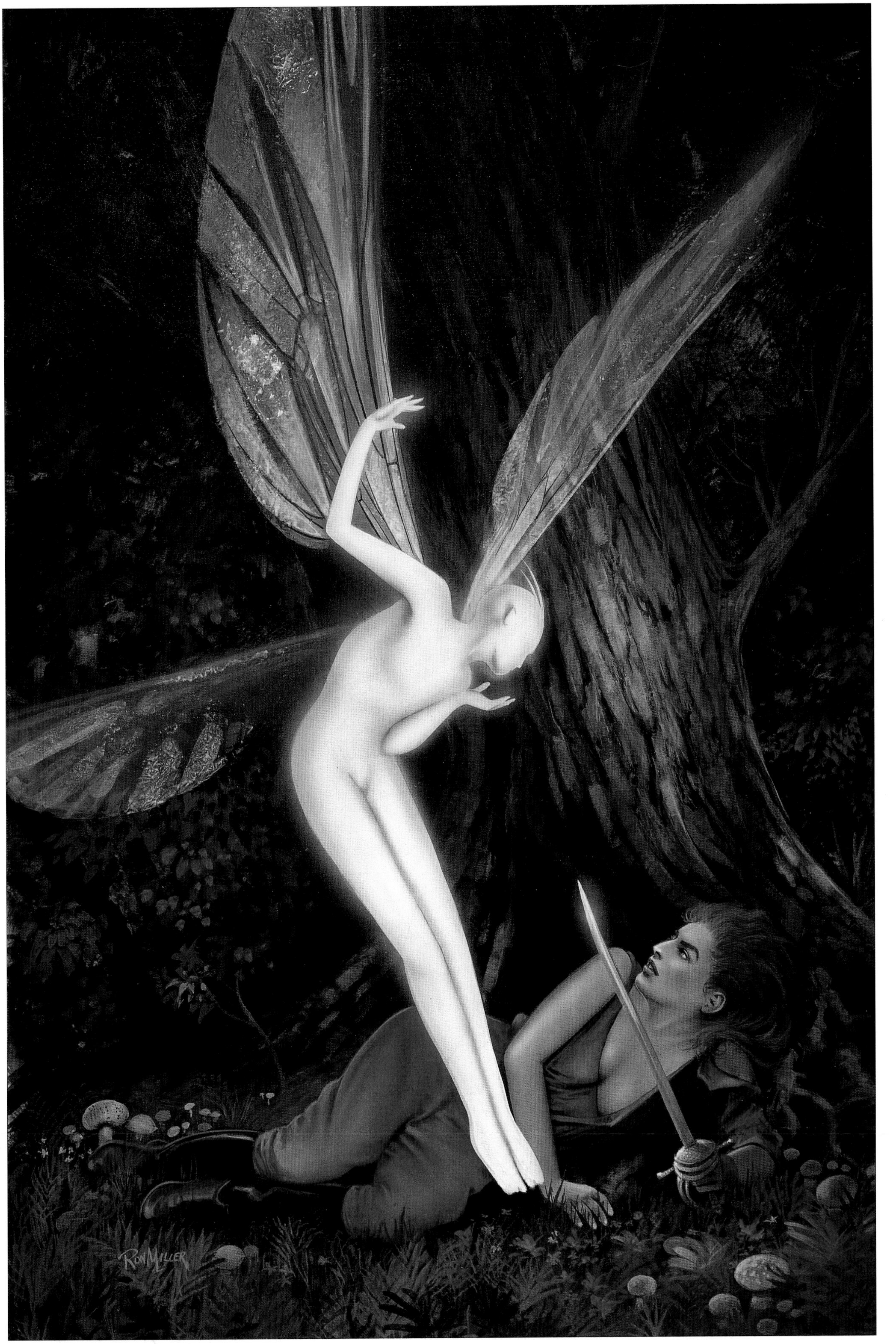
RON MILLER

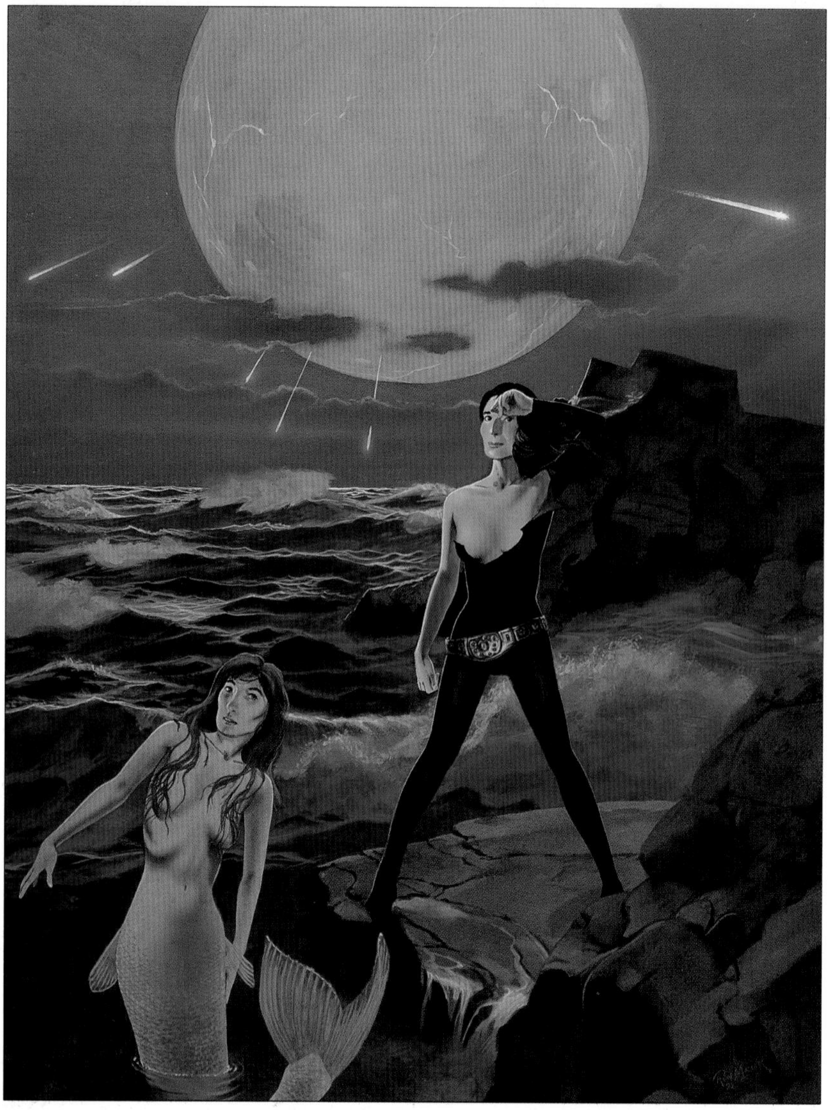

Bronwyn Tedeschiiy & Rykkla Woxen (left)
(*Palaces & Prisons*, *Silk & Steel*, *Hearts & Armor*, *Mermaids & Meteors*, Ron Miller, 1991-1995)
Rykkla, circus owner, acrobat and adventuress, through her friendship with the Princess Bronwyn becomes embroiled in a series of complicated and fantastic adventures and perils, from escaping a harem to leading a band of pirates.

with the first James Tiptree, Jr. Memorial Awards, given annually to science fiction and fantasy that expands and explores gender roles.

Greg Bear, another of the field's most prominent writers, won a Nebula Award for his novel *Moving Mars* (1993). With solid realism and an abundance of carefully developed details, Bear tells the story of Casseia Majumdar, her coming of age and her reluctant involvement in the politics of Mars and its century-old human settlements.

More and more science fiction writers are writing about women as human beings caught up in times and places unlike our own, as active people who affect and even change their worlds. In the process, they are shedding some light on what kinds of creatures we are. These writers are in effect undertaking a great experiment, a fact that might be better appreciated when one considers how few precedents exist for such portrayals of women in other literature. Joanna Russ, in her collection of essays *To Write Like a Woman* (1995), mentions the precedents for stories about women and boils them down to two basic plots: the love story and the story about a woman going crazy. Even the most old-fashioned space operas could, in the hands of ingenious writers, offer more story possibilities for their female characters than that.

It is unfortunate that so many people still retain an impression of science fiction as a literature primarily concerned with male characters when so many female characters can be found, especially in recent years. Unlike other forms of writing, science fiction and fantasy are not bound by the world as it is. The firebrands of science fiction, those vivid and powerful female characters that have become ever more numerous in the genre, exemplify our dreams, hopes, fears and deepest wishes for ourselves and our future. They show us what we are and what we might become.

Polgara the Sorceress (opposite)
(*Queen of Sorcery*, *Polgara the Sorceress*, 1987, 1997, David Eddings)
Polgara, the arch-sorceress, is the daughter of Belgarath the Sorcerer.

Moon Dawntreader Summer (page 108-109)
(*The Snow Queen*, Joan D. Vinge, 1980; also *The Summer Queen*, 1991)
The clone of Areinrhod, the Snow Queen, who rules the Tiamat, she is snatched from her world and must find her way back and to take her rightful place as Summer Queen.

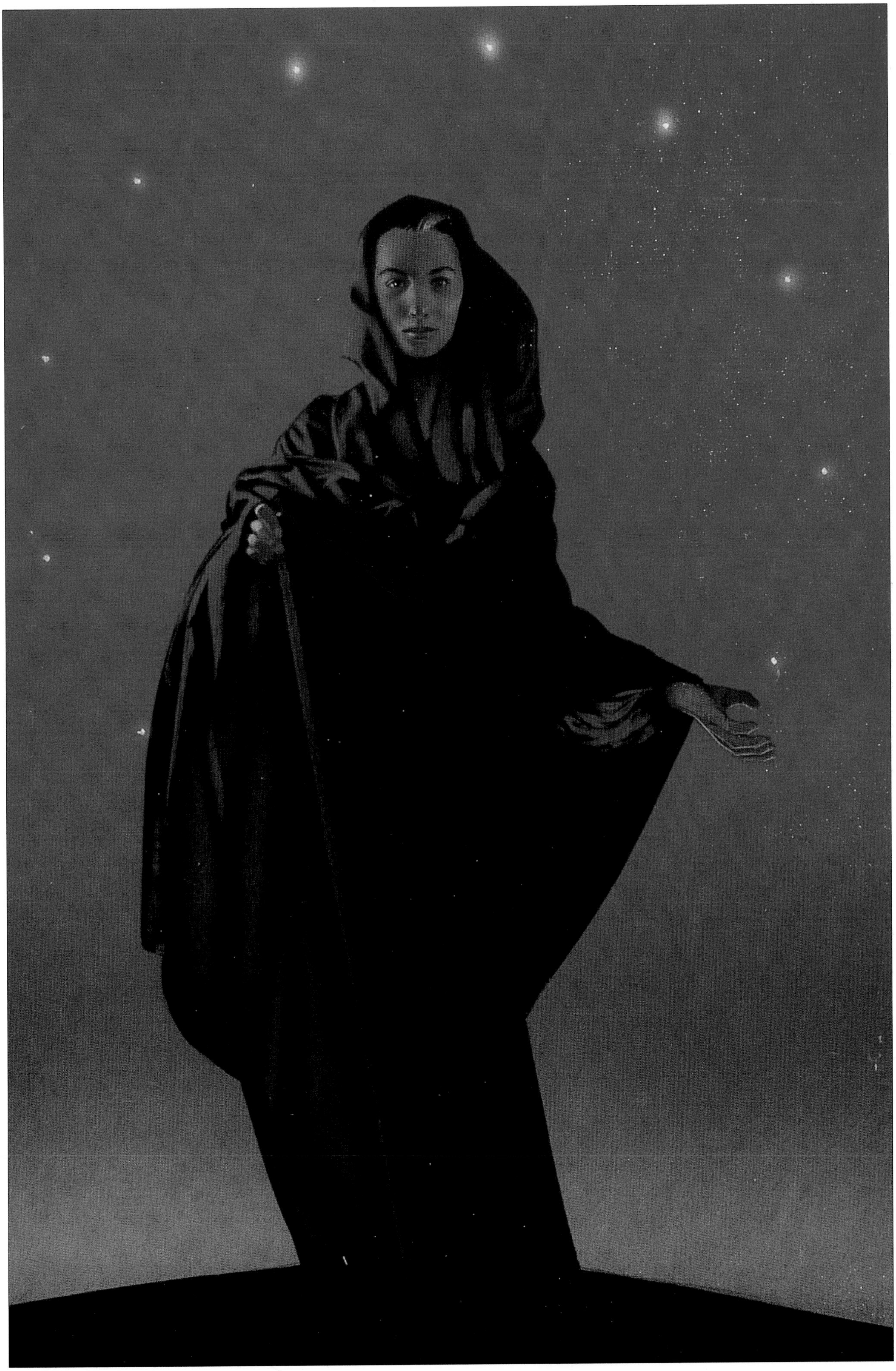

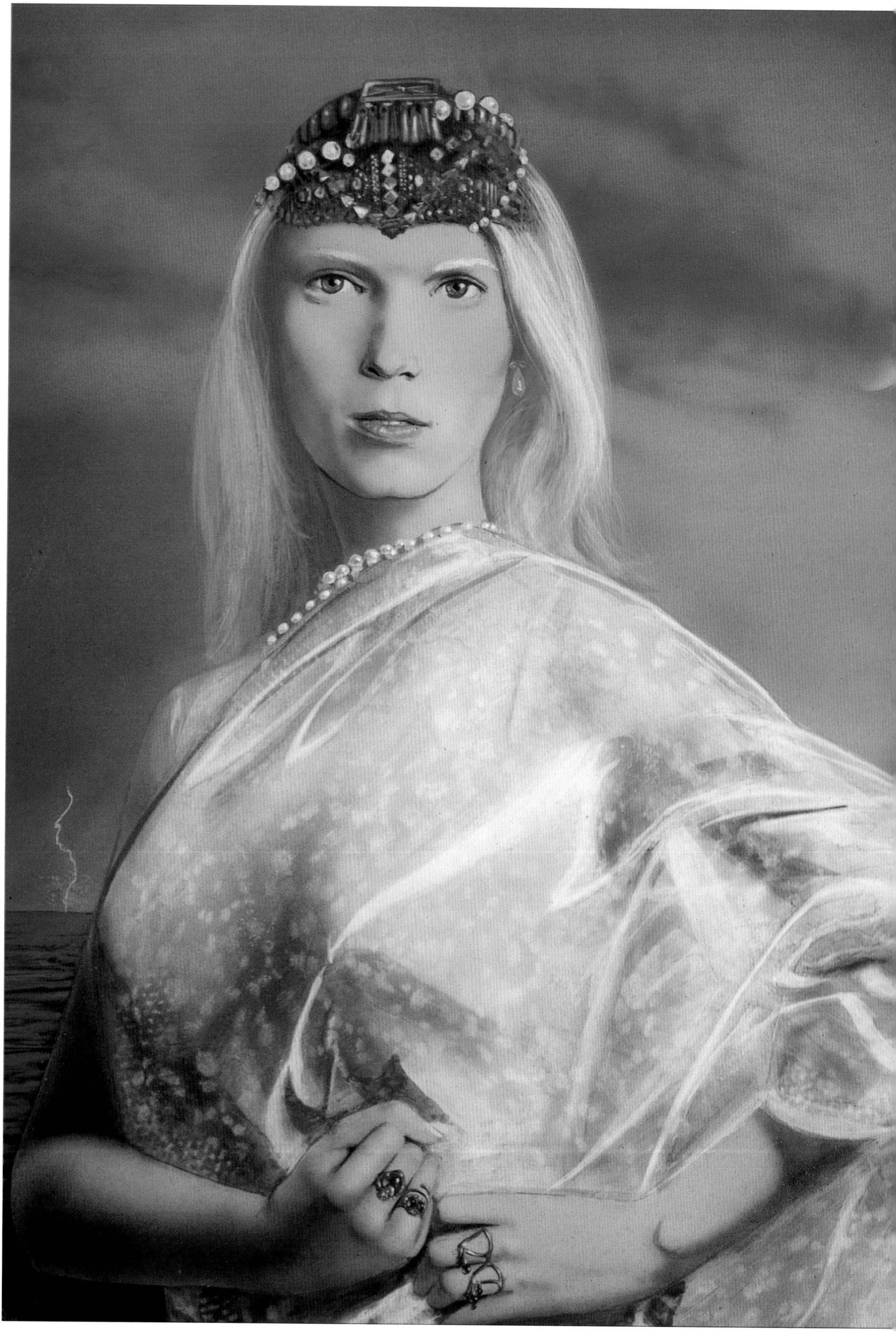

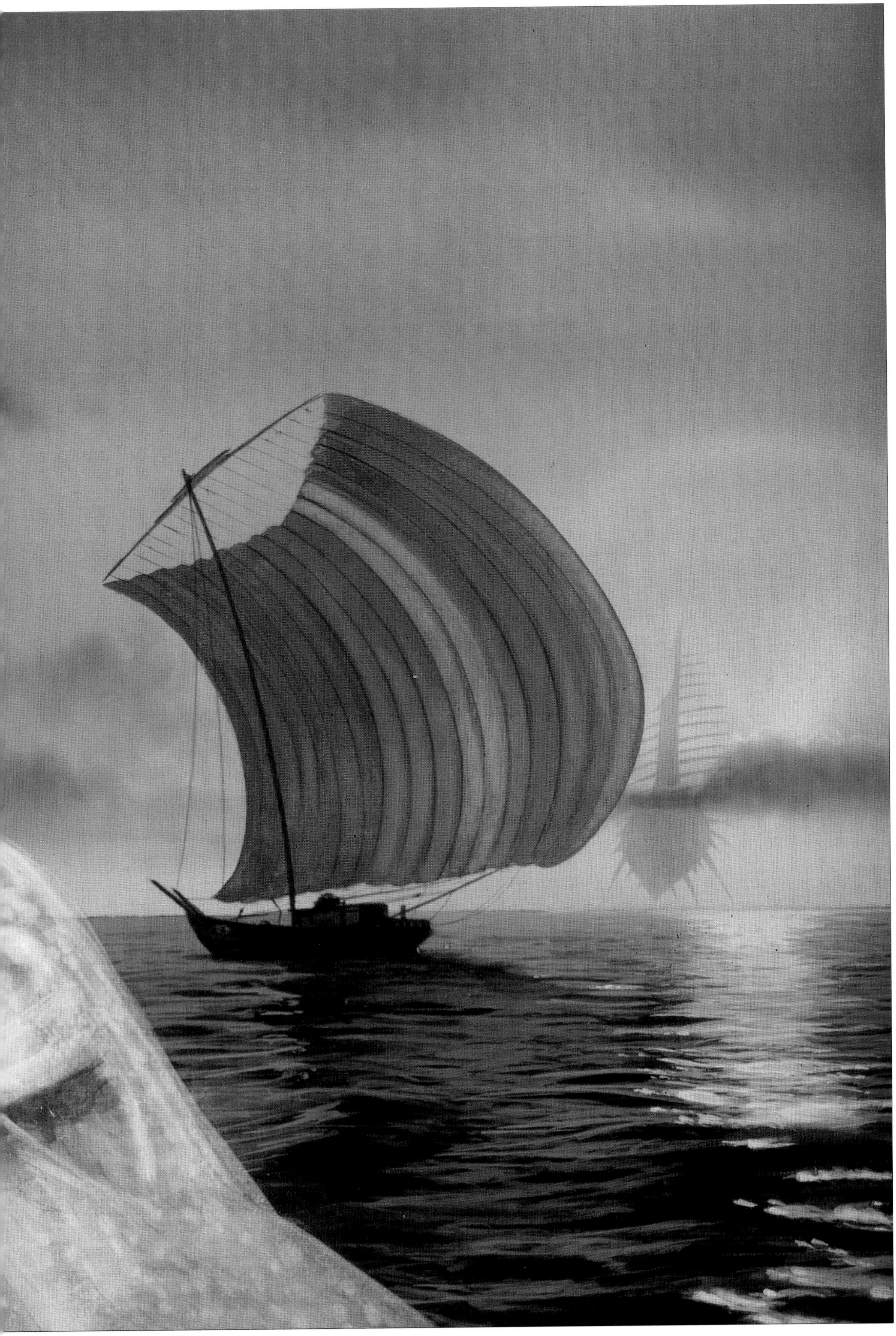

About the Authors

Ron Miller is an artist and author, specializing in the creation of illustrations for books and magazines about science fiction and astronomy. His work has appeared in books and on book jackets and in magazines such as *National Geographic*, *Reader's Digest*, *Newsweek* and *Scientific American*. Ron has also published almost twenty books, including the Hugo-nominated *The Grand Tour*, as well as magazine articles and professional papers. He has been a production illustrator for several motion pictures, notably *Total Recall* and *Dune* and has sat on the faculty of the International Space University (Strasbourg), lecturing on space art and history all over the world. Ron's original paintings are in numerous private and public collections, including the Smithsonian Institute and the Pushkin Museum in Moscow.

Pamela Sargent is a world-renowned science fiction writer whose works have been translated into eleven languages. Described by the *Washington Post* as 'one of the genre's best writers', she has won both the Nebula and Locus Awards and been shortlisted for the Hugo Award. Her novels include *Cloned Lives*, *The Golden Space*, *The Alien Upstairs*, *Venus of Dreams*, *Venus of Shadows*, *Alien Child* and *The Shore of Women*. *Earthseed*, a novel for younger readers, was chosen as a Best Book for Young Adults by the American Library Association. *Publishers Weekly* described her *Women of Wonder* anthologies of science fiction by women as 'essential reading for any serious SF fan.' She is also the author of *Ruler of the Sky*, a historical novel about Genghis Khan.

Veronica Cody

Jean Meredith

Acknowledgements

Judith Miller, model and moral supporter; Maria Schuchardt (who photographed most of the artwork); Pamela Sargent, indefatigably patient collaborator; Forrest J. Ackerman, advisor; models Patricia McFarren, Constance Johnson-Chapman, Claudia Dunaway, JulieAnn Fogarty, Donna Jo Duval, Sommer Browning, Erin Roth, Cathy Hovey, Kerah Hicks, Pamela Clouse, Krista Dyson and Catherine FitzMaurice; Betty King (author of the invaluable reference book: *Women of the Future* [Scarecrow Press, 1984], which was a goldmine of information); Mark Bennett; Janrae Frank and Jean Stine, George Zebrowski, for help with research; and those authors who not only gave their blessing to the project, but provided invaluable assistance in the depiction of their characters: Jack Chalker, Joe Haldeman, C. J. Cherryh, John Varley, Harry Harrison, L. Sprague de Camp, Vonda McIntyre, Larry Niven, Poul Anderson, Phyllis Ann Karr, F. M. Busby, Janet Morris, Peter S. Beagle, Anne McCaffrey, Joanna Russ, Marion Zimmer Bradley. Alexei Panshin, Joan Vinge, A. E. van Vogt and the late Frank Herbert, Robert A. Heinlein, Fritz Leiber and Isaac Asimov.

My most sincere apologies to those whose active enthusiasm had to be rewarded by having their characters – for one reason or another – not included in this edition.

(RM)

Tigerishka

Lady Amalthea

Index